Measuring Soft Power in International Relations

Measuring Soft Power in International Relations

Irene S. Wu

LYNNE
RIENNER
PUBLISHERS

BOULDER
BARNSLEY

To Joseph

Paperback edition published in the United States of America in 2026 by
Lynne Rienner Publishers, Inc.
1800 30th Street, Suite 314, Boulder, Colorado 80301
www.rienner.com

and in the United Kingdom by
Lynne Rienner Publishers, Inc.
47 Church Street, Barnsley, South Yorkshire S70 2AS
www.scriptbooks.co.uk/rienner

The publisher's authorized representative in
the EU for product safety is Authorised Rep Compliance Ltd.,
Ground Floor, 71 Lower Baggot Street, Dublin D02 P593, Ireland.
www.arccompliance.com

© 2024 by Irene S. Wu. All rights reserved by the publisher

ISBNs: 979-8-89616-679-5 (pb: alk. paper)
      979-8-89616-680-1 (ebook)

Library of Congress Cataloging-in-Publication Data
A Cataloging-in-Publication record for the hardcover edition of
this book is available from the Library of Congress.

British Cataloguing in Publication Data
A Cataloguing in Publication record for the hardcover edition of
this book is available from the British Library.

Printed and bound in the United States of America

∞ The paper used in this publication meets the requirements
of the American National Standard for Permanence of
Paper for Printed Library Materials Z39.48-1992.

5 4 3 2 1

Contents

List of Tables and Figures   xi
Preface   xv

1   **The Soft Power Rubric: Measuring Cultural Influence in International Relations**   1
    The Intuition Behind the Soft Power Rubric   2
    Openness to Foreigners May Be the Key to Soft Power   5
    Soft Power: When Foreigners Think of Us as "We" Rather Than as "They"   6

Part 1   Foundations of the Soft Power Rubric

2   **The Evolution of Soft Power as a Concept**   9
    Hard, Soft, and Cosmopolitan Power Approaches   10
    Power Resources and Relational Power   11
       Soft Power as Threat as Well as Reward   11
       Soft Power Agenda Setting   12
       Soft Power Shaping Beliefs and Preferences Through Communication   13
    Virtue, Virtuosity, Metapower, and Soft Power   14
       Virtue and Virtuosity   15
       Endearment and Emulation   16
    Japan's Soft Power Rise   18

3   **How Effective Is Soft Power?**   21
    What Influences Public Opinion About Foreign Countries?   24
       Direct Social Interaction Improves Foreign Public Opinion   24

       Effective, Visible Aid Programs Improve
         Foreign Public Opinion 24
       Foreign Policy Credibility Amplifies or Undermines
         Public Diplomacy 25
    What Are the Benefits of Soft Power Relationships? *27*
       Commercial and Business Benefits 27
       Trade Benefits 29
       Social, Cultural, Economic, and Political Benefits 30
       Political Benefits 31
    Soft Power Influence Flows in Many Directions *33*
       Countries with a Lot of Students Studying Abroad in
         Democracies Will Themselves Become More Democratic 33
       Western-Educated Leaders Are More Likely to
         Democratize 34
       Training That Includes Extensive Socialization Heightens
         the Influence of Sending Country Norms 36
       Migrants to Democratic Countries May Transmit Political
         Norms Back to Their Sending Countries 37
       Travel and Movies—Opportunities for More
         Quantitative Work 40
    Soft Power as a Mutually Beneficial Relationship and the
    Impact on the "Producer" Country *41*

4 Measuring Social Interaction   45
    Parallels Between the Soft Power Rubric and the
       Gross Domestic Product *45*
    Look to the Audience: Learning from Television,
       Social Media, and Studies of Discourse *47*
    Quantitative Perspective on Nationalism and Community
       Integration *50*
    Creating Culture, Building Trust, and Accumulating Social
       Capital Through Interaction *51*
    Thoughts on Measurement *54*
    Cautionary Lessons from the History of the GDP *55*

5 Connecting the Personal to the International   57
    The Push-Pull Model in International Education Studies *59*
    Individuals' Transnational Identity in Migration Studies *60*
    Place Identity and Destination Image in Tourism Studies *62*
    Systems and Structures in International Media Studies *64*
    Weaving Together Ideas from Migration, Study Abroad,
       Travel, and Movie Literature *65*
    A Narrow View Can Broaden Horizons *67*

Contents   vii

Part 2   Using the Soft Power Rubric

6   Movies and Popular Culture as Soft Power Indicators   69
    United States at the Center of the Global Movie Industry   70
    Other Major Movie Producers in the Global Market   72
    Netflix as a Comparison   73
    How Media Can Build Transnational Trust Communities   76
    Beyond Movies to Popular Culture   77
    Implications for Movies, Media, and Soft Power   78

7   The Power of International Education Hubs   79
    A Global View of International Education   79
    Australia—Global Leader in International Education   80
    What Motivates Students to Study Abroad?   85
    Foreign Students Who Interact with Host Communities
        Fare Better   88
    Avoiding the Trap of Treating Foreign Students as
        Pawns in Diplomacy   89
    How Travel Abroad and Hosting Foreign Students
        Transformed Australian Identity   90

8   Indian Emigrants as Drivers of Soft Power   91
    Exploring India with the Soft Power Rubric   93
        Foreign Audiences for Indian Movies   93
        Foreign Visitors, Students, and Immigrants in India   94
    Indians Abroad Building Soft Power Relationships   96
        Indian Students Abroad   96
        Indian Emigrants Abroad   97
    Soft Power Success: The G20   101
    Emigrants and Students Abroad as a Soft Power Resource   107

9   Russia's and China's Soft Power Compared   109
    China's State-Led Soft Power Campaign   109
    Russia's Soft Power Goal May Be National Security   110
    Postcommunist Cultural Nationalism as a Bulwark Against
        Foreign Influence   111
    Applying the Soft Power Rubric   112
        Immigrants   112
        Foreign Students   113
        Foreign Visitors   117
        Movies   119
    Russia's Long-Term Relationships and China's
        Recent Momentum   120

10 Understanding Soft Power in Southeast Asia — 123

Southeast Asia as a Foreign Policy Priority *124*
Southeast Asian Students Go Abroad *125*
People of Southeast Asia: Their Attraction to
  the United States and China, 2000–Present *127*
  Immigration 128
  Education 129
  Travel 129
  Movies 129
  Other Leading Countries 129
Southeast Asian Countries' Soft Power Influence:
  Foreigners Traveling to ASEAN *130*
  Immigration 131
  Education 131
  Travel 132
  Other Leading Countries 136
Spotlight on Malaysia as an Educational Hub *133*
Returning to the Culinary Scene *135*

11 The Soft Power Leaders: Global Rankings — 141

Why Are Rankings Important, or Not? *142*
Comparing the Soft Power Rubric to the
  Soft Power 30 List *143*
Soft Power Rubric—Using It to Rank Countries *144*
Beyond Rankings—Historical Application of
  the Soft Power Rubric *147*
Unpacking the Data for the United States, France,
  Germany, and the United Kingdom *147*
  *The US Share of Immigrants, Foreign Students,
    and Foreign Visitors 147*
  Comparing France, Germany, and the United Kingdom 151
South Africa: More Soft Power Than Their
  Hard Power Might Predict *154*
Toward a More Objective Ranking of Soft Power
  Relationships *157*

Part 3 Conclusion

12 Implications of the Soft Power Rubric — 159

Conceptual Foundations for the Soft Power Rubric *160*
Case Studies Applying the Soft Power Rubric *164*
  Japan 164
  Russia and China 164

India's Soft Power and the G20 and G7 165
  Southeast Asia: Great Power Competition, Transnational
    Identities, and Destination Image 165
  Movies 166
  International Education 166
  Ranking Soft Power Leaders 167
 Implications of the Soft Power Rubric for Foreign Policy 167
 How a Parsimonious Approach Opens New Vistas to
    Understanding Soft Power Relationships 169

Appendix 1: Calculating the Rankings of Soft Power Leaders   171
Appendix 2: Soft Power Leaders: Data Tables, 1960–2020   177
Bibliography   193
Index   205
About the Book   213

Tables and Figures

Tables

2.1	How Norms Develop in a Community	13
2.2	How Ethics Changes the Perception of Power	16
3.1	Foreign Public Opinion Response to US High-Level Visits	26
3.2	Effect of Foreign Public Opinion on US Foreign Policy Goals	32
8.1	India's Emigrant Community Compared to Other Countries' Total Population	99
8.2	Top Five Countries with the Largest Emigrant Communities Abroad	100
8.3	Brief History of G-Group Meetings	103
8.4	Top Countries by GDP, 1998	104
11.1	Comparing Soft Power 30 and Soft Power Rubric Rankings, 2010 and 2019/2020	142
11.2	Soft Power 30 Results, 2010–2019, Available Years	145
11.3	Soft Power 30: Selected Indicators	146
11.4	Soft Power Rubric Global Rankings, 1960–2020	148
11.5	South Africa: Indicators of Soft, Military, and Economic Power	154
11.6	Spain, India, and China: Indicators of Soft, Military, and Economic Power	154
A1.1	Soft Power Rubric Ranking, 2020	171
A1.2	Soft Power Rubric Data for Top Ten Soft Power Leaders, 2020	172
A2.1a	Top Countries Ranked by Soft Power Rubric, 1960	177
A2.1b	Number of Immigrants for Top 9 Countries, 1960	177
A2.1c	Number of Students for Top 9 Countries, 1960	178
A2.1d	Number of Visitors for Top 9 Countries, 1960	178

A2.2a	Top Countries Ranked by Soft Power Rubric, 1970	178
A2.2b	Number of Immigrants for Top 15 Countries, 1970	179
A2.2c	Number of Students for Top 15 Countries, 1970	179
A2.2d	Number of Visitors for Top 15 Countries, 1970	179
A2.3a	Top Countries Ranked by Soft Power Rubric, 1980	180
A2.3b	Number of Immigrants for Top 15 Countries, 1980	181
A2.3c	Number of Students for Top 15 Countries, 1980	181
A2.3d	Number of Visitors for Top 15 Countries, 1980	181
A2.4a	Top Countries Ranked by Soft Power Rubric, 1990	182
A2.4b	Number of Immigrants for Top 15 Countries, 1990	183
A2.4c	Number of Students for Top 15 Countries, 1990	183
A2.4d	Number of Visitors for Top 15 Countries, 1990	183
A2.5a	Top Countries Ranked by Soft Power Rubric, 2000	184
A2.5b	Number of Immigrants for Top 15 Countries, 2000	185
A2.5c	Number of Students for Top 15 Countries, 2000	186
A2.5d	Number of Visitors for Top 15 Countries, 2000	186
A2.6a	Top Countries Ranked by Soft Power Rubric, 2010	186
A2.6b	Number of Immigrants for Top 15 Countries, 2010	188
A2.6c	Number of Students for Top 15 Countries, 2010	188
A2.6d	Number of Visitors for Top 15 Countries, 2010	188
A2.7a	Top Countries Ranked by Soft Power Rubric, 2020	189
A2.7b	Number of Immigrants for Top 15 Countries, 2020	190
A2.7c	Number of Students for Top 15 Countries, 2020	191
A2.7d	Number of Visitors for Top 15 Countries, 2020	191

Figures

1.1	The Soft Power Rubric: Indicators of Social Integration Across Borders	3
2.1	Japan's GDP Growth Compared to Soft Power Rubric Indicators	19
3.1	Soft Power Resources: The Relationship Between Producer and Audience	22
3.2	Percentage of Students from Chile Abroad in Democratic Host Countries Compared with Democratic Levels at Home in Chile	35
6.1	US-Produced Movies as Fraction of Total Global Admissions, 2007–2017	70
6.2	UNESCO Movie Admissions, 2007–2017	71
6.3	Major Movie Production Countries, Part 1, Admissions, 2007–2017 (every odd year)	72
6.4	Major Movie Production Countries, Part 2, Admissions, 2007–2017 (every odd year)	73

6.5	Netflix Subscribers by Region, 2017–2022	74
6.6	Top 5 Production Countries in Netflix Library, 2021	75
7.1	Total Students Enrolled in Foreign Universities for a Degree, 1960–2020	80
7.2	Top Destinations for Foreign Students, 1960–2020	81
7.3	Top Destinations for Foreign Students, 2020	81
7.4	Australia: International Students, Top Ten Countries of Origin, 2020	84
7.5	Australia: Immigrants, Top Ten Countries of Origin, 2020	84
7.6	Students Enrolled in Foreign Universities for a Degree, by World Bank Country Income Classification, 2021	87
8.1	Foreign Visitors and Foreign Students in India and China, 1980–2020	94
8.2	India and China Immigrants, 1990–2020	95
8.3	Indian Immigrants: Top Ten Countries of Origin, 2020	96
8.4	Indian Students Abroad, 1960–2020	97
8.5	Indian Students Abroad by Country, 1960	98
8.6	Indian Students Abroad by Country, 2021	98
8.7	Top Ten Host Countries of Indian Emigrants Abroad, 2020	101
8.8	More Indians Abroad Than Foreigners in India: Migrants, Visitors, Students, 1960–2020	106
8.9	India's Soft Power Rubric Data Compared with France and Italy	106
9.1	Immigrants to Russia and China, 1990–2020	112
9.2	Immigrants to Russia: Countries of Origin, 2020	114
9.3	Immigrants to China: Countries of Origin, 2020	115
9.4	Foreign Students to Russia and China, 1980–2019	116
9.5	Foreign Visitors to China and Russia, 1995–2018	118
9.6	Russian Productions: Movie Admissions Outside Russia, 2005–2017	119
9.7	Chinese Productions: Movie Admissions Outside China, 2005–2017	119
10.1a	ASEAN Emigrants Abroad, 2000–2020	128
10.1b	ASEAN Students Abroad, 2000–2020	129
10.1c	ASEAN Visitors Abroad, 2000–2020	130
10.2a	Immigrants to ASEAN, 2000–2020	132
10.2b	Foreign Students to ASEAN, 2000–2020	133
10.2c	Foreign Visitors to ASEAN, 2000–2020	134
10.3	Foreign Students in Malaysia, Top 10 Countries of Origin, 2022	138
11.1a	Immigrants: US Fraction of World Total	149
11.1b	Foreign Students: US Fraction of World Total	149
11.1c	Foreign Visitors: US Fraction of World Total	149

11.2a	Immigrants in France, Germany, and the United Kingdom, 1990–2020	151
11.2b	Foreign Students in France, Germany, and the United Kingdom, 2000–2019	152
11.2c	Foreign Visitors to France, Germany, and the United Kingdom, 2000–2019	152
11.3	French, German, and British Immigrants to China, Japan, and Russia, 2020	154
11.4	French, German, and British Going to the United States, 2018 and 2020	155
A1.1	Total Number of Countries Reporting All Three Series: Immigrants, Foreign Students, and Foreign Visitors, 1960–2020	174

Preface

WHEN I REFLECT ON WHAT EXPERIENCES FORMED MY VIEWS of other countries, the most powerful influences were people. Growing up, my Spanish teachers were from Cuba; their families had fled Castro. My history teacher from Germany taught us that her Dresden had been bombed in World War II. My Turkish neighbors drank tea just as we did. Our friend from Lebanon shared a great cheesecake recipe. I first heard of Ramadan from my classmate from Persia. My South Korean friends' parents did not trust Japanese products, but my friends bought Sony Walkmans anyway. I felt solidarity with my Jewish classmates who had to go to Hebrew school on the weekend, like I had to go to Chinese school. All this occurred in a southern US town, not one of the big metropolises on the coast. Whatever I subsequently learned about these countries in books and lectures built on this knowledge from childhood. When I saw news about the countries, these past friendships brought the events closer to me.

Later on, as the internet transitioned from a science enterprise to a commercial service in the 1990s and early 2000s, I sat on several government committees and task groups seeking to understand its development, which included considering how to measure it. Many indicators I worked on with colleagues still stand today; many more proved less useful and have faded away. A result of this experience is that I tend to see measurements as outcomes of an effort to understand questions, rather than just as inputs into models. Every measurement has its history and its creators, with their particular intellectual concerns. Measurements emerge in order to address certain issues and evolve a kind of permanence based on whether they successfully contribute to solving problems.

This book merges my interests in international relations, foreign policy, economics, and communications policy. While my first public presentation on measuring soft power was in 2014, the research gained momentum only because of a fellowship from the Wilson Center for international scholars in Washington, DC, in 2017–2018. Stapleton Roy introduced me to the Wilson Center; Robert Litwack and Shihoko Goto at key moments kept the project rolling forward when it might have stood still. Blair A. Ruble, William E. Pomeranz, Monde Muyangwa, Elizabeth M. H. Newbury, Robert Daly, Michael Kugelman, Rui Zhong, Cynthia J. Arnson, Laura Dawson, Sandy Pho, Abraham Denmark, and Izabella Tabarovsky all shared their expertise. Other Wilson scholars gave timely comments and insight: Neeti Nair, Aynne Kokas, Elizabeth Stanley, Jeffrey Taliaferro, Wenhong Chen, Leaynet Yilma, Valerie Anishchenkova, Patrick McEachern, Ewa Bérard, Yasushi Watanabe, Amy Austin Holmes, Nobuhiro Aizawa, and Zuhamnan Dapel.

The Wilson fellowship also provided access to the Kluge Center at the Library of Congress. With the support of John Haskell and Travis Hensley, especially, I found the essential empirical data needed to build the Soft Power Rubric in the books of the library. I have relied on the openness of the library to scholars and the kind guidance of the reading rooms' staff ever since.

In the formative stages of creating the Soft Power Rubric, J. P. Singh's invitations to several conferences, especially the Dupont Summits of the Policy Studies Organization, and to his cultural studies program at the University of Edinburgh introduced me to a community of scholars interested in cultural, political, and economic issues. Without these discussions I would have doubted the project was worth pursuing. Also, Motohiro Tsuchiya invited me to Keio University and provided the opportunity to talk with Japanese scholars and students about what soft power means to them. Finally, Nanette Levinson and Henning Schulzrinne offered early, invaluable support. Carole Sargent was a great coach along the road to publication.

Several people in public policy organizations included me in conferences, where I had the opportunity to speak directly with government officials and policy analysts, including Emilia Adams, State Department Foreign Service Institute; David Montgomery, Minerva, US Department of Defense; Beverly Kirk, Center for Strategic and International Studies; Esther Brimmer, NAFSA Association of International Educators; and Adrienne Wu, Global Taiwan Institute. These conversations helped to me keep the Soft Power Rubric a practical undertaking and underscored the need for a measurement method based on open models and public data.

At the United Nations Educational, Scientific, and Cultural Organization (UNESCO), Lydia Deloumeaux and Chiao-Ling Chien advised me on how to best use their data. Maria Angeles Prieto and Laura Maria Munoz of the UN World Tourism Organization shared their data with me. Much of these organizations data are available online. I have posted some of their earlier data, mainly available in print, to DigitalGeorgetown, the university's digital repository (library.georgetown.edu/digitalgeorgetown). For UNESCO international education data from 1960–1990 and UN Population Division migration data from 1960–1980, which are primarily available in printed statistical books, I have made digital versions available at DigitalGeorgetown. Other data may be posted as permissions are granted.

One of the joys of working on this project was the chance to engage with specialist scholarly communities. Many shared their knowledge and read and commented on my work, including Renée Marlin-Bennett, Peter Rutland, Devesh Kapur, Naren Chitty, Giulio Gallarotti, Craig Hayden, Peter N. Stearns, Kiran Duwadi, Joseph S. Nye Jr., Elizabeth Gooch, Richard Kurin, Shoko Kiyohara, Ichiya Nakamura, Julie Baer, Jill Welch, Michael Kulman, Ang Peng Hwa, Dan M. Hausman, Miles Kahler, Kristen Hopewell, Laura Roselle, L. H. M. Ling, and Suzie Sudarman.

I am grateful to Lynne Rienner for recognizing the potential of this book, as well as to her staff and to two anonymous reviewers.

Finally, I thank my husband, Joseph Mok, for never doubting that this book would be published.

Note

This publication reflects my views only and not those of the US Federal Communications Commission, its members, or its staff.

1

The Soft Power Rubric: Measuring Cultural Influence in International Relations

WHEN THE BERLIN WALL FELL IN 1989 AND THE COLD WAR began to end, people walked westward, not eastward. One reason was the allure of popular culture, especially American, including movies, television, and particularly the music (Zhuk 2011). "From a rock concert to a student demonstration, from refusing to vote in the farcical elections to making an open speech at some official congress, or even a hunger strike," all these were ways for people to live within their truth, said Václav Havel in 1978; he was later elected president of Czechoslovakia (Havel 1985). In 1985, Mikhail Gorbachev lifted decades of active suppression of rock and roll; he and his wife both professed their love of the Beatles (Ryback 1990). Gorbachev later became president of the Soviet Union. In 1988 Bruce Springsteen sang Bob Dylan's "Chimes of Freedom" in East Berlin, a turning point in the end of communist rule, says András Simonyi, former Hungarian ambassador to NATO and the United States and himself a rock and roll guitarist (Kounalakis and Simonyi 2011). In the midst of Cold War politics, precisely because American rock and roll was not state sponsored, it was even more influential. Simonyi calls it the pull of the market overwhelming the push of propaganda.

Playing rock and roll equaled cultural and political resistance, says critic Peter Wicke (Mitchell 1992). Its American attitude of youth rebellion and independence was transplanted to Eastern Europe and grew in its own directions. Havel writes in 1968, "On the one hand, there was the sterile puritanism of the post-totalitarian establishment and, on the other hand, unknown young people who wanted no more than to be able to live within the truth, to play the music they enjoyed, to sing songs that were relevant to their lives, and to live freely in dignity and partnership" (Havel 1985).

Rock and roll, this style of music so closely identified with American culture, became deeply and fully integrated in the East European cultural scene.

Soft power, not just guns and money, closed the Cold War chapter in the twentieth century, yet there is no recognized method for measuring it. The Soft Power Rubric is one way forward. This book renews our understanding of soft power in a way that makes quantifying it possible, opening up the possibility of comparisons across countries and analyses across time.

The Intuition Behind the Soft Power Rubric

Suppose we think of soft power as generated not only by nation-states but also by ordinary people expressing their interest in foreign countries. Suppose further that our country has soft power when foreigners think of us as "we" rather than as "they." In effect, soft power relationships exist when others include us as part of their community; we become friends of their nation. People express interest in foreign countries by engaging in activities like watching foreign movies and traveling, studying, and migrating abroad. The Soft Power Rubric brings together relevant, observable, and measurable activity that captures a country's potential scope for soft power influence—the number of cross-border interactions its people have with foreign countries. While this parsimonious approach cannot capture the quality of the interaction, any more than gross domestic product (GDP) can capture the quality of production, it does outline the outer bounds of potential soft power and has the added benefit of measurability over time and across countries.

Reconceptualizing soft power in this way opens new vistas for future investigations. It offers the possibility of empirical measurement across countries and across time. It connects the lived experience of individuals to the collective understandings of communities, which in turn informs the behavior of states. These vistas combine to make culture and values as tangible as money and firepower in the study of international relations.

The Soft Power Rubric can track changes in the volume and direction of interactions that people have with foreigners. Three elements are direct people-to-people interactions: emigrating, studying abroad, and traveling abroad. The fourth element is a mediated interaction: watching foreign movies. Emigration reflects a person's ultimate integration in a foreign society, permanently moving family and home to another country. Studying abroad reflects a person's serious interest and commitment to understanding another society by spending substantial financial resources and formative time in a foreign country. Visiting a foreign country reflects a short-term interest in a foreign society. Watching a movie expresses an interest or curiosity about another country. For each of these series, government international institutions collect and publish quantitative data for many countries. Research on each of the four elements of the Rubric has central questions and themes that overlap with the others. For example, all four of these literatures discuss the dynamics that push people abroad and pull foreigners into a country. Also, each discusses the effect of transnational social interaction on shaping personal identity. Finally, each discusses the systemic structure within which these interactions take place; there are always some countries at the core, while others are at the periphery.

The Soft Power Rubric measures soft power resources, the potential for a country to have a soft power relationship with another. GDP, a measure of economic power resources, sums the financial value of goods and services produced by an economy. The numbers of military bases, aircraft carriers, or personnel are measures of military power resources (Global Firepower 2023). More resources likely mean more success, but there is no guarantee. A bigger GDP does not guarantee the upper hand in a trade negotiation. More military bases do not ensure victory in war. However, more resources make success more likely, and the depletion of resources heightens the risk of failure. Similarly, the Rubric reveals the volume and intensity of people-to-people interactions that form the basis of many individuals' views of foreign countries and the foundation of a country's soft power resources. More soft power resources no more predict greater political cooperation than more military resources predict victory in war. However, it is reasonable to expect that the presence of major soft power resources itself alters perception and behavior.

Figure 1.1 shows that these indicators range from short-term attraction, such as buying a ticket to see a movie from another country, to long-term attraction, such as emigrating to a foreign country. What matters is not how many movies a country produces but rather how many foreigners choose to watch them. Data for over 200 countries from around 1960–2015 are available from public sources.[1]

The quantitative data in the Soft Power Rubric reflects the extent one country is integrated with others. The change in the number of immigrants, combined with changes in the other indicators within the Soft Power Rubric, is the change in soft power relationship between countries. This measure of soft power makes it possible to discuss the United States' soft

Figure 1.1 The Soft Power Rubric: Indicators of Social Integration Across Borders

Short-term attraction	Watch a movie	Visit a country	Study abroad	Emigrate	*Long-term attraction*

power relationship with Canada as distinct from its soft power relationship with China, or with countries in Europe.

This book opens in Part 1 with recent conceptual developments on soft power. Soft power influence is a form of attraction that includes admiration for virtue and virtuosity and prompts endearment and emulation. Recent research unpacks how the effect of soft power can be documented, such as by public opinion, and its benefits measured, whether by trade or support or by agreeing on United Nations resolutions. Also, research shows that soft power influence flows both ways; interaction between and among countries influences all that participate. This interaction is at the crux of the Soft Power Rubric, which sums social interactions between nations as an indicator of how closely these societies can work together. There are some parallels here between how the Soft Power Rubric works and the development of gross national product as a measurement of national economies. Finally, Part 1 explores the implications of seeing soft power as measured by social interaction and how ideas from related fields of migration, education, tourism, and communications can expand the range of tools to study soft power.

Part 2 applies the Soft Power Rubric to a range of cases. Two chapters focus on specific Soft Power Rubric elements—movies, among the most widely discussed soft power resources, and popular culture; and international education, perhaps the most powerful of the four elements of the Rubric. The United States is still the center of the global movie industry and the international education sector, but especially in education, other countries are growing quickly. Three chapters compare one, two, and a group of countries' soft power influence. For India, the size of its emigrant community and even larger diaspora are perhaps the country's greatest soft power resource. Comparing Russia and China shows major divergences in their Soft Power Rubric indicators. The discussion of Southeast Asia shows how the Soft Power Rubric can be used to analyze regional changes over time, to show both how the members of the Association of Southeast Asian Nations (ASEAN) interact with countries like the United States and China, and the relationships of individual ASEAN countries with the world. Finally, Part 2 concludes with a global ranking of soft power countries, from 1960 to 2020. The recent rankings place the United States, Great Britain, France, and Germany in the lead—much like other soft power rankings based on public opinion surveys or other indicators—but the Soft Power Rubric can show changes over a range of several decades, demonstrating its unique power as an analytical tool.

The usefulness of the Soft Power Rubric relies on two strands of work. The first is the quantitative work discussed in Chapter 3. The popular opinion survey research by Goldsmith and Horiuchi (2009, 2012) shows a link between foreigners' views of America and cooperation with the United States in foreign policy, especially for issues that are high profile in public discussions. When those kinds of public opinion surveys are not available, Datta (2014) and Atkinson (2006, 2014) show that trends in international education and international travel can work as substitutes. Also, inside the fields of international education and migration, there is growing evidence that these international experiences influence values in the countries of both destination and origin.

The second line of work that validates the Soft Power Rubric is in Chapter 11 on global rankings. Using the Soft Power Rubric, the global rankings for 2020 are roughly similar to the Soft Power 30 Index, which is the most widely used soft power measurement at the moment. This comparison indicates that the Soft Power Rubric travels in the same direction as other measurements that rely on opinion surveys. The difference is, however, that while the Soft Power 30 is available for only a handful of recent years for a restricted set of countries, the datasets backing the Soft Power Rubric easily reach back to 1990 and for some countries as far back as 1960.

Openness to Foreigners May Be the Key to Soft Power

The Soft Power Rubric measures foreigners' attraction by their interest in engaging with a country, an engagement that can happen only if societies are open. Singh and MacDonald (2017) argue that the openness of a society directly affects its ability to influence other societies. Based on data collection of various international indicators, they empirically demonstrate that democratic pluralism, economic prosperity, and strong cultural institutions attract international students, foreign tourists, foreign direct investment, and influence voting in the UN General Assembly. This work highlights the challenges that authoritarian states face in building their soft power resources.

In parallel, some in the movie industry argue that American movies perform well in the global market because their home market is a diverse audience (Straubhaar 1991). Karl Deutsch in *Nerves of Government* (1966b) argues that for a society to adapt successfully to new challenges, it requires open and good information about itself, the past, and the outside world, and further, that communications transactions are evidence of whether a society is open or closed. Deutsch's work suggests that openness and communication are mechanisms for change. Governments are more effective steering societies that are open to good and accurate information; a feedback loop is necessary. Taking Deutsch's example of national adaptability and extending it to the international level, those countries more open to foreigners are likely to have better information on how the international community works and greater ability to influence it.

During the Covid-19 pandemic from 2020 to 2023, those countries most open to foreigners were the ones initially hit hardest. As a result, all face-to-face interactions across national borders paused—migration, education, and travel—while mediated interactions grew. The weak US domestic response to the pandemic tarnished the country's image of competence and at a practical level reduced the number of foreign visitors, students, and new immigrants to the country. When the pandemic subsides, the country-to-country relationships may or may not resume where they left off.

Soft Power: When Foreigners Think of Us as "We" Rather Than as "They"

Joseph Nye has won the argument that military, economic, and natural resources alone do not fully explain a nation's influence abroad. How attractive foreigners find its society and values also plays an important role in its soft power influence. However, the scholarly literature still lacks consensus on how to measure soft power, a gap that weakens soft power policies as an option in a realpolitik world. If it cannot be measured, how can we be sure it exists? Reconceiving soft power as when foreigners think of us as "we" rather than as "they," the ultimate empathetic posture, makes it possible to draw on several theoretical insights and empirical resources to connect quantitatively a country's domestic appeal to its international status.

First, understanding soft power means understanding those countries and peoples who are influenced by soft power, not focusing on the country "projecting" soft power. Second, the volume and direction of interactions between people across national borders over time are indicators of how integrated these societies are—a clue to how much they are "we." Third, culture is not an external and fixed factor but created by people through innumerable performances a day. Fourth, the trust necessary for cooperation is not necessarily an act of faith but can be a rational attitude based on a history of reciprocal action among people. Finally, if we accept that soft power resources are created through people's interaction with foreigners, a major implication of this work is that the more open societies are to foreigners, the more likely they will have soft power influence.

Based on these insights, the Soft Power Rubric is a framework that brings together four elements that represent different kinds of social interactions among people across national borders: migration, study abroad, travel, and watching foreign movies. Each of these brings to the soft power debate a literature that explores why people engage in these activities and a set of indicators published by international organizations, opening vistas for both qualitative and quantitative research.

On the quantitative side, the Soft Power Rubric takes people's transnational interactions as the main indicator of interest in foreign countries, much as GDP takes the financial value of goods and services as the main indicator of economic activity. For all four elements of the Soft Power Rubric, publicly available data for nearly every country in the world are available in time series from 1960 forward. It is possible to create maps illustrating the direction and volume of interactions. Also, these indicators point to changes over the decades and make possible nuanced comparisons among countries.

Beyond the four elements of the Soft Power Rubric, when large, multicountry datasets with long time horizons are not available, there may be other data with a small number or a pair of countries that reflect other types of transnational social interactions that build trust and willingness to cooperate. For example, sport and religion are cultural activities that bring together people and produce communities with strong identities. Members of sport and religious communities develop a sense of "we," a trust community forged from having many opportunities to interact, to work together, to depend on each other, and to act as a collective (Wu 2015). Cultural institutions, which are important actors in creating meaning and cultivating community identity by building relationships both at the professional level and through popular culture, are another field where soft power develops (Singh, Kaptanoglu, and Li 2023). While large datasets with long time horizons on these interactions may not exist, harnessing the available quantitative data and documenting the narratives of people's experience in these activities are one way forward in applying the Soft Power Rubric.

On the qualitative side, the specialist research around each of the four Rubric elements provides insight on how soft power processes work. Study abroad research shows the importance of investigating why people leave a country and move to another. At the level of the individual, migration studies investigate the development of transnational identities—when people's ordinary lives geographically take place in more than one nation. At the level of communities, travel and tourism studies highlight the synergy and tensions between the traveler's image of the destination and the host's identity of their own place. At the level of systems, movie and media studies still debate whether the US domination of the movie industry is simply a reflection of the technological and business cycle, with others rising up, or the capture of global cinema by American culture.

For policymakers, highlighting the importance of the four elements to soft power brings to the forefront arenas that are not usually the main focus of public diplomacy. While international education has long been an important long-run tool for building alliances and common worldviews, travel and tourism are usually treated as a commercial activity, not a central concern of foreign policy. Visiting is an intermediate step between forming an image of a foreign country based on movies and media, and making a bigger commitment like enrolling in a foreign university or migrating. Similarly, migration more frequently figures in foreign policy as a problem—a brain drain for some countries or a crisis for countries on the receiving end of many migrants. From the Soft Power Rubric perspective, both immigration and emigration are also opportunities to build transnational social relationships that have long-term consequences for how all countries involved view each other. Finally, movies do figure highly in soft power discussions, but mostly in how they are made, less in how they are distributed, and even less in audience reaction to them. Newer technologies like on-demand video platforms and social media are making it easier to shift focus to audience reaction, demand, and even participation in transnational media production.

The Soft Power Rubric's new approach, a combination of quantitative measures and qualitative investigation, is one step toward reinvigorating our inquiries to unpack the influence of culture and values and to demonstrate the impact of relationships, not just force, in the world. It also underscores how we are all involved in creating soft power relationships. How we welcome foreign visitors, students, and immigrants, and the decisions we make whether to go abroad, where to go, and for how long, all have implications for soft power relationships and the standing of the communities in which we belong.

Note

1. All the data used in the Soft Power Rubric are collected and published by international organizations and available for free (online for recent data and in yearbooks at public libraries for earlier data).
- Migration data: The UN Population Division publishes immigrant stock information in five-year increments for over 200 countries. The most recent publication is available at un.org/development/desa/pd/content/international-migrant-stock.
- Study abroad: UNESCO publishes online the number of foreign students enrolled in a country's universities, including the students' country of origin at data.uis.unesco.org. The specific series is "International Student Mobility in Tertiary Education—Inbound Internationally Mobile Students by Country of Origin." These data are for over 200 countries from 1999 onward. Earlier data are available in UNESCO Statistical Yearbooks from 1960 to 1999.
- International travel: The UN World Tourism Organization publishes visitor and tourism data at www.e-unwto.org/toc/unwtotfb/current?expanded=undefined. Country-specific data on outbound tourism are available from around 1999 onward. Earlier data from 1960 forward are published in the United Nations World Tourism Organization yearbooks and in summary form in UN Statistical Yearbooks, available online at unstats.un.org/UNSDWebsite/Publications/StatisticalYearbookPastIssue.
- Movies: UNESCO publishes online the top ten movies by admissions as reported by several dozen countries from 2005 to 2017 at data.uis.unesco.org. Prior years' data on the importation for foreign films are published in the UNESCO Statistical Yearbook from 1970 to 1999; however, these are data on production, not on audiences.

2

The Evolution of Soft Power as a Concept

"WHEN I FIRST RETURNED TO THE UNITED STATES FROM JAPAN in 1960, I had not even questioned the general superiority of American society and American institutions. In almost every field we were substantially ahead of Japan, our capacity for research and creativity was unexcelled, and our natural and human resources seemed more than adequate. By 1975, I found myself, like my Japanese friends, wondering what had happened to America," recalls Harvard professor Ezra Vogel in the preface to his book *Japan as Number One: Lessons for America*. He neatly captures the attitude of the moment that presumed the United States was the natural leader and the surprise that Japan was a real rival (Vogel 1980).

Japan's ascendance after World War II was driven by its rapid economic growth. In 1967, Japan's total gross domestic product (GDP) surpassed France and Great Britain. In 1972, it surpassed Germany, making Japan the second largest economy in the world. Vogel's 1980 book, and others of this period, extolled Japanese success in learning, meritocracy, communitarian sharing of wealth, and low crime rate (Vogel 1980). The US auto industry suffered against its Japanese competitors and anti-Japan feelings ran high. In 1982 former Chrysler employees murdered Vincent Chin, mistaking him for Japanese, whom they blamed for automaker layoffs (Lee 2015). Japan's per capita GDP exceeded that of the United States for the first time in 1988 and held for the next nine years. It was amid this American context of fear, loss, and lashing out against Japan that Joseph Nye published his first works on soft power in 1990, which framed US global influence as founded not primarily on economic strength (on the wane) but instead on soft power—its cultural and social superiority (De Gracia 2021).

Nye's work at its heart is concerned with the United States and its place in the world, while acknowledging that the theory and ideas he develops are applicable to other countries. In *Bound to Lead: The Changing Nature of American Power* (1990a), he addressed the question of the moment: Has Japan's economic success meant it will replace the United States as the world's leading power, and is the European Community a threat? Nye's answer is no, the United States has soft power that Japan has yet to develop, and the European Community, while it has potential, has yet to coalesce. After the collapse of the Soviet Union in 1991 and the United States' emergence as a unipolar power, Nye published *The Paradox of American Power: Why the World's Only Superpower Can't Go It Alone* (2002), in which he cautions the United States against a unilateralist path. After the 2003 US invasion of Iraq without the multilateral backing of the United Nations and with the decline of the US government's popularity abroad, Nye published *Soft Power: The Means to Success in World Politics* (2004a), a call for greater US investment in diplomacy and multilateral engagement. A few years after the great financial crisis of 2007, Nye published *The Future of Power* (2011b), which discusses the impact of the internet and technological change on the diffusion of power and returns to the question of whether the United States is in decline.

Hard, Soft, and Cosmopolitan Power Approaches

Nye's framework presents hard and soft power along a spectrum, with coercive tactics as hard and co-optive measures as soft. Hard power approaches could include coercion, threats, payments, and sanctions. Soft power approaches include conceptual frameworks, persuasion, and attractions. Nye (2011b) defines soft power as a country's ability to get other countries to do what it wants through attraction rather than coercion or payments. A country's soft power resources include (1) its culture, to the extent it is attractive to others, (2) its political values, when applied consistently domestically and abroad, and (3) its foreign policies, when it's seen to act with moral authority (Nye 2004, 2011b). Not only nation-states but also other organizations and networks can have soft power.

"Smart power," a country's ability to strategically balance hard and soft power, is the pragmatic response to the all-soft-power advocates (Wilson 2008). For Nye (2011a), smart power means abandoning neither hard nor soft power in developing effective strategies. Giulio Gallarotti (2010) takes this approach further with his idea of "cosmopolitan power," which considers how hard, soft, or combinations of both approaches empower actors rather than, for example, restraining adversaries. Sometimes exclusively using hard power is self-defeating, an outcome Gallarotti calls hard disempowerment. A typical example of hard disempowerment is when a country launches a violent attack that is militarily successful but a diplomatic disaster, and the final outcome is a weakening rather than strengthening of their international status. At other times using soft power includes involving and elevating other groups and their interests, who in turn are empowered (Gallarotti 2010). An example is Gandhi's nonviolent movement leading to India's independence from Great Britain, which has influenced political movements worldwide and, in turn, enhanced India's status in world history.

Power Resources and Relational Power

In general, Nye's framework includes two main categories: (1) power resources and (2) relational power, which in turn include three different objectives or "faces of power": (a) threats and rewards, (b) agenda setting, and (c) shaping beliefs and preferences (Nye 2011b). Power resources are the assets at a nation's disposal and are often quantifiable. General indicators include land, population, and skills such as literacy. For military power this may include number of personnel, budget, or number of warheads. For economic power, this may include gross domestic product (GDP) and GDP per capita. Nye (2011a) includes in this category indicators related to internet and technology access. For soft power, he includes top universities, films, and foreign students.

Relational power is about what kind of control a state has over other states' behavior. For Nye, relational power has "three faces." The first face of a state can use threats or rewards to make another state do something they would otherwise not do. The second face is indirect, influencing the agenda, which then influences other states' behavior. The third face is also indirect, shaping another state's beliefs and preferences, at which point the influencer's and influenced state's interests are aligned (Nye 2011a).

Soft Power as Threat as Well as Reward

The distinction between soft and hard power is that soft power is not coercive or violent. The rewards of soft power—collaboration and cooperation—are more widely discussed than the threats. However, this does not mean that soft power is normatively good. Nye is clear in his exposition of soft power in that it is not necessarily better to "twist minds than to twist arms" (Nye 2017). Renée Marlin-Bennett explores this concretely in her work discussing two cases—blood libel accusing Jews of ritual murder and the "Pizzagate" where Democrats in the United States were accused of child trafficking—in which communities were maliciously accused of heinous crimes with the goal of inciting violence against them. The malicious accusations successfully incited violent response because there was a receptive audience willing to act (Marlin-Bennett 2022). Janice Bially Mattern, in her more conceptual discussion, shows how soft power can become a kind of verbal fighting, in which rhetoric posits one worldview as right, suggesting other views and their holder be ostracized, a kind of intense peer pressure (Bially Mattern 2005). Grigas's account of Putin's support for the Russian Orthodox Church echoes this strategy. By promoting conservative social values as central to the Russian identity and institutionalized by the Russian Orthodox Church (Grigas 2016), there is an implication that those who disagree are not good Russians. As Marlin-Bennett notes, however, such communicative strategies only work if recipients are open to it.

Soft Power Agenda Setting

While Nye makes a conceptual connection between domestic issues—whether a country's domestic policies reflect its values—and foreign policy, his practical discussions of how to use soft power focus on public diplomacy, the programs run by foreign ministries to build relationships with foreign publics. What specific advice is there for building norms and influencing agendas? The work in international relations on how institutions shape norms fills this gap. Many political science scholars take as a point of departure that people's behavior is based on shared beliefs, which shape the interests they pursue (Finnemore and Sikkink 2001). From this perspective, there may be instances when culture, ideas, and identity explain people's and government's actions more than the military and economic calculations. Norms are one kind of shared belief; one definition is that a norm is a single standard of behavior, a value that guides people on how they ought to behave. By extension, then, institutions can be thought of as a system of norms. Finnemore and Sikkink (1998) describe "sovereignty" and "slavery" as two examples of institutions that are collections of norms about how actors ought to behave. As shown and expanded upon in Table 2.1, they also broadly describe norms as having a life cycle—a first phase when norm entrepreneurs work to persuade others to accept the norm, a second phase when the norm is accepted by communities, and a third phase when the norm is internalized by community members (Finnemore and Sikkink 1998).

In this arena of research, there are a number of areas where government action is better explained by norms than by other military or economic interests, such as opposing slavery and human trafficking, support for equality for women, and other action on civil and human rights. Major actors in these campaigns include transnational activist groups such as Amnesty International and international institutions such as the United Nations. In addition to these, there are "epistemic communities," groups of experts with specialized knowledge where members have been social-

Table 2.1 How Norms Develop in a Community

	Stage 1: Norm Emergence	Stage 2: Norm Cascade	Stage 3: Internalization
Actors	Norm entrepreneurs with organizational platforms	States, international organizations, transnational *activist* networks	*Epistemic communities*, law, *professional groups*, bureaucracy
Motives	Altruism, empathy, ideational commitment	Legitimacy, reputation, esteem	Conformity
Dominant mechanisms	Persuasion	Socialization, institutionalization, demonstration	Habit, institutionalization

Source: Expanded from Finnemore and Sikkink (1998).

ized through education and professional training. Such members act as norm entrepreneurs and the epistemic communities as networks for norm cascades. One example is that many of the internet's technical standards and behavioral norms for both creators and users were established through international, nongovernment expert networks (Mueller 2010; Musiani et al. 2016).

Soft Power Shaping Beliefs and Preferences Through Communication

Converting norms and institutions into political action is at the center of work on social capital and collective action, both major fields of study within social science. The idea of social capital is that when people join groups and interact with others over time, they develop enough trust to work together. When individuals agree to work together, setting aside individual benefit for the greater good, they are taking collective action (McAdam, Tarrow, and Tilly 2001).

My own work on technology's impact on politics shows that online groups that work with each other over time can forge trust communities with shared norms. Once established, these communities can switch goals together, such as a cultural community converting its efforts to a humanitarian service (Wu 2015). The idea of a nation is really held together in the imagination of its members—citizens who have never met each other are willing to go to war to defend them. They are motivated by a history of collective experience, from following the same daily news, the celebration of annual national events, and the shared belief that others in the past have sacrificed for their collective future (Anderson 1983). Interaction in person or communication mediated through technology is essential to developing a sense of common identity and community.

Communication and social interaction are at the core of soft power relationships, argue scholars like Marlin-Bennett, Craig Hayden, and Bially Mattern. It is only possible to have a soft power relationship between two countries if each has heard, spoken to, or seen each other by some means. This is why technology-enabled communication, which allows more people to interact with others around the world, has increased the importance of soft power; Nye's reflections on the importance of information technology and Hayden's focus on rhetoric reflect this insight (Marlin-Bennett 2022; Hayden 2012). Bially Mattern underscores the fundamental role of communicative exchange in creating attraction. Without some form of communication, attraction is not possible (Bially Mattern 2005).

In the search for a better way to measure soft power, I argue that soft power resources are the relationships people have across borders, and the best indicators of these are observations that reveal those relationships. It is not the movies that are the soft power resource, but the people who watch the movie and the people who make the movie. It is not the Olympics that is the soft power resource, but the opportunity for hosts and guests to meet.

Virtue, Virtuosity, Metapower, and Soft Power

Gallarotti and Naren Chitty also address the relationship aspect of soft power. When soft power audiences perceive virtue and virtuosity (Chitty 2017b) in the soft power producer, the recipients' own values and norms change, through the process of endearment and emulation. This Gallarotti refers to as a *metapower*. The soft power performer and audiences are embedded in a social relationship. There is a convergence of producer and audience norms and values to the point that it is no longer correct to say the audience is "following" the performance, but rather the audience is following its own adopted norms and values. Gallarotti describes this as the endogeneity of metapower (Gallarotti 2010).

In plainer language, in the education sphere this is quite a common phenomenon. Students who take classes from teachers they admire for either virtue or virtuosity or both, if all goes well, will become fond of their teachers and may emulate their norms and values. Over time, these norms and values become the students' own. Calling them simply "followers" of their teacher ignores the contribution of the students' own experience and relationships that inform their values. In time, the students may become teachers themselves. This example further clarifies that from the beginning the interests and proclivities of the students also influence the teachers. The social relationship in which the exchange is embedded is reciprocal. Further, it may be the case that teachers unwilling to accept the reciprocal nature of the relationship may find their influence reduced.

These ideas go beyond Nye's soft power framework to address the soft power audience's state of mind and behavioral response. While inspiring respect and admiration are important, virtue and virtuosity inspiring endearment and emulation is the sign that soft power relationships are developing. These are relationships that are reciprocal; they are dialogs among individuals and among communities. The Soft Power Rubric emphasizes the agency of all parties in the soft power relationship and brings forward the data that show how individuals act based on their views of foreign countries.

In general Nye is focused on the country seeking to influence, the soft power producer. However, the test of whether soft power has influence is not in the mindset or the actions of the producer but rather in the mindset and the actions of the receiver, or as is often said in the study of communications, the audience. The soft power producer performs, but the mark of whether the performance was successful is determined by the reaction of the audience. Beyond Nye's concerns are several other considerations that are important to understanding how soft power works.

Virtue and Virtuosity

Soft power is in the minds of the audience, not in the control of the soft power producer. Chitty (2017a, 2019; Wang and Chitty 2021) argues when a soft power producer's performance has virtue or virtuosity, then the audience may feel endearment and aspire to emulation. Chitty discusses a range of virtues that can be relevant. Aristotle identifies some as courage, gentleness, and justice; Machiavelli, justice and charity; Montesquieu, love of republic, moderation, and frugality. Chitty also points out composite virtues like civic, corporate, and military to refer to ideals held by communities. Virtues he holds up as particularly relevant to soft power are the ones important in citizen-to-citizen relationships across countries. These include listening, engaging in dialog, exchanging for mutual benefit, cooperating, and eschewing violence and coercion. When an audience perceives a soft power producer to have values that resonate with their own worldview, the audience feels contentment. A virtuosic performance embodies excellence of craft or technique, which also generates contentment in the audience.

Not all forms of persuasion are ethically identical, and when it comes to power in the international system, there is an important distinction between legitimacy and illegitimacy. For example, some scholars argue that the anti-Americanism that emerged after the end of the Cold War is due to the perception that US use of power is illegitimate. Ruth Grant's (2006) work provides a conceptual framework to evaluate legitimacy by differentiating ethical from unethical persuasion in the use of power. The same use of force may be perceived as either just or tyrannical depending on whether its exercise is considered ethical or unethical, as shown in Table 2.2. Similarly, the same persuasion campaign may be perceived as either rational or fraudulent, depending on whether it is considered ethical or unethical.

To have a choice, Grant argues, is not the same as to act autonomously, the latter of which depends on legitimacy and character. This affects how to view the voluntariness of a person or a people in being persuaded or participating in an exchange (Grant 2006). Calleo in *Follies of Power* (2009) argues that after the breakup of the Soviet Union, the world was multipolar—Japan was an economic power, Europeans successfully formed a single community, and China and India had developed their own political and economic identities. The United States was never the sole superpower, a belief he calls "the unipolar fantasy" (Calleo 2009). The wars the United States waged abroad, then, were not the "just wars" of American rhetoric, at the top of Table 2.2, but rather conquest and tyranny in the eyes of other countries.

Endearment and Emulation

Endearment and emulation are two manifestations of soft power in Gallarotti's idea of cosmopolitan power—a framework that draws on the competing political theory models of realism, liberalism, and constructivism. Endearment and emulation both evoke emotion and attachment by the audience country to the soft power producer. Like Chitty's virtue and virtuosity, Gallarotti's endearment and emulation are the audience's state of mind when contemplating the producer's performance.

Endearment parallels Chitty's contentment. Gallarotti describes the audience as feeling endearment to a producer's performance when it is attractive and charming, a reaction more emotionally weighted than simple respect or admiration. In international relations, endearment is important because it might lead other countries to more readily defer or avoid confrontation.

Table 2.2 How Ethics Changes the Perception of Power

	Coercion-Force	Bargaining-Exchange	Persuasion-Speech
Ethical ↓ Unethical	Just law	Negotiation and trade	Rational discussion
	Fair fight	Incentive	Begging
	Threat of unjust force (includes unjust law)	Bribe	Flattery or shaming
	Conquest	Blackmail	Incitement
	Tyranny		Fraud

Source: Modified from Grant (2006).

Emulation may follow from endearment. Emulation is when the audience country takes the producer country as a role model and adapts their behavior accordingly. Gallarotti highlights three major examples of emulation: Britain's system of free trade, the British gold standard, and the US dollar as currency. Admiration for these British and American economic approaches led other countries to emulate them, which led to the building of international systems that favored the British and later the Americans. Again, as with endearment, emulation is a step beyond respect and admiration; it is the transformation of the self in line with the role model. Gallarotti's work points to the connection between emotion and behavior in international relations, a well-known link in psychology (Gallarotti 2010).

Psychologists know that what people do is more related to how they feel than to how they think. "Emotional prejudices felt toward racial minority outgroups are more closely related to discrimination than are beliefs and stereotypes thought about them. . . . In fact, emotional prejudices are almost as closely related to discriminatory behavior as discriminatory intentions are," report Cara Talaska, Susan Fiske, and Shelly Chaiken in their 2008 review of fifty-seven studies of racial attitude and discrimination. They show emotional prejudices are twice as closely related to racial discrimination as stereotypes and beliefs. Their review focused on how majority members view minority members in peer-reviewed studies published in English from 1957 to 2002; most are about the United States, but a few studies from outside the US are also included. In international relations, foreigners are always a minority outgroup. This suggests that for the future, work from the field of psychology may clarify our understanding of how feelings affect people's behavior toward foreigners. Two further examples—the effect of an emotionally major event and the everyday aspect of emotion in persuasion—further cement its importance in understanding soft power (Talaska, Fiske, and Chaiken 2008).

The terrorist attacks on September 11, 2001, triggered an affective wave. In the United States this wave included a spike in people's concern for their own safety, government focus on avoiding new attacks, an increase in counterterrorism spending, a relaxing of the public attitude toward civil and human rights, including torture, and a general desire for revenge (Jun 2017). Outside the United States, the affective wave is revealed in the rhetoric of not only close allies standing in sympathy but also other countries throughout the world, including expressions of sympathy from China and Russia. Conceptually, Todd Hall and Andrew Ross (2015) describe three affect pathways—top-down from leaders, horizontally via peers, and bottom-up from the grassroots. The affective wave is one form; a second form they call emergent collective solidarities. Much research on social groups starts with members' common identity and asks how they share views and emotions. Instead, Hall and Ross argue that it can be a shared, emotional experience that brings a group of people together, who otherwise do not share an identity (Hall and Ross 2015).

From a public diplomacy perspective, Wang and Chitty (2021) are explicit about the dialog at the center of soft power relationships in their study of diasporas. In their work, they address the role of the Chinese diaspora living in Australia. Instead of the "Great Wall" approach, which uses legislation and other tools to ban Chinese government influence in Australia, they support a "Great Bridge" approach, whereby communities on both sides build their social capital with one another, and in particular a "Great Stories" approach. The Great Stories approach proposes to encourage the best narratives about the Chinese diaspora experience in Australia, stories that reflect the shared values of Chinese and Australian communities, as a deliberate effort to build a sustainable relationship based on friendship and hospitality. This also places a responsibility on the Australian public to welcome first-generation immigrants interested in learning about democracy's values, practices, and processes. In effective public diplomacy, emotion is the key link between soft power resources and long-term relationships. Touching emotions are part of argument and persuasion. Individuals are emotionally connected to political communities, and if public diplomacy wants to persuade people to new beliefs, these are the emotions they need to reach.

Japan's Soft Power Rise

This chapter began with Vogel's surprise in 1975 at Japan's economic rise. Reflecting the shift in Western popular sentiment, the *Financial Times'* Nick Foulkes also admits changing his mind from a 1960s "prejudiced belief that [Japanese watchmaker] Seiko, if not exactly the work of the devil himself, had certainly involved input from such deputies as Beelzebub" to in 2014 enthusiastically backing Grand Seiko's Hi-Beat mechanical watch for a Swiss watch prize, well ahead of European watchmakers (Foulkes 2020). What happened between the 1970s and the 2020s in both scholarly and pop culture views of Japan? Fear of Japan's economic power has now faded, although Japan's economy continued to grow and Japan is more powerful now than it was then. Looking at the Soft Power Rubric in Japan, its social interactions with foreigners grew markedly, as seen in Figure 2.1. In these intervening decades, more people had the opportunity to communicate with Japanese and learn about Japan, and vice versa.

Between 2000 and 2010, the number of foreign students and foreign visitors doubled and continued to rise thereafter, even as total GDP moderated after 2010. By 2019, the Soft Power 30 index listed Japan as the eighth

Figure 2.1 Japan's GDP Growth Compared to Soft Power Rubric Indicators

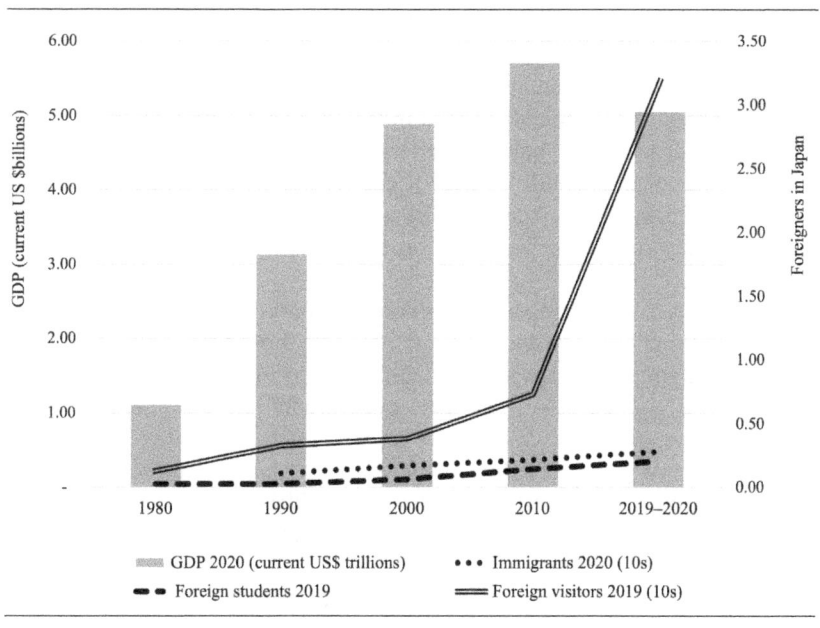

Sources: World Bank, UN Population Division, UNESCO, and UN World Tourism Organization.

most influential country in the world (McClory 2021). Even as its economic growth receded somewhat, Japan's soft power grew.

After the dissolution of the Soviet Union in 1991, there was a period of US triumph at the winning of the Cold War and the embrace of a unipolar vision. Simultaneously, there was a rise in anti-Americanism; this is the period when the French called the United States the "hyperpower," in part because of the rapid development of the internet and ubiquity of its popular culture (Védrine and Moïsi 2001). After the US invasion of Iraq in 2003, US soft power collapsed and anti-Americanism peaked. Nye responded with his book *Soft Power* (2004a), and smart power emerged as a way to articulate the need to balance between hard and soft power (Cohen, Nye, and Armitage 2007).

In the United States today, instead of Japan it is China's rise in power that is the center of policy attention. Chinese interest in soft power mobilized after 2007, when President Hu Jintao said to the Seventeenth Congress of the Chinese Communist Party that China needed to invest more in soft power. Chinese scholars and writers developed their own view of soft power and how China should develop and deploy it (Repnikova 2022). This has not only affected Chinese scholarship on soft power but spilled into US and Western scholarship assessing China's soft power, discussed further in Chapter 9, where I compare China with Russia.

Nye's work set out the importance of soft power—a noncoercive influence as important as economic and military power. Gallarotti, Chitty, and others point out that understanding soft power is more than understanding the soft power producer, but also understanding the reaction of others, the soft power audience. Marlin-Bennett, Bially Mattern, and Hayden underscore the centrality of communication and exchange in building the attraction necessary for soft power relationships to develop between producer and audience.

How do soft power relationships convert to preferred policy outcomes? Building a large military does not automatically convert to victory at war. Economic strength does not automatically convert to winning at trade negotiations. Hosting the Olympics does not automatically convert to other countries accepting your values. Nye suggests that power resources translate to relational power usually within a specific domain and for a particular outcome (2011b). Another set of scholars identified specific research questions to determine whether soft power has effects and sought out empirical data to test them. Chapter 3 discusses these several domains in which soft power relationships have influenced outcomes.

3

How Effective Is Soft Power?

A SUBSTANTIAL QUANTITATIVE RESEARCH LITERATURE NOW confirms that soft power is significant and can influence the direction of international relations. It also disabuses the notion that governments can simply command soft power at will. Soft power resources reside in civil society, in the minds of individual people, who are agents in their own right and not necessarily biddable by the state (Chitty 2023). In this section I review quantitative studies that show the channels that influence foreigners' opinions about a country, what observable actions foreigners take when they are attracted to a country, and the impact these actions can have on those foreigners' society. This review also reveals gaps in the research that are opportunities for future study.[1]

Figure 3.1 presents a map of the section and its underlying assumptions. Drawing on communications research, the country seeking to exert soft power is the producer and the target country is the audience. I first review studies that show certain actions by the producer can influence opinion in the audience, reflected by the arrow "A" in the diagram. Producer actions can include humanitarian aid, diplomatic visits, cultural programs, and related initiatives. Audience opinion in these studies is measured in public opinion polls. Second, I review studies that show the link between audience opinion and audience member action, reflected in arrow "B" in the diagram. Audience member actions can include emigrating to the producer country, visiting or studying there, watching its movies, trading or investing there, or other similar activities. Third, I discuss how audience member actions can influence norms and values in the audience country, identified on Figure 3.1 as arrow "C." Mainly, the research here focuses on the spread of democratic norms and values. Fourth, I discuss the effect that audience actions have on public opinion, and norms and values in the producer society, identified on

**Figure 3.1 Soft Power Resources:
The Relationship Between Producer and Audience**

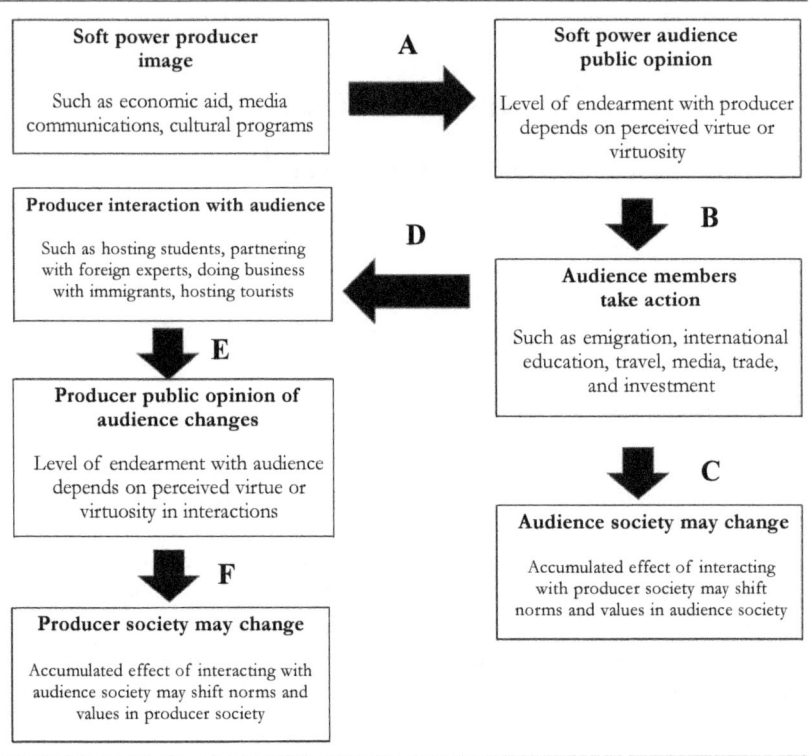

Figure 3.1 as arrows "D," "E," and "F." In the broader social science literature, outside of soft power research, there is evidence of these shifts. Finally, I address the question of measuring soft power. Using the Soft Power Rubric approach, which is built on the observable actions foreigners take when attracted to a country, is one way forward when public opinion survey data are scarce.

As discussed in Chapter 2 on soft power's history, in foreign policy, Nye (2011a, 2011b) views soft power resources as primarily a country's culture, political values, and foreign policies, when they are in turn attractive, authentic, and legitimate. Chitty theorizes that countries that exhibit virtue and virtuosity generate respect and contentment in audiences. In other words, when a country produces admirable ideas, behaviors, and objects, the audience respects the virtuosity of the skill involved and experiences contentment with the embedded virtuous values, if they affirm the audience's worldview. The soft power relationship is strongest with both respect and contentment (Chitty 2021). Similarly, Gallarotti (2010) discusses the importance of endearment, capturing the emotional as well as the material or practical attraction people of one country may have toward another. He identifies international systems like the British monetary standards of first pound sterling and later the gold standard as examples of soft power. He also emphasizes the popularity of US brands, corporations, and nongovernmental organizations as positive purveyors of American culture abroad (Gallarotti 2010). Grant's (2006) theory on ethics argues that in foreign policy the same persuasive measures are perceived differently depending on whether the persuader is seen as ethical or not, expanding on the notions of authenticity and legitimacy mentioned by Nye.

Research on culture and trust connects soft power with a broader social science literature on collective action, where people set aside their individual concerns to act for the greater good, a particular form of cooperation discussed further in Chapter 4. Fine (2012) reminds us that we create and perform culture as we interact with each other. His term, "tiny publics," builds on Alexis de Tocqueville's notion of "minute associations," small groups of people—like a book club or a team of video gamers—who work together, hold common values, share a past, and look forward to a future (Fine 2012). Ostrom's (2003, 2005) work emphasizes that people create trust through a series of reciprocal actions. She investigates how people with a common resource to share—like water or land—govern themselves successfully for the group's overall benefit. Ostrom's conception of "trust" is not simply an act of faith but a choice based on experience and self-interest (Ostrom 2003). Social science theory shows that small interactions accumulated over time build both culture—shared social meaning—and trust—the social basis for collective action. The aim of countries with soft power is to create the shared social meaning and trust that will lead to political cooperation.

The challenge of quantitative work is that in order to fashion a hypothesis that can be tested concretely with data, big ideas are reduced to very specific variables, and the complexity of the international system has to be reduced to a single scenario. These scholars examine whether changing the variables before yields different results after. More sophisticated studies run several variations of a single scenario. While in the scholarship of ideas, discussed earlier, the weakness is that no idea is really proved or disproved, the weakness in quantitative work is that sometimes it is too narrow to draw general conclusions that could actually be applied in policymaking. In this section, I review the quantitative literature with an eye to its applicability and ability to offer insight into real world politics. From the broad range of published scholarly work, I have selected those where the scenarios are close to real life experience and the variables connect to datasets large enough to encompass a wide range of countries and, therefore, speak to the international, not a regional or local, system. Unlike theory, which often has an evergreen quality to it, quantitative work can be disproved; therefore, reviewing it requires updating. This section presents a sample of the best work to date.

What Influences Public Opinion About Foreign Countries?

Many scholars rely on foreign public opinion data as a measure of soft power. There are several quantitative studies that address the factors that influence foreign public opinion. Three such factors are direct social interaction with foreigners, effective and visible foreign aid, and credibility in foreign policy.

Direct Social Interaction Improves Foreign Public Opinion

A survey of about 1,000 people in each of fourteen countries assessed the impact of US military presence on public opinion about the United States. The survey responders indicated whether they had personal contact with US military personnel, whether a friend or family member had contact with US military personnel, whether they personally benefited economically from US military presence, and whether a friend or family member benefited economically from US military presence—questions that assessed their opinion of US military forces in their country, of the US government, and of the US people. The results showed that having network contact with US military personnel increases the likelihood of a more positive attitude toward US military, government, and people, but direct contact is even more effective. Those who benefit economically are more positive toward the government, but not toward the military or US people. While it is possible that people who have contact with the US military are predisposed to like Americans, the authors also argue that people with the largest grievances also select to interact with the military (Allen et al. 2020).

Effective, Visible Aid Programs Improve Foreign Public Opinion

An analysis of the impact of the US President's Emergency Plan for AIDS Relief (PEPFAR) shows a positive effect on public opinion of the United States. PEPFAR comprised approximately 15 percent of the US development aid budget and is widely viewed as an effective public health program. Goldsmith and Horiuchi examine data on PEPFAR aid to seventy-nine countries for four years, from 2007 through 2010. The input variable is the amount of PEPFAR funds per capita in each recipient country. Other factors that were also considered were total US foreign aid, GDP per capita, World Bank governance indicator, Freedom House civil liberties score, whether the country is in Africa, imports and exports with the United States, and UN voting with the United States (Goldsmith, Horiuchi, and Wood 2014).

The results were that higher PEPFAR funding per capita is significantly correlated with public opinion approval of the United States. Doubling PEPFAR per capita funding for a recipient country increases by about 30 percent the approval/disapproval ratio. In other words, if the "approve" percentage was initially 40 percent, doubling PEPFAR per capita would increase it to 52 percent. PEPFAR was selected for analysis because the research literature identifies it as a program that has several important characteristics:

- Targeted at a widely understood need
- Delivered over a sustained period of time
- Effective
- Highly visible as a US government program

The results suggest that foreign aid programs with these characteristics can have a positive impact on a foreign country's public opinion of the United States, which is an important aspect of soft power (Goldsmith, Horiuchi, and Wood 2014).

This research resonates with the theory on trust by Ostrom (2001) and other scholars that more frequent, direct social interaction is likely to result in a more positive relationship, which is the theoretical foundation of the Soft Power Rubric. It is also consistent with Atkinson's (2006, 2014) empirical work on education discussed later in this chapter. When foreigners have an opportunity to interact directly, regularly, over time with people from another country, they are more likely to be open to that country's values.

Foreign Policy Credibility Amplifies or Undermines Public Diplomacy

The credibility of US foreign policy relates to foreign public opinion of the United States. Foreign public opinion about the United States was compared before and after a visit by the US president or US secretary of state, between 2001 and 2006. Goldsmith and Horiuchi collect their public opinion data from ten survey questions from nineteen studies conducted in sixty-one countries by six organizations: BBC World Service, Chicago Council on Global Affairs, Gallup International, German Marshall Fund of the United States, GlobeScan with the Program on International Policy Attitudes, and Pew Research Center for the People and the Press (Goldsmith and Horiuchi 2009).

To assess the credibility of US foreign policy, they searched the Factiva database for articles on the United States and terms like trust, legitimacy, and credibility. They divide the timeframe 2001 to 2006 into three periods, summarized quantitatively in Table 3.1.

- From 2001 to the invasion of Iraq in March 2003, US foreign policy is credible. In the Factiva database, there were very few and only sporadic articles on the United States and credibility. High-level visits increased positive public opinion of the United States and decreased negative public opinion.
- March 2003 to April 2004 when the Abu Ghraib prison scandal broke, US foreign policy is controversial. There are regularly around five or fewer articles on the credibility of the United States. High-level visits increased positive opinion only a little and had almost no effect on reducing negative public opinion.
- April 2004 to December 2006, US foreign policy is noncredible. There are regularly at least ten and often around twenty-five articles on the United States and credibility. High-level visits actually decreased positive public opinion and exacerbated negative public opinion.

Goldsmith and Horiuchi's final conclusion is that high-level visits by the president and secretary of state can have a significant impact on foreign public opinion of the United States; when US credibility is high, the impact can be positive. As their 2012 article shows, positive opinion of US foreign policy on major issues can lead to cooperation. However, when the United States is not credible, then high-level visits may have little or even negative effect on public opinion (Goldsmith and Horiuchi 2009). This work empirically supports Grant's theory discussed in Chapter 2 that the same persuasive measures are perceived differently depending on whether the persuader is seen as ethical or not. Here, the roughly similar high-level visits from US officials generate different responses depending on how credible the United States is seen as being (Grant 2006).

Like the 2012 article, this research is also focused on a narrow time period during the administration of President George W. Bush and Secre-

Table 3.1 Foreign Public Opinion Response to US High-Level Visits

Time Period	Perception of US Foreign Policy	Positive Public Response	Negative Public Response
2001–March 2003	Credible	+8.20%	−16.83%
March 2003–April 2004	Controversial	+2.42%	−0.07%
April 2004–December 2006	Noncredible	−1.07%	+2.95%

tary of State Colin Powell. Furthermore, the authors note that by gathering opinion data collected by six different organizations, there is less likelihood that any bias in a single organization would affect the results, but also, at a practical level, bringing together data in a consistent way is more challenging (Goldsmith and Horiuchi 2009).

As Grant (2006) predicts, Goldsmith and Horiuchi's data show the roughly similar high-level visits from US officials generate different responses depending on how credible the United States is seen to be. This also resonates with Chitty's (2017a) thesis that virtue, or lack thereof, is an important element of attraction. Ethics and virtue matter in soft power politics.

These studies show that foreign policy credibility, effective and visible foreign aid, and direct social interaction with foreigners are factors that improve foreign public opinion about the United States. There is room for further studies on countries other than the United States. Also, there are other factors that are no doubt also important influences of public opinion. One of the major constraints of this work is data on foreign public opinion. The United States is one of the most asked about countries in these surveys; more resources should be devoted to regular polling of public opinion on other countries as well.

What Are the Benefits of Soft Power Relationships?

Quantitative, empirical research shows that countries with soft power win more cooperation from and increased trade with other countries. Further, they attract more students, tourists, and foreign direct investment. This dynamic is reflected in Figure 3.1 as arrow "B." The accumulated results of these studies develop a short list of quantifiable, observable behaviors that reflect foreigners' opinion of a country's attractiveness. In the absence of direct public opinion polling, such behaviors can be used as a proxy to assess soft power.

Commercial and Business Benefits

Datta's book *Anti-Americanism and the Rise of World Opinion: Consequences for the US National Interest* (2014) includes a chapter on America as a brand. In the earlier literature review of ideas, one paradox that scholars like Ellwood and Védrine identify is that even when foreigners disagree with US foreign policy, they eagerly consume American popular culture (Ellwood 2012; Védrine and Moïsi 2001). Datta brings quantitative tools to bear for the period before, during, and after the George W. Bush administration (2000–2008), when anti-Americanism was high. He collects data on favorable opinions of the United States from several sources, including US

Information Agency Record Group 306, Pew Research Center, and Zogby International. There are 198 country-year observations for 2002–2011 across thirty-three countries. For this dataset, the mean for favorable opinion of the United States is 64 percent; the countries included lean pro-American (Datta 2014).

In particular, he analyzes the growth of Coca-Cola and Starbucks, two well-known US brands. For Coca-Cola, he has data on cases of soda sold for seventeen countries in four regions of the world: the Americas, Western Europe, Eastern Europe, and Asia. For Starbucks, he has data on the number of coffee shops in eleven countries in four regions of the world: the Middle East, Northeast Asia, Southeast Asia, and Western Europe. Holding other potential variables constant—such as GDP per capita, population size, or whether the country is primarily Muslim—there is no correlation between good public opinion of the United States and growth for either Coca-Cola or Starbucks. These two companies' growth appears immune to widespread anti-Americanism (Datta 2014).

As a comparison, Datta runs a similar analysis on two other economic activities—visiting the United States and studying abroad in the United States. By contrast, there is a significant correlation between a country's favorable view of the United States and whether its people visit or study there. Datta's data on visitors and their spending are from the US Office of Travel and Tourism Industries in the US Department of Commerce, covering 102 countries from 1985 to 2011. Datta finds there are several factors that influence whether people visit the United States, including the exchange rate, GDP per capita, and whether the country is part of the US visa waiver program. He concludes that if a country has a 10 percent increase in favorable opinion of the United States, there is a 6 percent increase in arrivals and a 6 percent increase in spending (Datta 2014).

Datta's analysis on education draws from the Institute for International Education's Open Door data from 1994 to 2011 for twenty-two countries. A 10 percent increase in favorable attitude toward the United States in a country predicts a 5 percent increase in student arrivals. Another factor that correlates to an increase in students going to the United States is if the country has a higher GDP per capita. Whether a country is Muslim has no correlation, but whether a student is from Europe has a negative correlation. Datta points out that the number of foreign students going to Great Britain increased significantly in this timeframe (Datta 2014).

Datta goes further with a qualitative investigation of the reasons behind the popularity of Starbucks and Coca-Cola in spite of rising anti-Americanism. He interviews both diplomats and representatives of Starbucks and Coca-Cola. The diplomats' views draw out the common phenomenon that foreign publics are happy to buy US brands even when they disagree with US policy. The businesspeople emphasized that both Starbucks and Coca-

Cola are products embedded in the local economies, and the products themselves are modified and targeted to local tastes.

Trade Benefits

The work of economist Andrew Rose shows that the more soft power a country has, the more it exports. His 2016 article, "Like Me, Buy Me: The Effect of Soft Power on Exports," and 2018 book chapter, "Soft Power, Sanctions, and Exports: Checking the BS in BDS," use public opinion data that asks people their views of other countries as either a mainly positive or negative influence in the world, and trade data from the International Monetary Fund.

The 2016 study concludes that if an importer perceives an exporting country to be a positive influence in the world, then the importer buys more from that country, holding constant other factors such as common language, common land border, membership in the same regional trade agreement or currency union, and a former colonial relationship. The 2016 study uses data from the BBC GlobeScan survey released by the Program on International Policy Attitudes and the University of Maryland. In 2006, the survey asked people in thirty-three countries their views of eight countries and Europe on whether they were mainly positive or negative influences in the world. Every year, the surveyed countries and the questions about countries varies. In the period 2006 to 2013, people from a total of forty-six countries were asked their views of a total of seventeen countries, for a total of around 2,700 observations. With some technical reservations, Rose concludes that a 1 percent increase in perceived positive influence raises exports by about 0.8 percent (Rose 2016).

Rose's 2019 study expands this work to compare the effectiveness of soft power with sanctions. His work on the effect of soft power expands in time; it now covers 1998 through 2013, continuing to rely on the BBC GlobeScan survey. Again, in total the survey asks people in up to forty-six countries whether up to seventeen countries are mainly positive or negative influences in the world. More specific than the 2016 study, in his 2018 work Rose shows that there are four country outliers. US and Russian exports are less affected by foreign opinion; Israel and North Korea's exports are much more affected by foreign opinion than most countries. Adding a new perspective to the work, Rose considers the effect of sanctions on exports, drawing on a 1998–2005 dataset on general sanctions, threatened sanctions, and economic sanctions. Rose's work shows that the effect of sanctions on exports is less than the effect of soft power, measured as public opinion (Rose 2019).

These articles by Rose illustrate how quantitative work builds and changes over time. The data show that there is a correlation between positive public opinion and greater trade between nations. While the relationship is not necessarily causal, it is stronger than competing correlations between trade and common language, trade and common regional trading area, among other factors. Beyond the scope of Rose's work is *why*. Why does soft power relate to trade more than sanctions, which are designed specifically to impact trade? What are the channels by which one influences the other? There is room for more work for others to do.

Social, Cultural, Economic, and Political Benefits

All the research discussed so far used public opinion surveys as evidence of US soft power, or lack of it, in other countries, but are there other ways to measure soft power? In general, soft power resources are those aspects of society that make it attractive to others—not foreign opinion, but the conditions or characteristics that lead to foreign opinion. Singh and MacDonald's (2017) study undertaken for the British Council identifies quantitative measures of society (e.g., level of democracy and GDP) as measures of soft power resources and tests for correlations with activities of foreigners (e.g., visits and foreign investment) that reflect their interest and attraction. Another goal of this study is to combine into one series of models the political, cultural, and economic dimensions of soft power attraction from 2000 to 2012 for forty-four countries, all members of the G20 and the European Union plus Switzerland. In their models, the soft power input variables include (1) political, such as the level of democracy, political and civil liberties, and foreign aid; (2) economic, such as GDP per capita and military expenditure as percentage of GDP; and (3) cultural such as cultural goods exports, literacy levels, and the number of its cultural institutions. The results indicators include (1) social, such as incoming international students; (2) cultural, such as incoming international tourists and expenditure; (3) economic, like foreign direct investment; and (4) political, such as voting in the UN General Assembly. The results are an assessment of the soft power attractions of the forty-four countries:

- To attract international students, the most important factors were democracy, GDP per capita and total GDP, cultural institutions, and internet users.
- To attract international tourists, the most important factors were whether the host country's cultural institutions had a presence in the tourist's home country, GDP per capita and total GDP, and internet users.
- To attract foreign direct investment, the most important factors were per capita GDP, population size, and cultural institutions. Every 1 percent increase in the number of outreach countries engaged by national cultural institutions correlates with a 0.66 percent increase in foreign direct investment.

- To increase political influence as measured by UN General Assembly voting, greater freedom of political rights and a country's cultural rank in the Good Country Index have the greatest correlation. If a country is in the top fifteen of the Good Country Index, then its political influence increases by 0.52 percent, which is greater than other factors in the model. The other influential factor is greater freedom in political rights, more than overall levels of democracy.

Overall, to attract more foreign students, tourists, foreign direct investment, and friendlier UN General Assembly voting, the main factors are greater democracy, economic prosperity, and international cultural institutions that are networked with other countries (Singh and MacDonald 2017).

This research addresses two policy-relevant questions: the position of China and suggestions for the United Kingdom. First, the report shows that China has invested unusually heavily in promoting its soft power; however, the returns so far are limited. With regard to the United Kingdom, it has amassed significant soft power assets over time—especially through its institutions and their international networks; however, its departure from the European Union has sent a signal that it may not be as open and welcoming a society as before (Singh and MacDonald 2017).

Political Benefits

If a country has the support of foreign opinion, then on certain big picture issues there are definite political benefits. To measure US soft power, Goldsmith and Horiuchi used data from three polls that asked people their opinion of US foreign policy, conducted in 2002–2003: Voice of the People included 27,000 people in thirty-seven countries; the Gallup International Iraq Poll 2003 included 28,000 people in forty countries; and the Gallup International Post-War Iraq Poll 2003 included 34,000 people in forty-five countries (Goldsmith and Horiuchi 2012).

They chose three foreign policy issues of importance to the United States: (1) joining US military forces in Iraq; (2) whether to enter into a bilateral immunity agreement with the United States, which protects certain US interests should issues arise in the International Criminal Court;[2] and (3) the proportion of voting decisions in the UN General Assembly that agreed with the United States in 2003. These three issues differ in their salience in public debate. To measure salience, Goldsmith and Horiuchi counted the number of articles on each topic in the world politics sections of the Factiva news database between May and December 2003. For example, in December 2003, there were over 2,000 articles on the Iraq War, around 250 on the International Criminal Court, and around 100 on the UN General Assembly (Goldsmith and Horiuchi 2012).

Table 3.2 captures their results. From the surveys, public opinion on US foreign policy was available from a total of fifty-eight countries. Countries with the highest opinion of US foreign policy included Albania, the Dominican Republic, and the Philippines; countries with the lowest opinion included France, Vietnam, and Türkiye.

On the most salient issue, countries with a high opinion of US foreign policy were far more likely to send troops to join the United States in Iraq. On the issue of middle salience, high opinion countries were more likely to support the US position on the International Criminal Court and have a bilateral immunity agreement with the United States. On the issue of least salience, public opinion on US foreign policy had little correlation with whether the country voted consistently with the United States in the UN General Assembly (Goldsmith and Horiuchi 2012).

Goldsmith and Horiuchi's final conclusion is that foreign public opinion is important mainly when issues are controversial and highly visible in the media, such as the question of whether to join US troops in Iraq. The weakness of the study is that the data are on very specific issues only during the period 2002 and 2003. The result is a correlation between public opinion and foreign policy, which is not a claim of causation. Both factors suggest caution in overgeneralizing results. However, viewed from today, the invasion of Iraq in 2003 is an event of primary importance in US foreign policy this century, and this analysis of foreign opinion covering nearly 80,000 people in fifty-eight countries is a major contribution to the field (Goldsmith and Horiuchi 2012).

Goldsmith and Horiuchi provide a roadmap for analytical tools that are available to any policymaker. First, their work shows it is reasonable to use public opinion data as an important factor in a country's willingness to cooperate with the United States. Second, they show how a news database—in this case Factiva—can be used to assess the salience of a foreign policy issue (2012) and the credibility of the United States (Goldsmith and Horiuchi 2009). Both are tools that policymakers can use in

Table 3.2 Effect of Foreign Public Opinion on US Foreign Policy Goals

Opinion of US Foreign Policy	Join US in Sending Troops to Iraq	Bilateral Immunity Agreement (BIA) with US for the International Criminal Court	Percentage of UN General Assembly Votes Consistent with US Vote
Top 29 countries	55% countries sent troops	31% countries have BIA	52% countries consistent
Bottom 29 countries	21% countries sent troops	10% countries have BIA	51% countries consistent

their daily work to add a quantitative, empirically based perspective to their analysis.

Rose and Goldsmith and Horiuchi both use foreign public opinion as their measure of soft power. Datta instead examines consumer spending, international travel, and international education as evidence of soft power influence. In a contrasting parallel argument, Singh and MacDonald look at the fundamentals of what attracts foreigners (democratic freedoms, per capita wealth, and cultural development) and how this affects their observed behavior (students, tourists, investments, and political decisions). All these scholars use overlapping indicators of soft power "success," political cooperation at the UN or other situations, attracting tourists and students, and bringing in trade and investment

Soft Power Influence Flows in Many Directions

In Figure 3.1, arrow "C" illustrates that foreign audience interaction with the "producer" country may influence the foreign audience society. A robust set of quantitative studies shows that when students go abroad to train in foreign democracies, their origin countries experience an improvement in democratic institutions in later years. Emerging studies seek to draw a similar connection with migration.

Countries with a Lot of Students Studying Abroad in Democracies Will Themselves Become More Democratic

Spilimbergo (2009) shows that when democratic countries educate foreign students, democratic political norms later develop more strongly in the students' origin countries. His quantitative study is based on UNESCO's international student data covering 183 countries from 1960 to 2005 and the Freedom House Political Rights Index. No other comparable study uses a dataset with this broad geographic scope and expansive time series. The input variables include democracy level in the student's sending country, the number of students abroad as percentage of the sending country population, and host country democracy level. The results variable is democracy level in the student's sending country five years later. To explore whether other factors explain democracy levels in the sending country better than the input variables, Spilimbergo also tested for democracy in neighboring countries, educational attainment, democracy in trading partners, and GDP per capita (Spilimbergo 2009).

The results are, for a sending country, if all its students abroad are hosted in democracies, then in the next five years its democracy index will increase by 25 percent. If half of a sending country's students abroad are hosted in a democracy, then its democracy index will increase by 8 percent in the next five years (Spilimbergo 2009).

To add further detail to this general result, in the paper's appendix, Spilimbergo provides specific country results for Chile, South Korea, Argentina, and Iran, showing when large percentages of students study abroad in democratic or nondemocratic countries, the sending country's political system shifts accordingly within years. Excerpted from the article is Figure 3.2 on Chile, a democracy before the 1972 coup and then again in the 1980s, as shown by the hyphenated line. The solid line shows that Chile's students who went abroad in the 1960s went to less democratic countries, and then shifted to more democratic countries in the 1970s, and sharply more in the 1980s (Spilimbergo 2009).

The strength of Spilimbergo's work is that it definitively establishes the relationship between democracy in the student's host country and democracy development in the student's sending country. Spilimbergo points out that while his work focuses on democracy, other kinds of regimes, including socialist and Islamic governments, have also followed a similar pattern of training young people with the goal of fostering likeminded countries with shared values. Further work is needed to show whether Spilimbergo's findings apply to political values generally or to democracy only. The other potential weakness is that students when selecting host countries for foreign study may embody political trends already present in the sending country. In other words, the fact that many students from a country choose to go to democratic countries may be a signal of political trends, and these trends may be the cause of political change, not the students' period of study abroad (Spilimbergo 2009). Further works by other scholars may shed light on this puzzle.

Western-Educated Leaders Are More Likely to Democratize

Pol Pot was educated in France, but instead of democratizing Cambodia, he established one of the fiercest genocidal regimes in modern history. The US Army's School of the Americas trained foreign soldiers and police, many of whom participated in torture, murder, and political oppression in Latin America (Gill 2004). There are many serious examples of Western-educated leaders who do not democratize, but what is the bigger picture? Gift and Krcmaric (2017) find that in the big picture, Western-educated leaders on the whole are more likely to democratize.

Their model relies on the Archigos dataset, which covers the entry and exit of world leaders in 188 countries. For those leaders in power after World War II for at least three years, Gift and Krcmaric find there are 566 total leader spells, of which 109 are Western-educated, 235 are non-Western-educated, and 222 had no higher education. Other factors in the model that

Figure 3.2 Percentage of Students from Chile Abroad in Democratic Host Countries Compared with Democratic Levels at Home in Chile

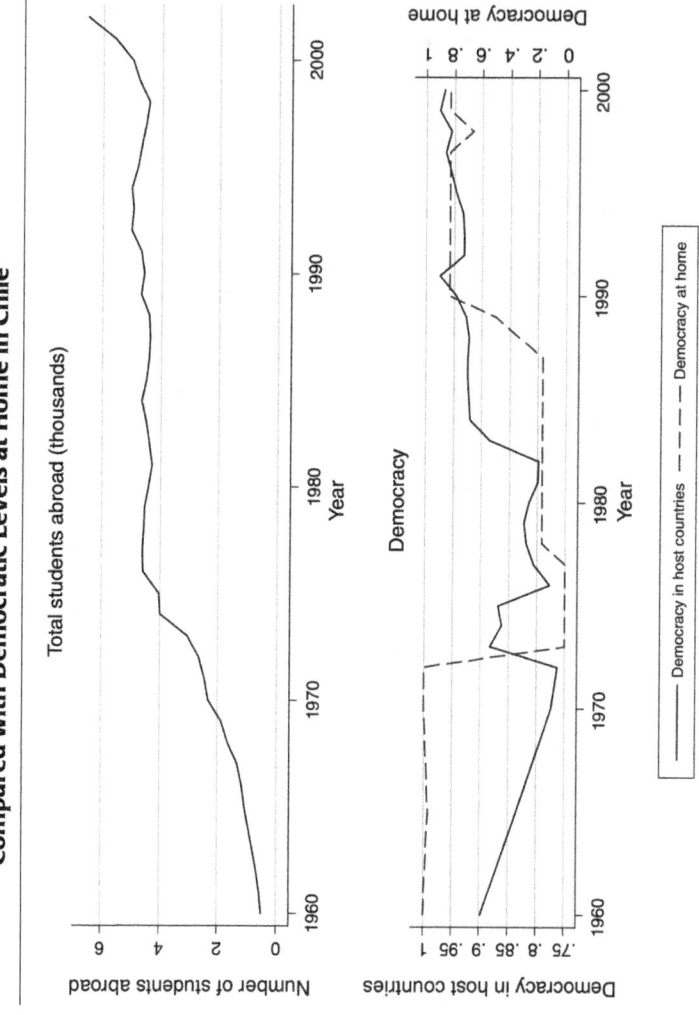

Source: Antonio Spilimbergo, "Democracy and Foreign Education," *American Economic Review* 99(1): 533. Copyright 2009 *American Economic Association*; reproduced with permission.

could explain the tendency to democratize included economic development, inequality, ethnic fractionalization, Protestantism, former British colony, US ally, aggregate student flows to democracies, executive constraints, and pre-existing democracy. Even taking into consideration these other possible factors, they still find that having a Western education statistically significantly predicts a leader improving democracy. The policy implication is that while there are always important and significant historical examples where students trained in democracies go home to oppress their people, a broad, quantitative analysis shows leaders who are trained in foreign democratic countries on the whole bring democratic norms home (Gift and Krcmaric 2017).

Training That Includes Extensive Socialization Heightens the Influence of Sending Country Norms

Atkinson's (2014) study shows that countries sending foreign military officers to US war and staff colleges also improve democratic norms in sending countries. Unlike the civilian students in the Spilimbergo study, many foreign military officers in Atkinson's study represent highly authoritarian political regimes with a vested interest in maintaining power. Her input factors include participating in US military exchanges, status as a former colony, economic development, and how long the regime has been in power. Atkinson runs her model for two sets of results. Her first results are measured by the Polity IV dataset, which includes 169 countries from 1972 to 2006, resulting in over 5,000 country-year observations. Polity IV categorizes regimes as coherent democracy, middle-ground regime, or coherent autocracy. Her results show that autocratic and middle-ground countries that participate in US military exchanges were more likely to acquire democratic political institutions than those that did not. For "coherent autocracies," such as South Korea, Mali, Paraguay, and Portugal, those that sent officers to US military exchanges were 2.8 times more likely to democratize than autocratic countries that did not (Atkinson 2014).

Her second set of results uses the Cingranelli-Richards indices, which cover data for 195 countries. These indices measure the degree to which governments respect citizens' physical integrity by not torturing, murdering, imprisoning for political reasons, or making them disappear, and respect basic empowerment freedoms including movement, speech, religion, political participation, and workers' rights. Her results show that countries that participate in US military exchanges are more likely to have a positive, systematic effect on government's respect for basic freedoms, but no significant impact on respect for citizens' physical integrity (Atkinson 2014).

Atkinson earlier undertook work to compare the effect of US military exchanges with civilian programs at US universities. Using a similar model for data 1980–2000, she finds that whereas countries participating in US military exchanges increased empowerment rights by nearly 8 percent, civilian exchanges increased by 2 percent. Further, she identifies reasons for the difference. First, US military exchanges are structured for extensive social interaction with Americans compared to civilian programs, which are less structured. Second, military officers have a high sense of common, professional identity that crosses national lines, which strengthens the socialization process. Third, military officers selected by their governments to train in the United States are likely to return to elite positions of responsibility and have greater, immediate influence (Atkinson 2006).

Going beyond only quantitative analysis, Atkinson also conducts a survey of graduates of five military academies: Air University, Army Command and General Staff College, Army War College, Marine Corps University, and National Defense University, including both US and foreign graduates. Their stories identify the major channels of influence that explain how studying in the United States can lead to more democratic approaches at home. This is discussed in more detail in Chapter 7 on international education and Australia.

The work on international education as a soft power resource that influences political norms in students' sending countries is mostly focused on the transfer of democracy. Whether this would apply to other kinds of political regimes is possible, but as of yet, under-researched. The Spilimbergo and Gift and Krcmaric works do not address whether students who choose to study in democracies abroad are predisposed to accept democratic norms even before they leave home. From a practical perspective for policymakers, the implication is that if there is high demand among foreign students to train in your universities, welcoming more of them will likely increase your country's soft power. However, if there is no queue of people applying for student visas, simply recruiting more will not necessarily have the same soft power effect. Atkinson's research mitigates this concern, however, because she observes the rise in democratic institutions in even authoritarian countries when they send military officers for US training.

Migrants to Democratic Countries May Transmit Political Norms Back to Their Sending Countries

A growing set of research shows that when democratic countries attract migrants, there may be several channels through which the migrants' origin countries also develop stronger democratic norms. Unlike the research in international education where there are comprehensive studies covering large numbers of countries across long periods of time, in the migration area, the quantitative research is in earlier stages focused on specific points in time and particular sets of countries. However, the evidence is building and there are several insightful works.

Beine and Sekkat's 2013 article "Skilled Migration and the Transfer of Institutional Norms" argues that when people from around the world emigrate to Organisation of Economic Co-operation and Development (OECD) countries, the governance of their sending countries improves—and this is especially the case if the emigrants are skilled. They include migration data for 1990 and 2000 covering all sending countries and thirty destination countries, members of the OECD. They also include governance data for 1994 and 2004 covering voice and accountability, which includes citizens' ability to select their government; political stability; government effectiveness, which includes the quality of the civil service; and regulatory quality, which includes the ability to implement policies that promote private sector development, rule of law, and control of corruption.

In Beine and Sekkat's modeling, a country that has more total emigrants to OECD countries is likely to have its institutions improve on all governance indicators except voice and accountability. If the sending country's migrants are skilled, this result is intensified. This is an interesting insight given the limitations of looking at just two years of data. Further work to clarify why "voice and accountability" does not change and why skilled migration may have more of an impact would be useful. As for how emigrants influence their sending country's political norms, there is a body of research examining specific country cases and timeframes that is offering useful ideas (Beine and Sekkat 2013).

Transnational households—families with at least one member who lives in another country—tend to have more conversations about politics in the home country and the destination country, shows Crow and Pérez-Armendariz's "Talk Without Borders: Why Political Discussion Makes Latin Americans with Relatives Abroad More Critical of Their Democracies" (2018). Their data come from the AmericasBarometer survey, which asks respondents to assess democracy in their own country on (1) how democratic it is, (2) whether they are satisfied that democracy is working, and (3) pride in their political system. It also asks if they have a family member abroad and how often they communicate; if they do have a family member abroad, is that relative in the (1) United States, (2) United States and other countries, or (3) other than the United States. These three sets of questions for 2006–2008 for twenty Latin American countries produce 28,000 observations (Crow and Pérez-Armendáriz 2018).

The results show that for Latin American households, the effect of having a transnational member in the United States compared to households with no transnational members is a

- 4.6 percent negative swing on satisfaction with democracy in their own country
- 3.2 percent negative swing on evaluation of democracy in their own country

- 6.5 percent negative swing on pride in one's own political system

There are no large effects for transnational households with family members abroad in the other two categories. Their conclusions show that emigration can affect the governance of the sending country through the channel of transnational family discussions about politics, especially if the destination country is the United States (Crow and Pérez-Armendáriz 2018).

Morocco's returnee migrants from Western countries are more likely to demand political change in Morocco than nonmigrants or returnee migrants from non-Western countries, and localities in Morocco with a high share of return migrants are more likely to have participated in the 2011 elections, according to Tuccio, Wahba, and Hamdouch's (2019) "International Migration as a Driver of Political and Social Change: Evidence from Morocco." The data on political attitudes come from a Moroccan government ministry survey conducted in August to October 2013 of 1,200 households, about a quarter of which had no migrants, about half had one or more members abroad currently, a quarter had returnee family members, and the remainder were foreign households. The survey asked several questions related to political norms, including, "Are you happy about how Morocco is administered?," "I think we should defend the traditional lifestyle in Morocco," and "We need to make more effort in order to treat everybody equally." The results show that returnees from Western countries are more likely to want change compared to returnees from non-Western countries or nonmigrants. Among households with current migrant abroad, there is less demand for political and social change; many current migrants are in Arab countries where political institutions and accountability are low (Tuccio, Wahba, and Hamdouch 2019). Typical Western country destinations include France, Belgium, Germany, the Netherlands, Spain, and Italy; non-Western, Libya and the Gulf. The survey also asks about open-mindedness; the responses show that returnees from Western countries are not more open-minded than other groups, which suggests that they are not predisposed to demand political change (Tuccio, Wahba, and Hamdouch 2019). Further data on political norms come from Morocco's census and the 2011 World Values Survey. The survey of 1,100 people asks whether they have confidence in the government. Districts with a greater share of return migrants are less likely to have confidence in the government (Tuccio, Wahba, and Hamdouch 2019). Data on voting behavior combine census data with Afrobarometer's Round 5 survey, which included 1,200 people in 2013 and asked whether they voted in the 2011 election. The November 2011 elections had been scheduled after pressure from large-scale demonstrations across the region during the "Arab Spring" earlier that year. The results show that people living in areas with more return migrants are more likely to have voted in the election (Tuccio, Wahba, and Hamdouch 2019). In summary, while returnees from Western countries are not likely to be more open-minded than other groups, they are more likely to have less confidence in the Moroccan government, to have voted in the 2011 election, and to demand political and social change.

These three studies represent the kind of work underway now in the area of migration and change in political norms. They build a picture of how migration can affect political attitudes and behavior in the home country. Baudassé, Bazillier, and Issifou (2018) provide a fuller review of this literature. While migration definitely has an effect, important variables include the politics of the destination as compared to the home country and the closeness and communication between the individuals with migrant experience and their community in the home country (Baudassé, Bazillier, and Issifou 2018).

Travel and Movies–Opportunities for More Quantitative Work

Two remaining elements of the Soft Power Rubric are travel and movies. Earlier in this chapter, Datta (2014) showed that foreigners' views of a country influence whether they travel there. However, does the travel behavior in return affect opinion or political attitudes? There are very few quantitative empirical studies on this question. One study by Arif and Hall (2019) tests tourist data from the UN World Tourism Organization for 149 countries in four years (1995, 2000, 2005, 2010) against Polity IV Index data on quality of institutions. They find no significant impact of international travel on the sending countries' political institutions. In terms of qualitative studies, however, Australians in the 1960s and 1970s found that traveling to Asia transformed their worldview and undermined their support for the restrictive White Australia policy, as discussed in Chapter 6. Also, Franco deliberately encouraged Americans to visit Spain as part of an all-out effort to win US support after World War II, as discussed in Chapter 11 on how the personal and political are connected.

In the movie arena, there are case studies that examine whether watching foreign movies changes audience views of the foreign country (Arif and Hall 2019). Car, Kos-Stanisic, and Viduka (2016) had 200 Croatian students screen five Indian movies followed by discussion. They found audience views of India changed little as a result, with the exception of *Pinjar,* a historical movie about a family during the Partition (Car, Kos-Stanisic, and Viduka 2016). Messaris and Woo (1991) asked Korean immigrants to the United States how they formed views of the United States before immigrating. More highly educated immigrants that relied on personal contacts as well as mass media felt they had a more accurate image of the United States before emigrating; those with views formed mostly by media had rosier views of the United States than reality. These results contrast, however, with qualitative studies discussed in Chapter 6 on movies, where my personal experience and fieldwork suggest an important link. From a research perspective, both travel and movies are areas that would benefit from larger-scale, quantitative analyses.

Soft Power as a Mutually Beneficial Relationship and the Impact on the "Producer" Country

Soft power thinkers comfortable with broad-brush policy discussions are often uneasy with the sharply defined and narrowly focused quantitative studies that establish a measure for every intangible factor and use numbers to rank the success and failure of policies and programs. This chapter shows that the range of the quantitative studies is indeed very narrow. So far, they focus primarily on the effect of democratic countries on others, and mostly of the United States and European countries on the rest of the world. Necessarily, the studies are limited to a few policy initiatives in specific timeframes. However, there has been substantial progress, and within these narrow constraints, there is positive evidence that certain kinds of government actions can influence foreign public opinion, that positive foreign public opinion benefits a country tangibly, that foreign public opinion influences foreigners' interest in traveling and studying in a country, that foreign students and immigrants abroad influence politics in their country of origin, and that countries who host immigrants and foreign students experience change in their own societies.

Stepping back from a narrow focus on foreign policy to look at all government policy holistically, the kinds of policies that increase soft power influence also have a direct influence on the "producer" society. Usually these changes to the producer country are not considered part of soft power discussions—debates about immigration policy, education policy, tourism, and national culture. However, drawing on these connections clarifies the mutually influential nature of soft power relationships. For example, in the United States, major immigration policy changes in 1965 resulted in a big influx of new immigrants from a wider range of countries, many of whom arrived as students, who now comprise one-quarter of the population. Spilimbergo's (2009) and Atkinson's (2006, 2014) work suggests this also supported the spread of US-style democracy in other countries. The main change, however, was in the character of US society and culture, as documented by Foner (2022). Another example is that in Australia, scholars show that the arrival of foreign students combined with Australians' change in travel patterns—to Asia, not just Europe—contributed to the decline of the White Australia policy, a shift in national identity (Darian-Smith and Waghorne 2016; Oakman 2001; Sobocinska 2013). Germany after the influx of Syrian refugees in 2015 may be undergoing a similar process now.

In Figure 3.1, these changes are reflected in arrows "D," "E," and "F." With this theoretical link drawn, it is easier to see why some countries pause when challenged to implement the most powerful policies to increase their soft power—opening their own society to more interaction with foreigners. Growing soft power implies a willingness for deeper connection with foreign societies and for the producer society itself to change.

The quantitative research shows that foreign public opinion can influence foreign policy outcomes for a country, especially on issues that are very prominently discussed in the media. Therefore, it is important to understand the factors and dynamics that influence foreign public opinion. Studies show that government initiatives like effective government aid, high-level diplomatic visits, and direct social interaction between people of the soft power producer and foreign audience all contribute to forming foreign opinion. When the foreign audience perceives these initiatives and interaction as having virtue, virtuosity, or both, then their opinion rises. When the audience perceives the producer's actions as authentic and legitimate, then their opinion rises in positivity. A producer action seen as legitimate by the audience will raise audience opinion positivity whereas the same action seen as illegitimate or hypocritical will lower audience opinion positivity. Said differently, to increase soft power influence, the producer needs to endear itself to the audience. In terms of room for further research, these studies so far look to general public opinion at the national level. Perhaps future work could examine the significance of a specialized community's opinion for foreign policy issues that are not so salient in the media.

If a foreign audience has a high opinion of the soft power producer, studies show that the audience members demonstrate this opinion through a variety of observable behaviors. These include traveling to, studying in, or migrating to that country. They include audience businesses trading with and investing in the producer country. By comparison, there appears to be a weaker link between a producer's brands located in the audience country. Audience dislike of a foreign producer country is not likely to affect their willingness to buy from foreign brands present in the audience's home market.

These observable behaviors are the basis for the Soft Power Rubric. The Rubric identifies four types of action people take when they are attracted to another country—emigrating, studying abroad, traveling abroad, and watching movies from that country. Data for these and other types of activities are available for a wider range of countries over longer timeframes than public opinion. The Soft Power Rubric approach opens the way to researching countries that are soft powers in their region, for example, or are members of a group, such as a trade or environmental group. Also, it allows the study of soft power relationships over time. The Rubric is flexible, and depending on the research question at hand, a different assortment of quantitative measures of social interaction may be appropriate to look for answers.

The social interactions between soft power producer and audience countries can have a lasting effect on the audience society. For international education, there is strong evidence that students from the audience country enrolled in universities in the soft power producer country do transmit the values of the producer country back to their home audiences. There is emerging evidence that immigration may produce similar effects. For both education and immigration, the quantitative evidence suggests there is correlation, while qualitative study shows how the personal relationships between student or immigrant and their network of friends, family, and colleagues can reshape the values of the audience country. The focus of research in these studies is the transmission of democracy from the United States and other wealthy countries. There is room for more work on whether other political values systems can be similarly transmitted, and for study of a wider range of soft power producer countries. On international trade and investment, the quantitative research suggests a strong correlation with high public opinion, but the reasons why are still unspecified. There is room here for both quantitative and qualitative inquiries into why businesspeople choose to work with certain countries but not others, and whether this has further effects on the scope of audience markets, the character of the economy, or perhaps the political regime.

When audience members interact with the soft power producer country, both the audience and producer are transformed. For example, when a producer country welcomes large groups of immigrants from audience countries, not only do the audience countries change through the transmission of values, but also the producer country identity may change. This is well-documented for both the United States and Australia and may be the case for other countries as well. There is room for further linking these areas of study with the soft power research, which in the past have been separated by academic disciplinary lines. For countries interested in growing their soft power resources, the policy implications are to open their societies to more social interaction with foreigners—immigrants, international students, visitors, and foreign media. Opening up more, of course, may mean that their own society may change as a result.

In conclusion, the current research shows that soft power is measurable by tracking social and cultural interactions among countries, and that these interactions cumulatively have an impact on the direction of international relations. The shortcoming of the research is that so far the work tends to focus on great powers in the international system, with many focusing on wealthy democracies. There is considerable room for further measurement and quantitative analysis of regional powers and those states with other forms of governance. These kinds of investigations will be essential to a fuller understanding of whether soft power is a resource peculiar to open societies or whether there are other measurable aspects not yet fully captured in the research work to date.

Notes

1. An earlier version of this chapter appeared in *The Routledge Handbook of Soft Power*, 2nd ed., edited by Naren Chitty, Lilian Ji, and Gary D. Rawnsley (London: Routledge, 2023). Used with permission of Informa UK Limited through PLSclear.

2. The International Criminal Court (ICC) entered into force after the treaty was signed by 120 countries and ratified by 60 countries in 2002. The United States in 2002 rejected joining the ICC and began a process of negotiating bilateral immunity agreements with individual countries to protect US citizens in military, civilian, and private capacities from being subject to the International Criminal Court (Goldsmith and Horiuchi 2012, 568–569).

4

Measuring Social Interaction

IN 1945 ECONOMIST JOHN KENNETH GALBRAITH ASKED PAUL Baran to kidnap Rolf Wagenführ from Soviet-controlled East Berlin in order to gather the necessary data to analyze Germany's postwar economy and construct its first gross national product (GNP) calculation. After interviews over a few days, Galbraith asked Jürgen Kuczynski to accompany Wagenführ back to East Berlin, where Kuczynski eventually relocated. Wagenführ eventually left East Germany and took a job with European Coal and Steel Community, a precursor to today's European Union (Lepenies 2016). Rest assured that no scholars were kidnapped in the production of the Soft Power Rubric.

Parallels Between the Soft Power Rubric and the Gross Domestic Product

This episode about GNP calculations illustrates a few important points about measurement and international relations relevant to the Soft Power Rubric. First, figures like the GNP, now more often calculated as the gross domestic product (GDP) and also known as national income, seem as though they have existed forever but actually are a relatively recent development. The first modern calculations in the United States are from the 1930s, and it was applied to other countries starting after World War II.

Second, political goals matter and influence both the models and the calculations. The pioneer of national accounting, William Petty, calculated England's national income in the seventeenth century to show that the tax base could be broadened to include workers, lessening the burden on landowners like himself. In the United States, Simon Kuznets was for the first time able to show in figures the dramatic fall in employment between 1929 and 1932 due to the Great Depression—government calculations we take for granted today. Later, his research showed how income inequality can increase during periods of economic growth. During World War II, US economists calculated national income to determine whether increased war production would put pressure on the quality of life of ordinary people by decreasing private consumption. They found it did not, which led to large growth of wartime production, possibly influencing the outcome of the conflict. Galbraith's team developed Germany's national income calculations as part of postwar planning including the Marshall Plan (Lepenies 2016).

Third, another parallel between the GDP and Soft Power Rubric, which is both an advantage and disadvantage, is their reductive simplicity. As Lepenies (2016) describes it, "The idea of GDP is based on the supposition that one can grasp all the goods produced and services in a country as a single aggregated asset, the monetary value of which can be calculated. . . . Here, 'value' simply means monetary units. It is not the quality of the product or the services that are relevant for GDP, but the accumulated price of all goods produced." GDP is calculated by summing and comparing sums of three sets of data: (1) all production, (2) all income, and (3) all expenditure. While in practice they are not equal, if correctly calculated, they should be roughly similar and thus lend credibility to a final GDP figure. The intuition is that (1) all the work I produce should be roughly the same value as (2) the income I earn and (3) the amount I spend. Similarly, the intuition behind the Soft Power Rubric is simple. If I am interested in a foreign country, activities like watching movies from there, visiting there, going to university there, and migrating there are observable behaviors that reflect my attraction to that country. Similarly, the Rubric sums the total number of observable behaviors; these data reflect the quantity of activity, not the quality of it.

Finally, there is the question of the unit of measure. GDP is calculated in monetary units like the US dollar; the Soft Power Rubric elements are calculated per behavior—the number of social interactions with foreigners. Each has its strengths and controversies. With GDP, this requires the development of currency converters, including models like purchasing power parity. The Soft Power Rubric assumes that social interactions with foreigners are the currency of soft power based on the social science research that suggests such interactions are the foundation of trust, social capital, collective action, and, ultimately, governance in society. The rest of this chapter sets forward this argument.

There is a wealth of scholarship on political communications, trust, and social capital that provides both ideas and empirical strategies that could inform how people in one country develop and change their views of another with consequences for international cooperation and conflict. Several scholarly traditions suggest observing people-to-people interactions is likely to shed light on country-to-country politics. Two insights from political communications apply. The first is conceptual. When studying media broadcasting, political communications scholars are as interested in the reaction of the audience as the intent of the producer. Instead of approaching the study of soft power from the perspective of the government influencing foreign countries, suppose we flip the dynamic and define soft power as present when ordinary foreigners think of us as *we*, not *they*. That is the ultimate form of foreigners accepting our point of view. The second insight from political communications is empirical. We can detect the level of social integration among communities, in other words the extent and depth of "we," in changes in the direction and volume of communication activity between people.

From the study of culture and trust, two additional insights connect social interaction to possible cooperation and influence. One is that culture is not a force external to society; on the contrary, it is a world of meaning that is performed and created as people interact with each other. Therefore, transnational interaction is a basis for creating transnational culture, reflecting influences from all societies participating. A second is that trust between people is not necessarily only a matter of faith, but can be an attitude that grows through repeated, reciprocal interactions. Furthermore, this practical form of trust is one foundation of social capital, an important basis for cooperation. These two insights suggest that a country does not so much have soft power *over* another country, but rather countries have soft power relationships *with* each other. Getting to *we* and *with* suggests these societies are integrated, in whole or in part.

The Soft Power Rubric considers the experiences people have that inform their long-term view of foreign countries. The Rubric's elements each quantify some type of interaction with foreigners. In this section I consider the fundamental importance of communication in society and culture, which tie together all the Rubric elements. In the next section I explore each Rubric element's own research literature and how their main concerns relate to soft power and the international system.

Look to the Audience: Learning from Television, Social Media, and Studies of Discourse

In political communication, research is just as focused on how people receive and understand a message as it is on how people send a message. One of the turning points in communications research was Ang's study of Dutch viewers' reaction to the hugely popular US soap opera *Dallas* in the 1980s. At its peak, it broadcast to over ninety countries; in the spring of

1982, half the population of the Netherlands watched the show weekly. *Dallas* is a family drama, centered on the Ewings, their relationships and betrayals, hardships and deceptions. In every episode, the ideal of family life harmony is shattered in the sun-drenched, ultra-glamourous setting of oil-rich Texas (Ang 1985).

Ang's investigation springs from the irony of *Dallas*'s super popularity in the face of Western European political and intellectual elite criticism that the show was yet another example of American cultural imperialism—an antagonistic view of US soft power. Ang posted a short notice in a Dutch magazine inviting people to write to her about how they felt about *Dallas*, resulting in forty-two letters. Her correspondents revel in the tension between reality and the fiction on television—here the glamour of a fantasy America comes into play. Many are drawn by the tragic melodrama—characters who ought to be happy but are caught up in situations where tragedy and heartache are inevitable, episode after episode. Yet another group were caught up in the frustrations of the show's women; most of Ang's correspondents were women themselves. Finally, those letter writers who were angry with *Dallas* drew on an ideology of mass communication—that commercialized programming was trash and an affront to national culture, echoing American elite criticism of its own popular culture. In this particular case of *Dallas* in the Netherlands in 1982, the American character of the television show does not seem to be the main draw, although it does appear to be the main basis for criticism.

Ang's methodological insight is that she showed how revealing it is to ask the viewers. It is a technique valuable not only to marketers but also to political and other social scientists. In the study of soft power, examining how soft power initiatives are perceived and received by the intended audience is as or *even more* important than intent. Ang's work in the 1980s preceded the internet and social media and, therefore, emphasized reception. The viewers of *Dallas* might find themselves transformed by it, but there were few direct mechanisms for them to turn that influence back to the United States, to the producers of the television show.

By contrast Singh (2013) writes about the power of the feedback loop between content producer and audience, as a forceful influence itself. He argues that large groups of people experience transformations in their identity based on ideas and information communicated through technology; these new meanings he calls "meta-power" (Singh 2013). This metapower stands in contrast to identities and meanings created by nation-states or conveyed by hierarchical institutions to their members. Television and movies are asymmetrical communications in the sense that producers create stories for audiences, but audiences talk back mostly indirectly—through ratings or advertising sales that in the long run feed into whether the same producers are able to pursue their next project. Internet technology makes symmetrical communication possible; feedback is faster. A change in the technology's affordances, or functionality, can alter the technology's meaning in a user's life. An example would be that as my social media platform makes more kinds of interactions possible, my account is no longer just a place where I share messages with friends, but instead becomes an integral part of my identity, how I see myself, and how others see me. Technology makes it easier for people to interact across borders. The more they interact, the more their view of others and their view of themselves changes. Audiences no longer just receive, they also produce. Individual changes taken together have a collective impact on soft power relationships among countries.

These concepts of producer and audience extend to strategic communications in international relations. Roselle, Miskimmon, and O'Loughlin (2014) describe the elements of international discourse in terms of narrative formation, projection, interaction, and reception. At the simplest level scholars examine one country's speeches, look at its interactions with other countries, and whether those interactions produced the intended results. At the most complex, the relationships are recursive; there is not just a one-way directionality, but the discourse between and among countries influences and changes all parties. Roselle and colleagues define a strategic narrative as the stories people tell when explaining the relationships between their own country and others. A strategic narrative includes a plot, the characters, the obstacles, and endings that explain history, wars, disasters, or the economic events. An example is Huntington's *Clash of Civilizations,* which essentially tells the story of the world as conflict between communities with fundamentally different worldviews (Roselle, Miskimmon, and O'Loughlin 2014). Nye in his work for the general public, often writes that having soft power is telling the story that wins (2004b).

Any public diplomacy or soft power strategy takes place within the context of such strategic narratives, and there are many approaches to understanding them, argue Roselle, Miskimmon, and O'Loughlin (2014). For example, many international relations scholars view the world as an interstate game or a two-level game of elites and domestic forces. Critics of this approach, like Nye and Strange, take this framework as a point of departure but argue that other forces—in Strange's case, money and wealth (Strange 1986); in Nye's case, social and cultural influences (Nye 2004a)—are also important and sometimes dominant. A different approach uses institutions or specific elite communities (NGOs or journalists, for example) as a level of analysis. Singh's soft power study, which includes cultural institutions, is an example (Singh and MacDonald 2017). A yet more diffuse approach is to include all actors and practices as influential in the discourse.

Understanding of the development and application of soft power benefits from this more complex view of communication production and reception. Some research questions will lend themselves to the simplest or thinnest of these interactions; others will require what anthropologists call a thick description, where the actors in the discourse influence each other and the actors themselves may be individuals, organizations, or more diffuse communities.

Quantitative Perspective on Nationalism and Community Integration

In the mid-eighteenth century, there were more pieces of mail between the various colonies in the United States and the United Kingdom than there were between the colonies themselves. However, by the early nineteenth century, the volume among the US states grew to be greater than the mail between it and the United Kingdom (Merritt 1966). The change reflects the greater integration of the states with each other. In addition, Merritt discusses how better roads eased travel and the movement of ideas, and grew the market for news among the colonies. Regardless of the content of the mail or the newspapers, the change in volume and direction of communications is evidence that certain communities are more connected to each other than before. This is one way in which quantitative data on communications can provide insights into social integration. The Soft Power Rubric follows in this path.

Merritt builds on Deutsch's idea that the volume and intensity of social interactions reflect the degree of cultural integration. In *Nationalism and Social Communication* (1966a) and *Nerves of Government* (1966b), Deutsch suggests that in looking for empirical evidence of ethnic and cultural communities, they can be thought of as observable networks of community channels. This is a particularly apt technique useful in digital communications, where the type and quantity of one person's interaction with another are traceable. However, Deutsch does not argue that numbers alone tell the story; he also argues that learned habits, preferences, and symbols are necessary to understanding the degree to which communities are integrated with each other (Deutsch 1966a, 1966b).

Deutsch raises the example that while many Swiss speak German, they may find it easier to communicate with their fellow French-speaking Swiss than with people from German-speaking Austria. He reports German-Swiss and French-Swiss may use different words for the same concepts, whereas German-Swiss and Austrian use the same words for different concepts. Deutsch argues that "Membership in a people essentially consists in a wide complementarity of social communication. It consists in the ability to communicate more effectively, and over a wider range of subjects, with members of one large group than with outsiders. This overall result can be achieved by a variety of functionally equivalent arrangements" (Deutsch 1966a, 71).

Anderson in his work *Imagined Communities* (1983), also on the subject of nationalism, points to the rise of printing, especially the development of newspapers in the eighteenth century, as critical to developing national consciousness. The regular act of reading a newspaper connected people together—cultivating a common language, symbols, and memories—creating a community of the mind, "imagined," if you will, rather than a community defined by physical boundaries (Anderson 1983). In my earlier work, *Forging Trust Communities* (2015), I take this concept into the twenty-first century. The more recent technologies of telephones, televisions, mobile phones, and internet each in their turn create the potential for new communities. This potential is converted into actual communities when the people included interact, reciprocate, and build trust (Wu 2015).

This work on community and nation building through communication has fundamental ties to the communications work on production and reception. Just because a postal system is created, does not mean that colonies become more integrated; the evidence of that integration is that people use the system to send mail. Just because a newspaper is printed and distributed does not automatically create an Andersonian "imagined community"; what creates the imagined community is that people choose to read it regularly. Finally, just because there is a social media platform available does not mean there is a "trust community"; when people form ties with each other through regular interaction, that is what forges a trust community.

Creating Culture, Building Trust, and Accumulating Social Capital Through Interaction

Culture, Fine reminds us, is not an outside force that is a catch-all for everything else unexplained by other means. People create and perform culture as they interact with each other. His term, "tiny publics," builds on Alexis de Tocqueville's notion of "minute associations," small groups of people—like a book club or a team of video gamers—who work together, hold common values, share a past, and look forward to a future. He argues that big social forces get started in small-scale places. To understand how cultural forces came to be, we must start tiny and work our way up to big (Fine 2012). To understand global dynamics of influence and attraction among countries, we must start with individuals interacting with others on the other side of national borders.

Research on trust and social capital focuses on the ties that bind people together and that improve cooperation in society. Elinor Ostrom's work emphasizes that people create trust through a series of reciprocal actions. Ostrom's conception of "trust" is not simply an act of faith but a choice based on experience and self-interest (Ostrom 2003). One of Ostrom's major contributions to economics and political science is her insight into the rules that work when people manage common-pool resources like water for farming irrigation, grazing lands, or fisheries—resources that are highly subtractable (if I catch a lot of fish, that's less fish for you) and highly difficult to exclude beneficiaries (if half of us hold back livestock from grazing in the town pasture, that's beneficial for the other half even though they are not sacrificing anything).

Based on her study of hundreds of case studies throughout the United States and other countries, she found that in a situation where the resource system itself and who has rights to the resources are clearly defined, certain principles enhance collective governance. Some of her findings may seem obvious. For example, the benefits of participating exceed the costs; there should be clear ways of resolving conflict; and complex resources may require complex coordination with overlapping institutions and layers of governance. Less obvious but grounded from the experience gleaned from fieldwork are principles like the ability of participants to modify the rules themselves, monitoring systems that track the common resource and keep participants accountable, and sanctions that are graduated—minor punishments for minor infractions, and major sanctions for big violations (Ostrom 2005).

In addition to fieldwork, Ostrom also conducted lab experiments to test how strangers build trust or not. She and James Walker demonstrate that when participants are negotiating over commonly held goods, the more rounds of activity and the greater the communication, the more likely they were to cooperate and to cooperate efficiently. For two groups, one with communication and one without, after ten rounds of action, the cooperation rate was between 0 and 50 percent. For the next ten rounds, the group without communication continued similarly, but the group with communication rose to over 90 percent in round eleven through the end (Ostrom 2003). Research on social capital shows that it is accumulated over time as people experience working and being together.

Additional research by scholars like Yamagishi (2003) show that American and Japanese participants in the same experiments demonstrate different baseline levels of trust. While anthropological work characterizes Japanese culture as more collectivist in orientation than US society, the trust experiments show Japanese baseline trust level in strangers is lower than Americans'. Yamagishi shows that the Japanese participants prefer to rely more on monitoring for accountability, one of the design principles Ostrom identifies, which is premised on strong interpersonal commitments. In terms of further expanding work to understand soft power, then, fieldwork and lab experiments on trust can all contribute to greater empirical understanding of cultural nuances (Yamagishi 2003).

Also relevant to understanding the effects of interaction and communication is the substantial research literature on social capital. Putnam (2002) and other scholars focus on the kinds of bonds that hold society together and enable people to work together. They explore several types of bonds among people that can lead to cooperation: formal and informal, thick and thin, inward and outward, and bonding and bridging. Inward focuses on helping members of the group; outward on achieving a public good. Bridging social capital is among people who are different; bonding among people who are similar. My own work *Forging Trust Communities* shows how this social capital, built through reciprocal actions over time, including transnational communities, can be created for one purpose, like a cultural festival, and quickly refocus on another goal, like humanitarian work (Wu 2015). Soft power relationships among countries reflect their willingness to work together based on trust accrued through positive, reciprocal interactions in the past, not only between states but also among ordinary people. Soft power relationships are the social capital among nations (Wu 2015).

Let us use a story to connect ordinary people's interactions with a country's soft power. Suppose an American student goes to see an Iranian movie. We know from Ang's work on *Dallas* that we should focus on the student's reaction. From Singh's work we expect that if she becomes a fan of Iranian movies, this interaction will influence her worldview—perhaps she will pursue an interest in Hafez's poetry or Middle Eastern politics. Following Deutsch and Merritt, we will observe whether the number of foreigners watching Iranian movies rises or falls, and which foreigners from where are watching them. Fine encourages us to explore whether any small associations form, perhaps the North American–Iranian film festival club, which organizes screenings of one country's films in the other. In the club, people can work together across national borders; they build Ostrom's trust and Putnam's social capital. Such phenomena happen every day but are rarely captured in our understanding of political relationships among countries. The Soft Power Rubric opens a path to bring to the fore these interactions and their meaning.

These social science findings based on extensive fieldwork and experimental evidence are consistent with the intuition of diplomats professionally engaged in persuasion and the exercise of soft power. These practitioners write about building narratives by setting the scene; identifying main actors, major institutions, and relevant forums; and preparing communications tools and instruments (Cooper et al. 2013; Chitty 2017a; Snow and Taylor 2009). Communication is the main focus of Craig Hayden's *Rhetoric of Soft Power: Public Diplomacy in Global Contexts* (2012), which compares Japanese, Venezuelan, Chinese, and US approaches in particular. The importance of these insights and the descriptive documentation of diplomacy at work are largely supported by the empirical science.

Thoughts on Measurement

Having established that reciprocity and communication are fundamental to cooperation and worth quantifying in order to understand soft power better, there are two additional questions to address. First, is the Soft Power Rubric a set of dependent or independent variables? Second, when social interactions are negative, how can that affect a country's soft power?

On the first question, I suggest that the role of the Soft Power Rubric in international relations is similar to the role of gross domestic product in economics. Before the methods were established for measuring GDP, it was not meaningful to ask whether it was the cause or result of economic development. The usefulness of GDP in its early stages was to describe one country's economic production compared to another, or to compare one country's economic production over different periods of time (Kuznets 1934; Lepenies 2016). The production of cars, one element of the GDP, was affected by many factors—social, economic, and political. The production of soybeans, another element of GDP, is affected by these factors and the weather. Once a GDP figure is produced, it feeds into other figures, which in turn are used to explain other events. GDP per capita, or an individual's income, is used to explain levels of education, the state of their health, and other phenomenon. GDP is in some analyses the result of forces, in other analyses the cause of forces. Similarly, the Soft Power Rubric data reflect social, political, and economic dynamics in society. At the same time, it can be used to show the accumulated effect of soft power resources—like one country supporting another country in crisis, but not supporting a third.

In other words, the GDP model is useful when it simultaneously achieves two goals: first, it is consistent with people's intuition of what matters in measuring economic production; second, it reveals insights into the economy that would be invisible without the model. With GDP, the insight is that economic production is a key activity fundamental to the economy, fundamental enough that nearly every economic activity results in production of something for money. The Soft Power Rubric's key insight is that interaction between people is an essential aspect of building and sharing social capital, and that in a crisis people stand with those they feel are more like themselves. First, the Soft Power Rubric assessments are largely consistent with other rankings of country soft power, described in more detail in Chapter 11. Second, the Soft Power Rubric's new contribution to the field is the ability to conduct cross-country and historical comparisons.

Another challenge to the Soft Power Rubric is that not every transnational interaction is a positive experience—how can having more interactions equal a stronger soft power relationship? There are two responses to this question. First, like other time series data, the Soft Power Rubric numbers should be taken into consideration over time. If most foreign students in China have a good experience, they will tell their friends and more foreign students will continue to go. If the experience is not good, then fewer students will go in the future. Similarly, with GDP data, all car sales are included—even sales of lemons. However, if there are a lot of lemons sold, then over time, sales should decline. Another response is more complex. US movies abroad are very popular, although it is very common for the United States to be portrayed negatively in the movies. Perhaps the hero is waging battle against a corrupt military-industrial complex, greedy Wall Street, or power-hungry city council. Yet, movies are generally regarded as a US soft power asset. Negative images and experiences can, but do not necessarily, diminish a person's regard for a foreign country. Another example is that foreign visitors are rightly shocked by the number of homeless people living on the streets of US cities. Do the visitors experience enough positive to balance the negative? Here, quantitative analysis falls short, and only a carefully considered qualitative analysis can unravel the threads.

Cautionary Lessons from the History of the GDP

The history of the GDP also offers salutary cautions. First, Kuznets created the GDP method out of an interest in welfare, not wealth. He objected to the use of GDP as a proxy for economic well-being because he thought many things important to well-being were not included in GDP. For example, he had wanted to add to the sum of production a factor for "income enjoyed," introducing a subjective element to the mix. Soft power measurement to date has been used to rank countries in terms of soft power prowess. For example, the Soft Power 30 Index may have this unfortunate effect that countries that are diverse and complex are flattened in order achieve a rank. This builds on Nye's original use of soft power to explain why the United States was not at risk of "losing" to Japan in the 1990s. Soft power comparisons can take on aspects of a beauty contest—which countries are most attractive. This should not be the main point of measuring soft power or the Soft Power Rubric. Instead, the purpose of measuring soft power is to understand the depth and breadth of social, cultural, people-to-people relationships among countries, with the larger goal of improving cooperation among nations.

Second, in Kuznets's landmark letter to the US Senate, he identified up front several categories of economic production that were not counted in GDP such as family care, casual work, and work considered illegal. In short, economic production by those at the margins of society—those caring for children and other family members at home, odd jobs work, volunteer and charitable work, undocumented work—is all real work not quantified and reported to the government and is, therefore, left out of GDP calculations. In other words, whatever hierarchies of status and prestige exist in a society are directly replicated in its measurements, including the GDP. Kuznets left his job at the US Commerce Department in part because the government refused to include these, but his insights later informed his work on income inequality (Lepenies 2016).

There are similar risks for the Soft Power Rubric, which is built on quantitative datasets already created by international governmental organizations related to the United Nations. They have done important work in defining categories in ways that allow for harmonizing national data across borders. However, when using these data and the Soft Power Rubric it is important to remember that while the figures may look simple, the reality behind them is complicated. The fundamental insight is that social interaction among people creates the opportunity for cooperation and that social interaction may not be captured in the international datasets; in many instances it may defy quantification. Are all immigrants captured in the United Nations population data? Are all movie audiences included in UNESCO's data? Of course not. The Soft Power Rubric is not meant to include exclusively only four indicators. The four indicators are just a beginning. The essential insight in understanding soft power resources is to understand what kinds of interactions people have with other people—whether directly or mediated—that potentially change their view of other countries. There is room for more indicators, and I look forward to others proposing them.

In some respects, the Soft Power Rubric is conventional. It relies on indicators already collected by established international organizations. However, the Soft Power Rubric is radical in other ways. The Soft Power Rubric assumes that power embodied in human relationships is as important as power embodied in money or in a gun, and as worthy of quantitative and historical assessment. The Soft Power Rubric suggests that soft power is not primarily the domain of high art, elegant diplomats, and clever cultural outreach programs but rather the everyday, mundane interactions among ordinary people across national borders. Like the free market forces in economics, government policy has a major role in shaping conditions but does not ultimately control them. The Soft Power Rubric brings people's life experience into the analysis of foreign policy.

5

Connecting the Personal to the International

THE PERSONAL STORIES OF THREE AMERICAN ICONS WHO studied in France—Jacqueline Kennedy Onassis née Bouvier (1949–1950), Susan Sontag (1957–1958), and Angela Davis (1964–1965)—capture the place France holds in the American imagination (Kaplan 2012). They are drawn to the promise of Paris, eager to shed the constraints of American life. Does the France of reality live up to the one of imagination? How does the experience change how they see themselves and their relationship to the world? How does it change the collective relationship between France and the United States? Through their stories we can see how disparate elements of the Soft Power Rubric overlap and tease out the concepts that connect individual experiences to relationships between countries.

In the fields of migration, international education, travel, and movies, there is fundamental concern around people's interactions with each other across national borders, which leads to strikingly interrelated questions. This chapter samples just a few, but further study would uncover more interconnections. For example, from the field of international education, scholars use the push-pull model to explain students' decisionmaking process, inquiring about what pushes students abroad and pulls them toward certain destinations. Migration scholars place a high priority on understanding the transnational identity of those whose everyday lives regularly reach across borders. From the field of tourism come the ideas of destination image, what travelers think about a locale, and place identity, how those who live in a locale think of their own community. From the research on movies arises the debate over whether the success of cultural productions in world markets is explained best by understanding the international core-periphery power structure or as subject to regular business cycles. Each of these concerns is relevant to phenomena in the other three fields.

Bouvier's junior year abroad was an opportunity to explore her own French ancestry, which her grandfather had glorified, and likely exaggerated. She lived with a French host family, friends of her mother's, and mixed with both aristocratic society and ordinary Parisians. A keen observer of history and literature, her year abroad was the foundation for a career in US society, during which she brought French elegance to the White House as first lady, and later French history and literature to American audiences as a noted book editor (Kaplan 2012). The year abroad cemented her transnational identity.

The France of 1949 was far from the elegant society of American fantasy, at least in material terms. Still suffering the scars of war and German occupation, the French families who hosted Bouvier and her fellow juniors needed boarders to keep their households together. Bouvier herself had a coffee and sugar ration card. She and her friends visited the remains of the concentration camps as France debated whether to preserve them and, if so, how. Henrietta Nicom, a young French woman during this time, noted that French themselves had become "realists" about their traditions, and it was really the young Americans who sought to carry them on. They drank the French orange bitters and lemonade while the French drank Coca-Cola. The American girls wore laced sandals and long straight hair not seen in France since 1900, and the young men dressed like garret painters and brought back into fashion the nineteenth-century mustache (Kaplan 2012). American students held a certain destination image of France, one that contrasted with the French's own place identity.

Susan Sontag, a precocious student who graduated college aged eighteen, always dreamed of traveling to Europe but never had the resources to go. Finally, she won a fellowship to study in Great Britain in 1957 and, after finding England dull, abandoned it for Paris. In Sontag's imagination, Europe was a place of moral freedom without puritanical American constraints. To come to Europe, she left behind both husband and son and was free to renew and discover lesbian relationships that were to shape her future personally and intellectually. Sontag taught herself French while there and, in time, became a window into French intellectual thought for American audiences. Later in life, she would regularly return to Paris, often spending her summers there and becoming, in her own words, a "self-Europeanized American" (Kaplan 2012). Like Bouvier, Sontag's Parisian sojourn allowed her to create a much longed for transnational identity.

When Angela Davis was a teenager in Birmingham, Alabama, pretending to be a French-speaking foreigner from Martinique gave her a few moments' relief from the Jim Crow laws that prevented her from shopping at the front of the shoe store. Paris in the 1950s held Black writers and artists like Richard Wright, James Baldwin, and Josephine Baker in special high regard and so for Davis—like Bouvier and Sontag before her—studying in France promised an escape from American constraints. Unlike Sontag and Bouvier, however, Davis arrived in Paris with an advanced mastery of French, prepared to immediately engage in philosophical debate and using that time to expand her interests to German language and philosophy (Kaplan 2012).

The year Davis was in Paris (1964–1965), France's empire had disintegrated and the country was building a new narrative for itself. Bouvier's France was recovering from war; Sontag's was shaken by Algeria's call for independence. By Davis's year abroad, Algeria was independent. Decolonization was a searing experience, and there were racist attacks on Algerians in France. James Baldwin wrote of the experience, "I live among the les Misérables, and the les Misérables are the Algerians." Although African Americans in France were relatively privileged in France compared to the United States, they could see French racism on full display (Kaplan 2012). For Davis, while living in France afforded a respite from American Jim Crow oppression, the hierarchical structure of oppression was only temporarily dislocated, not disappeared.

Davis returned to the United States, continued her studies, solidified her communist thinking, and as part of her activism became an advocate for George Jackson, a political writer whose career developed during the decade he spent in jail for driving the getaway car for a gas station robbery. In 1970 Jackson's brother stormed the courtroom with guns and took several hostages. In the end, four were dead, including Jackson's brother and the judge. The guns were registered to Davis, and she was put on trial for murder. During her trial, 60,000 people in Paris marched on her behalf. She was the most famous communist intellectual in the world. Acquitted of murder, she returned to Paris to promote her autobiography and her story passed into myth—a young African American woman studies in France, learns from its decolonization struggles, and returns to the United States triumphantly to challenge the powers that be. Her story, Kaplan records, is retold by intellectuals, filmmakers, taxi drivers, secretaries, and ordinary French citizens. Davis's story is a myth of freedom and how the French see the connection between themselves and the United States (Kaplan 2012).

Bouvier, Sontag, and Davis's stories of sojourn and return illustrate the interwoven concerns in the overlapping research interests on migration, international education, travel, and movies. In the next sections I explore each of these fields to further develop the connections.

The Push-Pull Model in International Education Studies

All cross-border transactions are motivated to some degree by the pull toward the foreign and the push away from home.

Interviewed for a research study, one Japanese student in the United Kingdom complained, "In a way, I escaped from Japan. I didn't like social relations in my graduate school there. I was the only female student in my seminar group. Therefore, making cups of tea was my job. When we went for a drink, I had to pour sake for my male colleagues. If I didn't do that, they would make a fuss behind my back afterwards. One of my male seniors even told me to wear a skirt for the seminar" (Habu 2000). Once in British universities, others found the rigorous standards at their university refreshing and challenging. Yet others felt they were revenue generators for the university and not treated the same as British students (Habu 2000). Encapsulated in these studies are their reasons for leaving Japan and going to the United Kingdom.

In international education, the push-pull model of Mazzarol and Soutar (2002) is the touchstone for a large body of case studies examining both why students decide to pursue education abroad and how they select their destination. The motivations that push them abroad reflect some dissatisfaction with university education at home. Scholars observe that for some students another push is the idea that study abroad is a kind of consumption that reflects the family's status and prestige. International education is not simply of practical use to the student but also of symbolic value to the family that may be important to reproduce over generations (Pimpa 2005; Tsang 2013).

Chapter 8 on India's soft power contains the results of this kind of push. The number of students from India who went abroad to train rose from 52,000 in 2000 to 350,000 in 2018. Common factors that pull students to a particular foreign country and university include previous knowledge and awareness of the country; personal recommendations from family and friends; cost, financial and social, including crime and discrimination; environment and lifestyle concerns; proximity to home; and whether they already have family or friends in the foreign country. People making decisions whether to emigrate, to travel, and even to watch a movie follow a similar push-pull pattern of decisionmaking. Chapter 7 on international education discusses Australia's pull as a major international hub, in 2017 overtaking France in the number of international students. At a regional level, Malaysia is also pulling a greater number of international students, as described in Chapter 10.

Returning to Kaplan's history, Sontag and Davis were eager to leave behind the constraints of US society for the greater freedoms promised in France. They and Bouvier were attracted to France as a land that conferred a seal of sophistication that secured their futures as members of the American elite.

Individuals' Transnational Identity in Migration Studies

An important concept in the migration literature is the idea of *transnationalism,* in which a person's identity, institutions, and cultural and information networks span two or more locales in different countries. These are people who, in the ordinary course of everyday life, routinely reach across national borders. For example, immigrants commonly have transnational identities. Transnational life can be passed down through families for many generations. Also, people can create a transnational identity through intercultural learning, contact, and exchange. Markers of transnational life include travel, language, education, affinity for television programs and movies and other entertainments, religion, and cuisine (Golbert 2001; Robins and Aksoy 2001; Vertovec 2001). If soft power is about foreigners thinking of us as "we" not "they," then understanding the transnational communities that exist within a country provides a map of important soft power relationships. Chapter 9 draws contrasts between China and Russia's history of immigration. Russia has been open, especially to its neighbors, while China remains relatively closed to immigrants, although welcoming to visitors and students. Whether this means foreigners are less likely to think of "we" when it comes to China as compared to Russia would be an interesting area to research.

Ethnic identity connects individuals to foreign policy. Interviewed for a research study, a London teenager reflected,

> What brought me my culture, to my spiritualism, was going to Cyprus when I was thirteen. I was old enough to realize. Then I knew that was my spiritual homeland. Sometimes when I watch television I can feel it, but I don't feel it until I am there, starting to listen to music, and hanging around with Turks, their parents, watching Turkish satellite.... So I never got my realization, my culture, through the television. But I can understand how, for a lot of people, it has brought them closer to who they are. (Robins and Aksoy 2001)

As a child she had rebelled against being Turk, against being Cypriot, but she changed her mind. She mainly watches British television and thinks the older generation who watch mostly Turkish television are living in a dream world. She speaks Turkish, but not fluently, and now thinks of herself as both Turkish and British (Robins and Aksoy 2001). This young woman, a British-born citizen in London, thinks of Turks as "we" not "they." At a community level, Chapter 10 discusses similar complexities in the Thai-American community. On some issues, the Thai government is willing to step in to represent the community, and on others it is not. In yet other areas, the community learns to mobilize politically to participate in Los Angeles local politics.

Susan Sontag wanted to become a "self-Europeanized American." She absorbed the French language, culture, intellectual trends, and debates and became a conduit for French ideas to American society. Bouvier explored her French ancestry on her travels, an identity that grew in importance during her life and career. Kaplan suggests her French identity contrasted with her husband John Kennedy's Irish American identity. In her public persona as first lady, she is still remembered today for bringing French panache to the White House (Kaplan 2012). In the earlier discussion of soft power's history, Gallarotti (2010) and Hall and Ross (2015) argue that emotional reactions that individuals and communities have to events in foreign countries reflect those countries' soft power. Identities like these are the foundations of such emotional reactions.

Place Identity and Destination Image in Tourism Studies

While transnationalism brings attention to the hybrid identities of individuals, destination image and place identity speak to how communities view themselves and are viewed by others. A researcher interviewed a Chicago man about his neighborhood: "Tourism can bring exposure to our culture, food, music . . . giving them [the tourists] an opportunity to see our experiences. . . . They can see our museums, art, music . . . those speak of the struggles we have faced. They'll be exposed to aspects of our culture. That is what we are doing . . . we are exposing them so they can tell about our resistance." He continued, "So when we put up the steel flags . . . ahhhh [a sigh of joy] . . . they are Puerto Rican symbols. These polls they shine, they show that is our community. They show who we are. Puerto Ricans are people who have a long sense of their history, a great deal of pride, and we want them to understand it" (Almeida Santos and Buzinde 2007). He talks about Humboldt Park in Chicago, a neighborhood that in the face of impending gentrification created Paseo Boricua, an avenue anchored by two large metal Puerto Rican flags among buildings painted with cultural murals (Almeida Santos and Buzinde 2007).

"Place identity" is how the people who are residents or who host a destination feel about that place. For people who have strong attachments to a locale, talking about place often becomes talking about identity. This intangible community spirit lends authenticity to a place as a travel destination. In some cases, communities whose identity is suppressed, successfully attracting tourists can boost their place identity (van Rekom and Go 2006). For influence in the opposite direction, Chapter 7 discusses how Australians who began traveling more to Asia, rather than just to Europe, began to perceive differently Australia's place identity. Over time, Australia is more integrated now with its Asian neighbors.

"Destination image" is another idea from the tourism and travel research literature. Why people travel to a place depends greatly on the image they have of a destination (Karl, Reintinger, and Schmude 2015). Three types of information feed this image: organic, autonomous, and induced. First, organic information is noncommercial information from word of mouth such as reviews by previous visitors. Second, autonomous information is from sources that are commercial but independent of the destination's tourism industry, such as new reports, education materials, popular culture, and movies. This information can be very influential if it is considered credible. Third, induced information is promotion material marketed by the destination's tourism industry. Induced material is least influential in putting a particular place on a traveler's awareness list. Instead, information from user-generated sources considered reliable and independent is far more important (Tasci and Gartner 2016). Finally, conflict between the tourists' image of a destination and the hosts' own place identity can cause problems.

    A historic example of destination image as foreign policy strategy is Spanish leader Francisco Franco's sweeping campaign to change how the United States perceived Spain immediately after World War II. Rosendorf (2013) documents how in December 1945, only six months after Germany surrendered, Franco began courting US journalists and emphasizing Spain's interest in building a good relationship with the United States. Part of building this relationship was welcoming US tourists to visit Spain in the hope that on their return these visitors would advocate for Spain, increase its prestige, and also bring in much needed foreign currency. In 1948, Spain opened its first tourism office in New York City. In 1952, it eliminated the visa requirement for US visitors. Beyond tourism, Franco welcomed Hollywood movie producers to film in Spain, turning it into one of the world's leading film production centers in the 1950s and 1960s. There was a direct public relations campaign, including *Spanish Newsletter* in the 1960s. Spain's 1964–1965 pavilion at the World's Fair was the most visited exhibition at the fair, with over 22 million visitors. Rosendorf documents as well how Franco lifted its suppression of non-Catholic religions in part due to critical US public opinion. This campaign continued through the 1960s and built such a foundation of exchange and commerce between the two countries that when Spanish politics changed and turned away from liberalization, Americans continued to visit through the 1970s, and it remains a major European destination for Americans today (Rosendorf 2013).

    In Bouvier's time abroad just after World War II, young American students' reverence for French style and society actually revived old fashions in hairstyles and mustaches, a gap between their fantasy destination image and a more prosaic place identity of the hosts. Seen in the broad sweep of US-French relations, Bouvier and Sontag opened for Americans a wider window into French society and thought, shaping the idea of France for an American audience. Davis, however, reaches further, influencing how the French see themselves in relation to Americans. Her triumphs at home were for the French an affirmation that they had useful lessons for Americans—

that they were instrumental in the heroic success of the marginalized over the powers that be—a contribution to French perceptions of themselves, their place identity, and their influence over others (Kaplan 2012).

The distinction between destination image and place identity helps clarify the value of feeling and sentiment in understanding soft power. For example, some may argue that people who migrate to join family members abroad are deciding based on personal factors while others who are deciding where to go on holiday are making a more impersonal, and therefore more objective, assessment of how attractive a country is. If a country's soft power was the same with every other country, then a less personal assessment might be more useful. However, if soft power is when foreigners think of us as "we," not "they," then personal ties matter more than those freighted with less emotion. For an immigrant who returns regularly to visit her home village, in her mind, the village's destination image and place identity may fuse together. The immigrant who never returns holds on to an ancient place identity; the traveler who visits once holds only the destination image.

Systems and Structures in International Media Studies

In the soft power literature, the popularity of US movies is seen as both a strength of US soft power and an emblem of its cultural imperialism, not only by rivals but also by allies. Canadian and European restrictions on the import of American programming into their film and television markets reflect this anxiety. As the movie data presented in Chapter 4 suggest, one major question is, Why is the United States so dominant? American movies' presence in the world market is far more central than the United States in travel, study abroad, and immigration. Is the US movie industry an imperialist empire or a product of business and technology cycles? Building on the structural core-periphery dependency theories of Fernando Henrique Cardoso and others, the idea of cultural dependence is one important explanation of this phenomenon. Transnational companies, headquartered in the United States, leverage the structural advantages of access to capital, technology, and a large domestic audience to produce programming at a far lower cost than other countries could produce for themselves. Further, these companies also control global distribution channels at a scale that companies from other countries cannot rival. Cultural dependency predicts that US hegemony in movies and other content production can only be challenged with structural change (Straubhaar 1991).

A possible example of ongoing structural change is China's entry into the global movie market, especially after it gained access to more markets after joining the World Trade Organization in 2001. Kokas details the beginning years of this transformation in *Hollywood Made in China* (2017).

Chinese companies eager for access to the global movie market are making major investments in US movie productions. The Chinese government reduced restrictions on American collaborations with domestic producers, and across the board—movies, television, anime, and other content—the frequency and intensity of collaborations are growing. Kokas notes the Chinese market itself is highly attractive motivation for US producers and investors to collaborate. The changes that result in both markets—whether more liberal or with greater accommodation of domestic content standards—will change movies not for just these two countries but also for the rest of the world. Chapter 6 presents the data on movies released in theaters, showing only a handful of countries produce films that are widely watched abroad.

In contrast with Cardoso's core-periphery view is another put forward by Ithiel de Sola Pool and others that domination of the global movie industry reflects a business cycle that favors the United States but that will favor others over time. This approach underscores the important role of audiences in market demand. As local producers of programming and content compete, the business cycle approach predicts that audiences will prefer movies and TV programs that are culturally proximate over US products (Straubhaar 1991). The earliest example is in Straubhaar's study of the Brazilian television market. By the 1980s, Brazilian television powerhouse TV Globo had not only significantly decreased the volume of television programming imported from the United States but had also itself become a major exporter of telenovelas in Latin America and other regions (Straubhaar 1984). Other regional media centers include the rise of South Korea in the 1990s. The Korean pop culture wave or *hallyu* began to sweep through Asia and other regions. Its foreign impact began with television dramas around 1995, K-pop music in the late 1990s, and has evolved to include broader elements of fashion and lifestyle (Jun 2017).

Another dynamic is that the cost of technology to both produce and distribute content is declining. This lowers the barrier to those who wish to produce movies and programming and provides an opportunity for audiences to seek new sources of entertainment without relying on traditional distribution systems like movie theaters. While these technological changes do not sweep away the structural issues that enable the US industry to dominate the market until today, there are prospects for significant change.

Weaving Together Ideas from Migration, Study Abroad, Travel, and Movie Literature

The Soft Power Rubric identifies a simple set of elements that mark the outlines of the soft power relationships among countries. However, to fill in the contours of the relationship requires concepts that interrogate the details. The push-pull model encourages balanced investigation of both host and destination countries. Transnationalism brings attention to the multiple, hybrid identities of individuals. Destination image and place identity underscore the importance of how communities see themselves and are viewed by others. Theories of dependence, business cycles, and technology change link individual cross-border interactions to broader social structures. These are just a few examples of how individuals relate to the world, how locales relate with each other, how transnational interactions shape individual and community identities, and how broad social structures shape individuals' and communities' choices.

The push-pull model from the education sector applies to other areas as well. Migrants are pushed out of a country by war, economic crisis, or political turmoil. They are pulled into a foreign country by an oil boom or the outbreak of peace. Tourists are pulled into traveling with big cultural or sporting events or an advantageous exchange rate. Sontag could not wait to leave the confines of American morality to experience the bohemian lifestyle of Parisians.

The destination image of a country influences not only tourists but also students considering a foreign degree and migrants looking for a new country to adopt as home. Place identity influences how locals welcome foreign students who are temporary neighbors or immigrants who are permanent. Davis left for France, a culture that she knew from childhood could provide a respite from US racial prejudice, and through her career and professional triumphs became a symbol in France, a reminder to the French of the power of their own revolutionary history.

Transnational identity is important not only in the study of migration but also in understanding how viewers select which movies to watch, or which holiday destination to choose. People often choose the culturally familiar, or they might choose based on the preferences of others in their family or community. There are many layers and paths that connect people to culture (La Pastina and Straubhaar 2005). For Bouvier, France was enshrined in familial memory. For Sontag and Davis, a stint in Paris nurtured their transnational identities—ones they chose rather than were born into.

Finally, all the Rubric elements are influenced both by practical cycles of business and technology and broader structures of core and peripheral power. Students decide where to study abroad based not only on practical considerations of curriculum, cost, and proximity to home, but also on whether foreign degrees will bring them prestige and open successful career pathways. Travel and migration are influenced by business and technology cycles, whether it's changes in the cost of travel or shifts in the latest fashionable destination.

In just this chapter's brief discussion, the Japanese student expresses pain at discrimination, the London teenager grapples with her growing identification with Türkiye and Cyprus, the Puerto Rican host is frustrated with how his community is often perceived. In these examples, we glimpse conflict, trauma, and historical tragedy. Soft power in international relations is usually discussed in terms of promoting a better image, or projecting a vision of a happier way of life. However, if soft power is about bonds among people, then shared hurt and pain are also paths to seeing others as "we" rather than as "they." From a scholarly perspective, the research on international migration, education, travel, and movies grapples directly with the richness of human experience and the forces that shape how we see each other. Exploring soft power from these perspectives will deepen our understanding of how countries connect and communicate with each other. The case studies that follow in the next chapters bring together these complex human narratives while using the Soft Power Rubric data as anchors for comparing countries and groups of countries with each other and over time.

A Narrow View Can Broaden Horizons

The four chapters in Part 1 show that a narrow view of soft power as ultimately built on people-to-people interactions can broaden horizons for future work. Building on the idea that soft power is about a country attracting and persuading other countries to its point of view, scholars now know that a country's virtue and virtuosity, its ethics and legitimacy, are all important aspects of its soft power influence, as discussed in Chapter 2. A country's soft power actually resides in the minds of foreigners and their view of the world, not the hands of government officials. Those countries that can inspire endearment and emulation in others have the opportunity to cultivate their soft power.

Given that soft power resides in the minds of foreigners, how can it be measured? By observing the actions of the foreigners, shows Chapter 3. The Soft Power Rubric is built on the assumption that when foreigners are interested in a country, they take actions like watching its movies, traveling there, studying at its universities, or perhaps emigrate there for good. This is a sequence from considering those in that country as "they" progressing to the point that "they" become "we," a process of social integration.

In order to develop measurements, the Soft Power Rubric takes a narrow, parsimonious approach, focusing only on social interactions between societies across national borders, as discussed in Chapter 4. This stands in contrast to most soft power measurement strategies, which develop baskets of indicators that reflect some transnational link. While the basket approach is fruitful in generating discussions about what kinds of links are interesting to study, the advantage of the Rubric's narrow approach is clarity and the promise that data can be reasonably compared across countries and across time. The Rubric data are only social interactions—of various intensities and levels of commitment—but just one category of data that can reasonably be summed, weighted, and analyzed against each other. Therefore, even though the Rubric approach is narrower, it opens doors to a range of useful comparisons.

Further, each category of social interaction in the Soft Power Rubric has an established literature that explores major issues, causes, and effects, and creates a library of concepts that link areas that are usually of domestic concern to international relations and foreign policy as discussed in Chapter 5. While the Soft Power Rubric data serve as a point of departure for setting historical context and country comparisons, it is the qualitative, often historical discussion that gives meaning to the data. At the core of immigration policy are issues of national identity. Education at its heart is about the transmission of culture and values from one generation to another, from one community to the next. When searching for channels that convert soft power relationships and resources into foreign policy action, these are likely to be the most useful areas to explore.

6

Movies and Popular Culture as Soft Power Indicators

WHETHER IT IS A SMILING JAPANESE PIKACHU PLASTERED across a transoceanic airplane full of fans or American singer Cher blasting "I believe, I believe, in love" over the radio in a Beijing taxi, the possibility of popular culture building bridges among strangers is undeniable. Movies are a major focus of the soft power literature. Nye (2004a) and many other theorists discussed in Chapter 2 argue that American popular culture, with movies as its marquee product, is one of the United States' most influential sources of soft power. Films from India, Nigeria, and South Korea, for example, all have many fans in their respective regions, and many scholars argue they are essential to these countries' soft power (Jang and Paik 2012; Onishi 2016; Tharoor 2007). One motivation for Chinese investment in global movies is the government's perception of a "cultural trade deficit" with the United States and the need to create an alternative global discourse (Kokas 2017).

A look at the available data, however, shows that the list of countries that produce widely watched movies is very short compared to those that attract a lot of international students, and especially compared to the long list of countries that attract substantial visitors and immigrants. Admittedly, the United Nations' statistical agencies' data on movies is far more recent and narrowly focused than on travel, education, and migration, but over time this series and perhaps other series for other popular culture media may deepen and grow. The very short list of blockbuster-producing countries does inspire the question—is pursuing popular culture success an essential soft power strategy? It can be an important strategy for some countries, but may not be essential.

What is important to look for in movies with potential for soft power influence? The Soft Power Rubric emphasizes the importance of the audience—how many foreigners watch a movie, rather than how many movies were produced. If the goal of soft power is to build a community of "we" rather than "they," then movies can be a gateway to building communities of trust. In my earlier work on trust communities, I show that social interaction mediated by technology—whether the telegraph, satellite television, or social media—where people have an opportunity to be with each other repeatedly over time, can turn a group of strangers into a community, a community that can be directed to social and political action (Wu 2015). Perhaps not one movie but a number of movies over time that bring people together across national lines can build a trust community. That is the kind of transformation that can lead to soft power influence.

United States at the Center of the Global Movie Industry

Rather than emphasizing movie production, the Soft Power Rubric looks to the audience. From this perspective, audience figures count more than the number of films. The following set of charts show data reported to UNESCO on how many tickets people bought to see foreign movies. These are tickets sold in foreign markets. For example, for a US-produced film, the number of admissions captures how many tickets were bought by people outside the United States. The results put into perspective for which countries movies really are soft power engines. Figure 6.1 shows that in

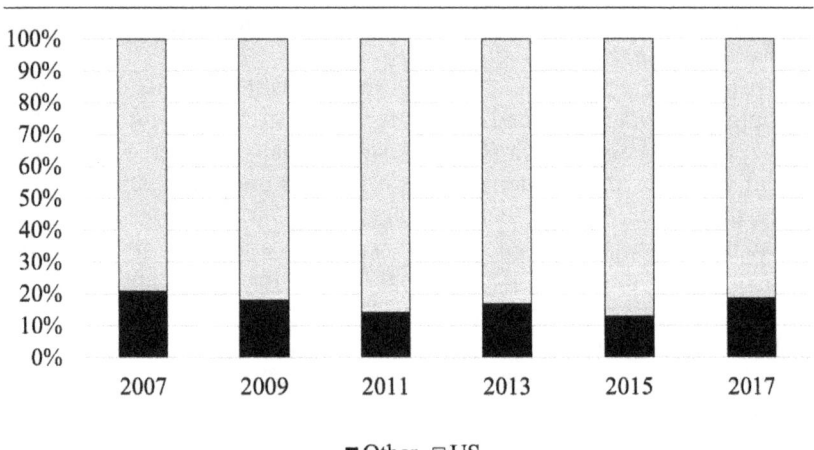

Figure 6.1 US-Produced Movies as Fraction of Total Global Admissions, 2007–2017

most of the selected years, US-produced movies represent around 80 percent of the admissions reported to UNESCO. US production still dominates the traditional movie business worldwide.

Note these data collected by UNESCO are limited to tickets sold in movie theaters that are reported in government data, and the world of movies is much larger than that. For example, there is video streaming on demand on platforms such as Netflix, which has subscribers, and YouTube, which is free to anyone who joins. Also, movies are shown for free on advertising-supported television and bundled into cable, satellite, or internet television subscriptions. However, so far, only UNESCO publishes time series data on countries around the world and its data to the public are free on its website. More data from a variety of sources will come out in the future, and this chapter lays out possible tools for analysis.

Figure 6.2 provides an overview snapshot of the UNESCO data. Between 2007 and 2017, the number of countries reporting admissions data ranged from twenty-nine to thirty-eight, and not every country reports in every year in this sample. The total number of admissions reported by this set of countries varies from 580 million in 2007 to 3 billion in 2011. Compared to the other Soft Power Rubric elements—migration, international education, and travel—the data on movies draw on a smaller set of countries over a shorter period of time.

Figure 6.2 UNESCO Movie Admissions, 2007–2017

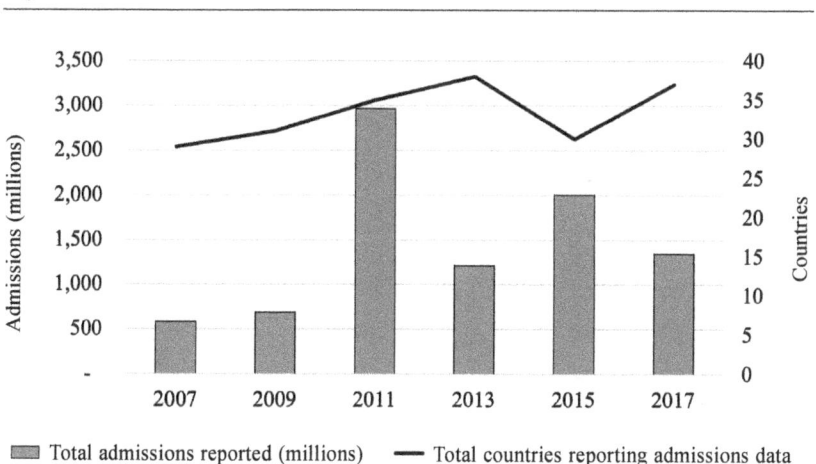

Source: UNESCO Institute of Statistics.

Other Major Movie Producers in the Global Market

While keeping in mind their shortcomings, it is still revealing to delve deeper into these data. Recall that in Figure 6.1, US-produced movies account for around 80 percent of all movie admissions outside the United States tracked by UNESCO. Figures 6.3 and 6.4 reflect the countries that produced the remaining 20 percent. Figure 6.3 shows the first set of movie-producing countries, the United Kingdom and France, which are second and third to the United States. Between 2007 and 2017, UK movies sold between 33 million and 181 million tickets outside the United Kingdom; France, between 22 million and 162 million outside of France. Movie ticket sales vary considerably from year to year, depending on which movies become hits. For example, 2011 is the release year for *Harry Potter and the Deathly Hallows (Part 2)*, a UK and US coproduction that was in the top three movies in twenty-eight out of forty-five countries reporting that year, either in terms of tickets sold or box office revenue.

Figure 6.4 shows the next largest producers of movies over this time period, and how many tickets those movies sold outside their home market: India, Germany, China, Spain, Australia, and Russia. These countries over time steadily produce movies that reach foreign audiences, sometimes on their own, sometimes in coproduction with other countries.

Again, the data are highly variable from year to year, reflecting individual movie hits.

The results show that for a small number of countries, their movies reach a sizable foreign audience, and there is a possibility these films could influence foreigners' view of the country. In broad terms, there are three

Figure 6.3 Major Movie Production Countries, Part 1, Admissions, 2007–2017 (every odd year)

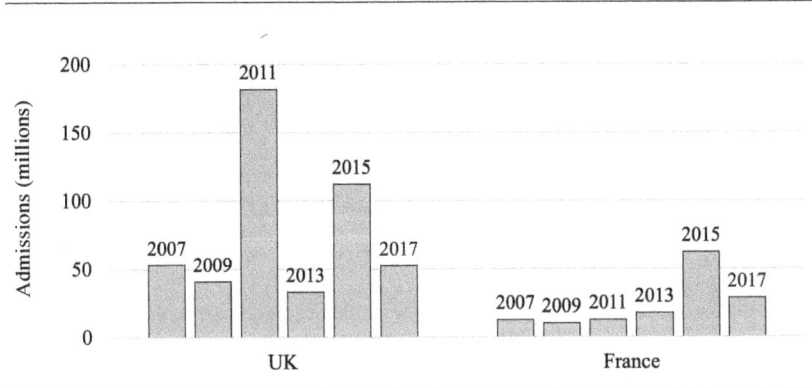

Source: UNESCO Institute of Statistics.

Figure 6.4 Major Movie Production Countries, Part 2, Admissions, 2007–2017 (every odd year)

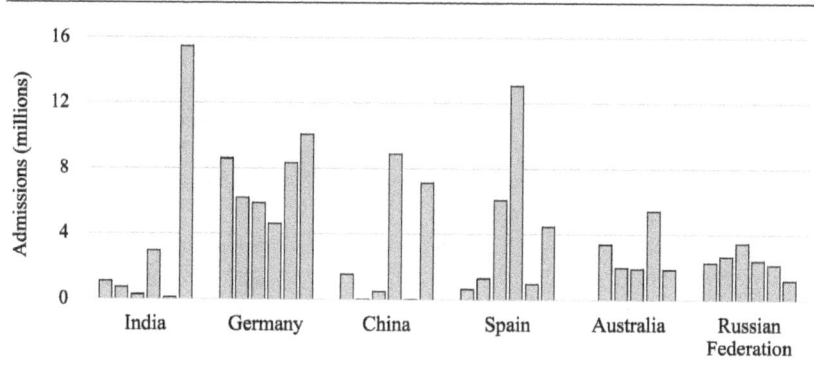

Source: UNESCO Institute of Statistics.

tiers. US production dominates, with the United Kingdom and France in the second tier. The third-tier countries of Australia, China, Germany, India, Russia, and Spain are big enough producers to show prominently in the global data. Compared to immigration and international education, movies are a relatively recent phenomenon. In general, the media research literature points to a general trend that as technology to produce and distribute content grows cheaper and movie markets deepen, more countries will participate in film production (Straubhaar 1991).

Many people watch movies in contexts that are not captured in official counts. While this is also true for international visits, study abroad, and migration, it is possible the extent of the issue is greater in the movie area. For example, Indian and Nigerian movies are all widely viewed outside their respective countries, especially and possibly mostly in informal markets, but these data are scarce. Therefore, while official data show total US domination as producer of the most popular movies in the world, reserving judgment is wise. Another concern is whether the data will be kept current. UNESCO has released data through 2017, but, as of 2023, they have not been updated.

Netflix as a Comparison

While the UNESCO data tell an interesting and important story, Netflix is a useful comparison. Though it is only one company, it is a growing business and globalizing rapidly. Netflix is an online technology platform that allows subscribers to watch movies on demand; once subscribers log on to the platform, they can select from a library of movies (Lobato 2018). They can watch as many movies as they want for no additional fee, and they can watch anytime at their own convenience.

Starting in 2015, Netflix began expanding beyond the United States to other countries. Figure 6.5 shows total subscribers doubling from around 110,000 in 2017 to 230,000 in 2022 (Netflix 2020, 2023). As of 2022, its largest regional market is "Europe, Middle East, Africa," and the fastest growing market is Asia Pacific. Subscribing to Netflix is an observable action people take to show they are interested, one analogue to buying a ticket to see a movie at the cinema.

Ideally, data that showed which movies Netflix subscribers watched, by audience nationality and movie country of production, would provide a contrast to the list of movie admission powerhouses shown in the previous section. However, Netflix does not release these data. What is available indirectly is information on Netflix libraries. Each of Netflix's national markets has its own library of movies available to subscribers, according to analysis by Amanda Lotz, Oliver Eklund, and Stuart Soroka (2022). Using data purchased from Ampere Analysis, they analyzed the seventeen libraries in Netflix and identified movies' country of production. Figure 6.6 shows the countries that produce the most movies that are included in the seventeen libraries combined.

Like the results from the UNESCO movie data in Figure 6.1, the United States is far and away the leader. In contrast with the UNESCO

Figure 6.5 Netflix Subscribers by Region, 2017–2022

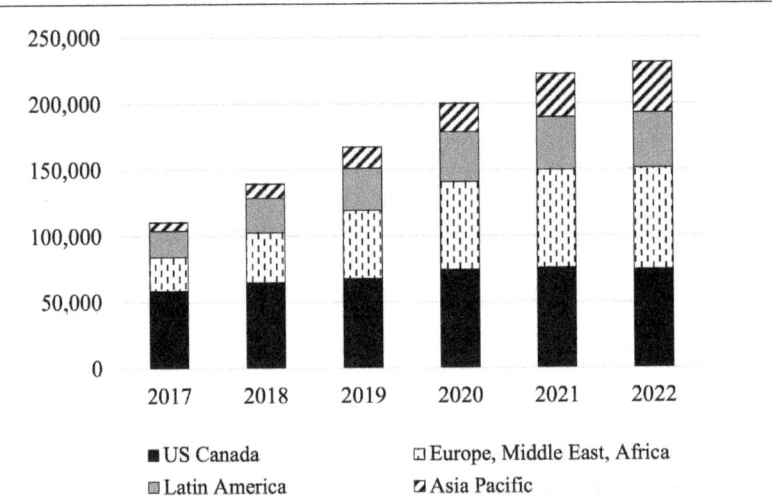

Source: Netflix Annual Reports 2019 and 2022 (Form 10-K), https://ir.netflix.net/financials/annual-reports-and-proxies/default.aspx.

Figure 6.6   Top 5 Production Countries in Netflix Library, 2021

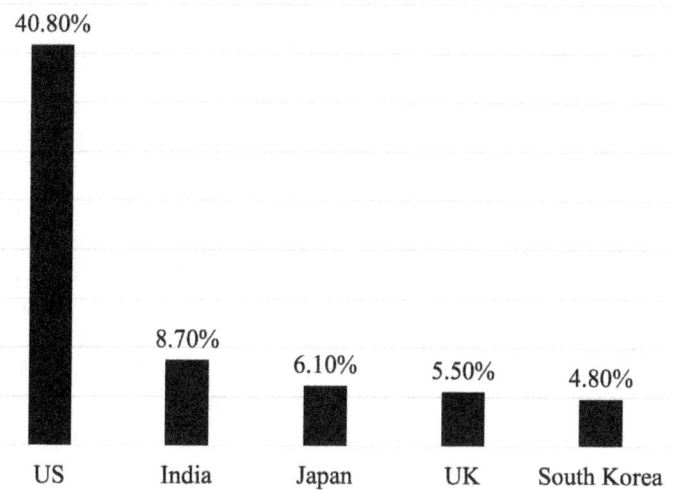

Source: Amanda Lotz, Oliver Eklund, and Stuart Soroka, "Netflix, Library Analysis, and Globalization: Rethinking Mass Media Flows," *Journal of Communication* 72(4) (2022): 511–621.

data, however, the second group of top-tier countries is quite different. The United Kingdom is still in this second group, but not France and Germany. Instead, India, Japan, and South Korea are leaders.

Figure 6.6 considers the seventeen Netflix libraries together. However, no single subscriber has access to all seventeen libraries; a subscriber only has access to the library in their own national market. Lotz, Eklund, and Soroka's (2022) analysis shows that within any single library, about 35–45 percent of the titles on offer are produced in the United States. This means over half the titles in every library are from other countries, a service unique to Netflix that stands in contrast to other services like Disney+ that offer primarily US content. Lotz and colleagues also note that some libraries primarily offer domestic content to its subscribers—the United States, Japan, South Korea, India, and the United Kingdom—while in other markets the Netflix library is primarily a way to access international movies. Netflix libraries cater to the interest of the customer (Lotz, Eklund, and Soroka 2022).

Netflix is only one streaming platform. There are several others based in the United States with global reach such as Prime Video and Disney+, and there are many more with more specialized reach. Lotz and Eklund (2024) highlight sixteen major non-US-based streaming platforms that reach more than one national market, including Globoplay (Brazil), Viu (Hong Kong), Zee (India), and ShahidVIP (Saudi Arabia). Their analysis of the libraries of these various platforms suggests a range of business strategies that can compete with or complement global platforms and existing multichannel video providers like cable and satellite television (Lotz and Eklund 2024; Lobato, Scarlata and Cunningham 2023).

How Media Can Build Transnational Trust Communities

In the eighteenth and nineteenth centuries, the daily mass ritual of reading the newspaper built in people's minds a consciousness of belonging to a particular nation, according to Benedict Anderson (1983). A nation is an *imagined community* of citizens who share similar concerns and interests and are bound together tightly enough to defend their nation against others. In my book *Forging Trust Communities*, I show that subsequent communication technologies like the telegraph, television, and social media create the possibility of similar *trust communities*, groups of people tied by common interests and concerns with the potential for collective action, either political or social (Wu 2015). I show how a group of bloggers from around the world came together online to run a cultural program, then quickly transformed themselves into an international humanitarian force when a large tsunami struck India and Southeast Asia. If people use communication technologies to interact, to exchange information and ideas, over time total strangers may become fellow travelers, who may over more time become important friends and colleagues (Wu 2015).

Similarly, movies support soft power relationships between countries when they serve as a gateway to social connection. Rather than a direct person-to-person interaction, movies and other cultural forms provide a mediated interaction between people of different countries. Over time, frequent and meaningful mediated interaction can lead to relationships that feel more like "we" than "they," or they can lead to direct interaction like travel, education, and migration. Movies and culture contribute to soft power relationships not as one-way broadcasts of a powerful country to the powerless, but when movies speak to a foreign audience and often listen back.

The opportunity to produce shows for Netflix gives producers in some countries the chance to reach a large, global market previously closed to them. This exemplifies how commercial investment can amplify diverse cultural voices, as Singh discusses in *Globalized Arts* (2011). At the same time, for some, these opportunities can be an incentive to pick certain stories or adapt narrative strategies that make them more legible to foreign audiences, a dynamic that can work with or against diversity of voice (Lotz 2023). Technological and economic change makes it easier for producers around the world to reach a larger audience, and this may transform what they decide to create. The interaction is not just or even primarily commercial, however.

Orlando Patterson (1994) documents how early roots of reggae music came from Jamaican disc jockeys who added their own rhythmic patterns and live performances to imported records. Reggae developed into its own distinctive form with a global audience and in particular spread into the United States with a large migration of Jamaicans in the early 1960s (Patterson 1994). When looking to movies and culture as an indicator for soft power relationships, it is important to look for the flow and movement of ideas and values, the social interaction among people, rather than the one-off productions.

Beyond Movies to Popular Culture

For media and popular culture, national-level data on audience and engagement harmonized at an international organization like UNESCO are rare. It is much easier to collect data on how much is produced and revenue earned than on how many people watched. In order to understand empirically the connection between media and soft power, faced with a choice between using producer data, as is so common in the research literature for understandable reasons, or letting go of the nation as the main unit of analysis, I lean in favor of the latter. For example, in a recent work I examined patterns of foreign visitors and visiting foreign staff at the Smithsonian Institution, the national museum of the United States (Wu 2023c). It was possible to identify some museums, such as the Smithsonian Air and Space Museum, as much more popular among foreign visitors than others, such as the American History Museum or American Art Museum, both of which have extensive collections of memorabilia from popular culture like movies and television shows. The Smithsonian Institution is just one set of museums. If over time there were further studies of more museums in more places that examined visitor data and other kinds of engagement data, a picture might emerge of what interest areas attract foreigners in different countries. A similar thematic approach could be taken for other categories of institutions—sports leagues, for example, or religious institutions. Who runs the international network? Who are the teams and players? And the fans, or the believers—who are they, and where do they come from?

Another approach is to examine cultural events. These have time boundaries, and often are in series—happening regularly on a fixed schedule. The Edinburgh Festival features music, theater, and dance, attracting performers and audiences from around Europe and the rest of the world. Mega sports events like the Olympics, or various World Cups for sport often generate discussion on the soft power benefits for the host. However, there are also soft power implications for the teams, and the fans—in person and watching on television or online—should also be part of the analysis (Wu 2023b). Videogaming, which can involve multinational networks of players and fans, is another possibility. Data on movies viewed outside cinemas, television programming, and other media events are also candidates. The challenge here is to connect individual cultural happenings to a larger claim about national soft power and how that translates into foreign policy influence. It is easier to make that claim for American movies and American soft power because of the US dominance of movie theater exhibitions worldwide for several decades. As technology and changing tastes transform the movie market, however, there is room to inquire whether other countries can successfully leverage blockbusters into political power.

Implications for Movies, Media, and Soft Power

The research shows that among the four elements of the Soft Power Rubric, international education is the one that most clearly transforms relationships with the host country of the university, as discussed in Chapter 3. Migration may work similarly, and the evidence for foreign travel and foreign movies is still emerging. As a thought experiment, if four different countries were invaded by their neighbors and asked my country for support, which ones would I help? The country where relatives had emigrated to (or where my family immigrated from), a country where I had studied at its university, a country I had visited on holiday, or a country that produced movies I liked? All other things being equal, very likely I would support helping the countries where I had the closest personal ties. Movies and other cultural forms, therefore, may be important contributors to soft power insofar as they create this sense of personal relationship; this might be in a story that resonates, in a presentation where there is more audience participation, or in some kind of direct engagement with the movie makers and the audience.

Among the four metrics of the Soft Power Rubric, whereas the other interactions are face-to-face, movies are a mediated interaction, the technologically newest, most transient, and most volatile from year to year. Trends in immigration and international education shift slowly; trends in international visits and movies change more quickly. This suggests that some aspects of people's relationships to foreign countries have long time horizons and others are faster to change. Among communications technologies, of course, films are the ancient ancestor of television, videogames, and online videos, which are now integrated into a range of social media platforms. Seen in this context, the UNESCO data on the top movies watched around the world, with its ten-year history, is a well-established series. Clearly, there are many opportunities for more research on newer media, transnational social interactions, and their relationship to soft power. Chapter 7 addresses another element of the Soft Power Rubric, international education, where the research shows a rich connection to building soft power relationships.

7

The Power of International Education Hubs

DURING THE COLD WAR, AUSTRALIA'S COLOMBO PLAN BROUGHT Asian students to its universities as a way to influence the elites of neighboring countries, while its White Australia policy restricted immigration to maintain its European identity. Ironically, the success of the Colombo Plan undermined domestic support for White Australia, according to many Australian scholars. Abandoning the idea of White Australia was part of the country's reorientation of its foreign policy toward Asia. Now students from around the world, especially from Asia, flock to its universities. This growing foreign student population is the factor that raises Australia's standing in the Soft Power Rubric measurements. Notably, the motivation behind the increase is the growth of higher education in Australia, funded in part by foreign student fees. In other words, the soft power gains appear unintentional. This case study begins by taking a global look at international higher education, and then I discuss Australia's developments in particular.

A Global View of International Education

Figure 7.1 shows the dramatic increase in students enrolled in foreign universities for a degree since UNESCO began collecting data in 1960s. In 1960, the number of foreign students worldwide was fewer than 150,000; by 2020 it was over 6 million.

In this book, "foreign students" are defined as those who enroll in foreign universities for a degree, the UNESCO definition of "international mobility" for students. This captures only a subset of the larger number of students who study abroad more informally, for example, for a year or two without pursuing a degree, or perhaps for language or cultural learning.

Figure 7.1 Total Students Enrolled in Foreign Universities for a Degree (millions), 1960–2020

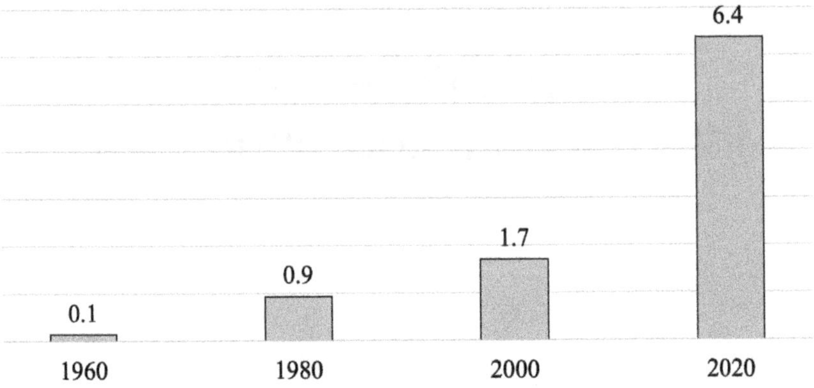

1960	1980	2000	2020
0.1	0.9	1.7	6.4

Source: UNESCO.

While degree-pursuing students are more likely to integrate more fully in the host society, even short stints have an effect. For example, Europe's ERASMUS program, which encourages cross-cultural understanding by funding students from Europe to travel to other parts of Europe for short periods of time, is sometimes described as academic tourism. While there is no measurable, direct educational or career benefit of participation in ERASMUS, the benefits of improving understanding, building greater cross-cultural confidence, make continuing the program worth it to the European Union (Lesjak 2015; Messer and Wolter 2007; Rodríguez González, Bustillo Mesanza, and Mariel 2011; Botas and Huisman 2013).

Figure 7.2 shows the five most popular destinations for foreign students from 1960 through 2020. Several countries consistently attract an increasing number of foreign students—the United States, the United Kingdom, France, and Germany. Between 2000 and 2020, Australia surpassed both France and Germany in the number of foreign students it attracted.

Figure 7.3 shows the top ten destinations for all foreign students in 2020. It also shows Australia ranked as the third most popular destination for foreign students, well ahead of France and Germany.

Australia–Global Leader in International Education

Historically, Australia's great international student program was the Colombo Plan. The Colombo Plan grew out of a foreign ministers' meeting in Ceylon, now Sri Lanka, in 1950 with the objective of improving cultural and educational exchange between Asia and Australia (Oakman 2001).

Figure 7.2 Top Destinations for Foreign Students (thousands), 1960–2020

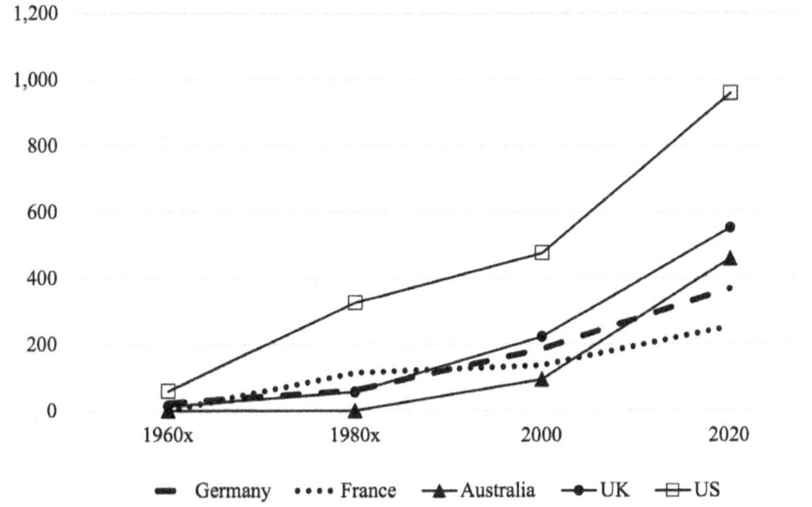
1,200
1,000
800
600
400
200
0
1960x
1980x
2000
2020
Germany
France
Australia
UK
US

Source: UNESCO Institute of Statistics.

Figure 7.3 Top Destinations for Foreign Students, 2020

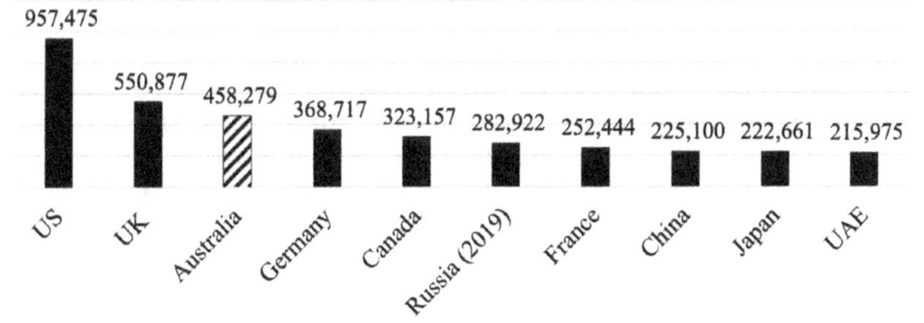
957,475
550,877
458,279
368,717
323,157
282,922
252,444
225,100
222,661
215,975
US
UK
Australia
Germany
Canada
Russia (2019)
France
China
Japan
UAE

Source: UNESCO.

The plan had supported over 20,000 foreign students in Australia by the time it ended in the 1980s. In the early years, driven by Cold War concerns, Australia was especially eager to build ties with friendly, anticommunist countries. The Colombo Plan was a major way to build relationships with foreign elites and impress upon them the excellence of Australian culture.

The Colombo Plan is an example of academic diplomacy, a practice with a long history. Going back to the end of World War I, the foundations of US-French student mobility were the US soldiers stationed in France between the 1918 armistice and the 1919 peace treaty. Many passed the time studying in French universities, and after they returned home, more American students flowed to France; in contrast, prior to World War I, most American students in Europe studied in Germany on the strength of its superior educational system. After World War II, US and Allied countries deliberately promoted transatlantic study. French and British universities adopted the PhD system to attract American students. US universities rolled out Western Civilization courses to bolster interalliance consensus (Irish 2015; Walton 2005).

During the Cold War especially, US and Soviet governments hosted foreign students with the goal of building ties with students' home countries. Imperial countries of the nineteenth century commonly hosted promising young colonials in their universities to improve administration of their empires. In the United States, academic diplomacy, which encompassed government programs and policies that supported student and faculty exchanges, was key to establishing its leading role in the North Atlantic community (Adam and Lerg 2015). Professors went abroad representing their university, their discipline, and also their government and country. The debates around the Fulbright program, which supports US scholars abroad, reveal the multiplicity of interests at play. Sometimes Fulbright programs were housed in a government department more responsible for propaganda, other times in a department with greater focus on cultural diplomacy (Bettie 2015).

In more recent times, there are programs that send students abroad with explicit international relations goals. The ERASMUS program is designed to support student travel within Europe in order to foster stronger European identity (Lesjak 2015; Messer and Wolter 2007; Rodríguez González, Bustillo Mesanza, and Mariel 2011; Botas and Huisman 2013). For students from Saudi Arabia, the King Abdullah Scholarship Program began in 2005 to improve Saudi Arabia's image abroad, enrich the country's human capital, and establish a path for long-term cultural change to lessen the influence of the ultraconservative religious establishment (Hilal, Scott, and Maadad 2015; Koch 2014).

While launching the Colombo Plan in the 1950s, Australia simultaneously maintained a strict immigration policy known as White Australia, which banned Asian immigrants from the country. The effect was that Colombo Plan graduates could not stay in Australia but were required to return home. However, the Colombo Plan students were in laboratories and lecture halls on campus. They often lived with host families. Ironically, Colombo Plan scholars were one of the main paths for Australians and Asians to socialize, build friendships, and learn about the other's culture (Darian-Smith and Waghorne 2016). Australian scholar Daniel Oakman describes it:

While publicly government officials and politicians cited the mutual understanding likely to stem from a mixing of Asians and Australians, such internationalization, was intended to reinforce the racial boundaries of the nation-state not remove them. The cultural negotiations fostered by these personal exchanges ultimately had the opposite effect, challenging imperial accounts of Asian dependence and inferiority and replacing them with more complex and intimate appreciations. That the presence of Asian students played an important role in the eventual demise of the White Australia Policy remains as one of the great unintended and unanticipated consequences of Australian foreign policy. (Oakman 2010)

By 1955, around the time the first cohort of Colombo scholars graduated, university activists were organizing against the White Australia policy. In 1960 the landmark pamphlet *Control or Colour Bar? A Proposal for Change in the Australian Immigration System* marked a public shift in attitude that welcomed a more open immigration system (Darian-Smith and Waghorne 2016).

Australians' love of travel was another important contributor to the unraveling of the White Australia policy. Travel guides and memoirs were among the most popular genres in the 1950s and 1960s. On the one hand, some professional writers were very aware of the Cold War foreign policy mandate to build better ties with fellow anticommunist countries. They called Asians "neighbors" and emphasized how Asians had everyday concerns just like Australians, an effort to persuade Australians to view them as "we" rather than an exotic "other." On the other hand, memoirs of this time recount not only Australians' shock at the poverty in many Asian countries, but also their positive impressions of the high standards of service, people's work ethic, and, in the case of Japan, the advanced technological gadgets of the time, like color televisions. Australian historian Manning Clark, author of the seminal *History of Australia,* recounts that a four-month visit to Indonesia, Singapore, and India reshaped his view of Australia's place in the world. Colleagues regularly asked him about Australia's complicity in the British colonial system, why it continued to rule over Papua New Guinea, and the reasons for the White Australia policy. This prompted him to note that many, but not all, Australians hated England—thus aligning Australia more with its neighbors in postcolonial history than with Europe (Sobocinska 2013). While Asia was not a major destination in 1955, in 1970, 35,000 Australians visited Singapore—a rise of 1,200 percent in fifteen years. In the 1970s, travel agents promoted package holidays to Asia; in 1973 more Australians went to Asia than to Europe, and since 1981 this has remained the case (Sobocinska 2013). With more regular and frequent contact with Asians—whether in Australia or abroad—Australians developed more complex and nuanced views; knowledge ultimately undermined the premise of the White Australia policy. A multicultural policy replaced White Australia in 1973.

84   *Using the Soft Power Rubric*

Drawing on the Soft Power Rubric, Figures 7.4 and 7. 5 show Australia's social network in Asia today. Figure 7.4 shows the main origin countries in 2017 of foreign students enrolled in Australian universities for a degree.

In 2020, Australia hosted 130,000 students from China and 84,000 from India. The other top sending countries are also from Asia. Australia's relationships with Asia continue to grow. The Soft Power Rubric data show the recent deepening of these relationships. Figure 7.5 shows immigration for Australia. Among immigrants, the largest community is from Great Britain at 1.3 million in 2020. Chinese immigrants numbered 653,000; New Zealanders 611,000; and Indians 580,000.

In Figures 7.4 and 7.5, the striped bars mark those countries that are in the top ten as a source of immigrants and students. This includes China,

Figure 7.4   Australia: International Students, Top Ten Countries of Origin, 2020

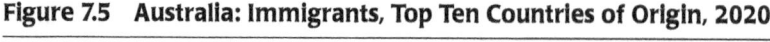

Source: UNESCO.

Figure 7.5   Australia: Immigrants, Top Ten Countries of Origin, 2020

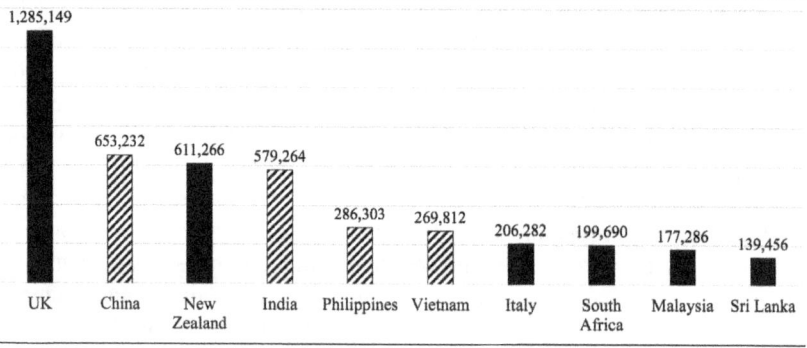

Source: UN Population Division.

ranked first among students and second among immigrants; India, second among students and fourth among immigrants; the Philippines, ninth among students and fifth among immigrants; and Vietnam, fourth among students and sixth among immigrants.

The Colombo Plan ended in the 1980s, and today Australia's higher education sector seeks foreign students for commercial, not political, reasons. The New Colombo Plan established by the Australian government in 2016, rather than bringing foreigners to Australia, instead supports Australians who study abroad (Australia, Government of 2021; Laifer and Kitchen 2017).

Australia spends relatively little on typical soft power projects. It has no cultural missions and no cultural centers abroad (Wang and Chitty 2021). Compared to its neighbors like Japan, China, and South Korea, with extensive cultural programs abroad, Australia's approach is distinctly laissez-faire. In this policy context, then, it is not surprising that Australian scholar Naren Chitty has developed the idea of "soft [power]," which is unintentional, which contrasts with "soft power," which implies it is backed by some kind of directed intent (Chitty 2019, 2023). The original Colombo Plan that was designed to influence neighbors instead was a major factor in transforming Australia itself. Now education growth driven by domestic interests contributes to Australia's soft power rise. The unintentional seems as or possibly more powerful than the intentional. Today Australia appears in rankings like the Soft Power 30—ninth in 2019. This is higher than Japan, China, and South Korea, with their better funded and more finely strategized soft power policies.

What Motivates Students to Study Abroad?

Australia's transition to a major international education hub follows several larger global trends. As a framework for organizing motivations, education scholars use the push-pull model, inquiring about what pushes students abroad and pulls them toward certain destinations (Mazzarol and Soutar 2002). The motivations that push them abroad reflect some dissatisfaction with university education at home. Scholars observe that for some students another push is the idea that study abroad is a kind of consumption that reflects the family's status and prestige. International education is not only of practical use to the student but also of symbolic value to the family that may be important to reproduce over generations (Pimpa 2005; Tsang 2013). Common factors that pull students to a particular foreign country and university include previous knowledge and awareness of the country; personal recommendations from family and friends; cost, financial and social, including crime and discrimination; environment and lifestyle concerns; proximity to home; and whether they already have family or friends in the foreign country. People making decisions whether to emigrate, to travel, and even to watch a movie follow a similar push-pull pattern of decisionmaking (Wu 2020).

Many students are pushed abroad because the training available at home universities is limited in some way. Mainland Chinese students go to Hong Kong and Macau because seats at Chinese universities are limited or they want instruction in English (Li and Bray 2007). Habu (2000) finds that Japanese women may want to escape the extreme gender bias pervasive at Japanese universities. Studies of Korean students find some chafe at the intensity of private tutoring necessary to gain admission to Korean universities when the quality of foreign universities is similarly high (Park 2009). Yet, the number of students from China, Korea, and Japan is declining compared to before, as their home universities improve (Kim and Roh 2017). The drop in Japanese and Korean students is already very pronounced, and a similar decline in Chinese students can be reasonably expected, a shift that is worth more investigation.

Beyond the practical gains, one pull of international education is an opportunity for students to acquire cultural capital and develop a transnational identity. Kaplan shares the stories of Jacqueline Bouvier, Susan Sontag, and Angela Davis—three American women whose identities and careers were strongly shaped by the year they spent in France. France shaped Bouvier's sense of style, Sontag's philosophy of life, and Davis's politics and language. In turn, each influenced US society: Bouvier, later Kennedy, as US first lady; Sontag as a leading writer of the feminist movement; and Davis as a major scholar and civil rights activist (Kaplan 2012).

Another pull is that international education is of symbolic value to the family and may be important to carry over generations. Baker's (2014) study of Canadian teenagers, Pimpa's (2005) research on Thai families, and Li and Bray's (2007) and Tsang's (2013) study of families in mainland China all show similar findings. Families and communities imbue with prestige certain universities in certain countries—values that young people accept and pass on to others. For some families, their children pursuing studies abroad fulfills one aspect of their self-identification as cosmopolitan elites who live transnational lives. Windle and Nogueira's (2015) study shows that Brazilian elite families strategically internationalize their children to ensure they have the "cosmopolitan cultural capital, most visible in the fluency of English." This strategy includes extended overseas school exchanges, short language courses and tours abroad, overseas holidays, and taking family on travel for work (Windle and Nogueira 2015). Travel, another element of the Soft Power Rubric, is aligned with education as one way for families to realize their transnational identities.

The research on migration brings insights to international student mobility. Empirical work on global migration between 1960 and 2000 shows that the largest number of migrants come not from the poorest countries but rather from middle-income countries (Czaika and Haas 2014). Migration transition theory argues that as a country modernizes, economic and technological change result in both domestic migration—from rural to urban areas—and also emigration abroad. As the economy industrializes, the labor pool shrinks and wages rise, then emigration flows transition to immigration flows (Haas 2020). In middle-income countries, more than in low-income countries, people have the resources, education, and information that feed their aspirations to migrate (Czaika and Haas 2014). For families from low-income countries, migration is a very difficult proposition, and those from high-income countries can expect slimmer gains. In international education, similarly, it is middle-income countries that are most likely to send young people abroad for training. Figure 7.6 shows that 70 percent of foreign students in the world originate from middle-income countries; of these nearly 40 percent are from China and India. About one-quarter of foreign students are from high-income countries and less than one-tenth are from low-income countries.

The higher education literature makes a distinction between global and regional hubs that rests on how economically developed the host nation is and the composition of foreign students it attracts—from nearby regions or from around the world. Reflecting on student motivation, researchers find foreign students from less economically developed countries than the host often have economic goals, while those from wealthier countries tend to

Figure 7.6 Students Enrolled in Foreign Universities for a Degree, by World Bank Country Income Classification, 2021

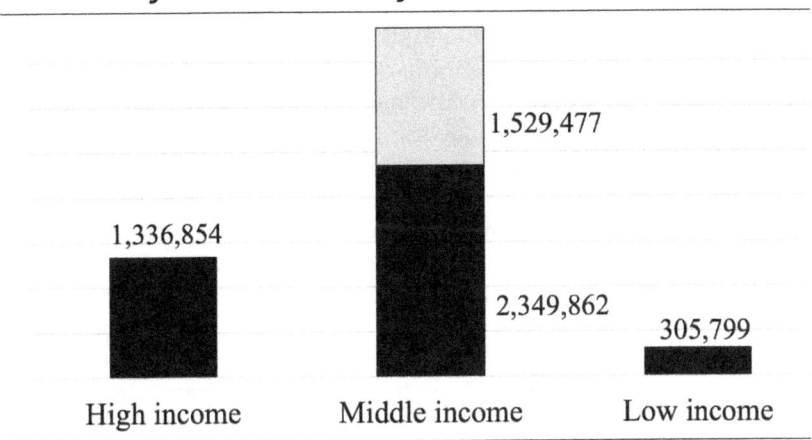

Source: UNESCO Institute of Statistics.
Notes: World Bank classifications are Low, Low Middle, High Middle, High. India is Low, Middle. China is High, Middle.

pursue cultural interests. In Korean universities, Asian students have specific educational, economic, and utilitarian goals; they are motivated by the ease of obtaining a visa, lower cost of living, and safety. Foreign students from North America or Europe tend to come for short-term exchanges and primarily are interested in Korean culture (Jon, Lee, and Byun 2014). In Mexico, Latin American students were the most academic oriented; they were more interested in quality of teaching and research in Mexico, the wealthiest country in the region. European and North American students are more interested in learning the culture without any specific educational or professional benefit (Cantwell, Luca, and Lee 2009). Similarly, in Türkiye, foreign students from wealthy countries had personal goals, while those from developing countries came for economic and academic reasons (Kondakci 2011). Students from less economically developed countries seek professional advancement from study abroad, while those from wealthier countries primarily seek personal growth.

Foreign Students Who Interact with Host Communities Fare Better

The Soft Power Rubric counts the volume of students; the data do not reflect the quality of the educational experience or whether the host country leaves a positive impression on the guest. There is research on when foreign students have poor or frustrating experiences abroad. For example, when surveyed, foreign alumni of Chinese military training regret that there were few opportunities to talk unofficially with instructors or with People's Liberation Army officers (Van Oudenaren and Fisher 2016). Foreign officers were unlikely to be able to speak Chinese and were segregated on different campuses from Chinese military officers. In the civilian world, in France's elite Grandes Écoles, while international students receive the same training as French students, they are flagged as foreign, given different degrees upon graduating, and are excluded from professional opportunities available to their French classmates. These practices tend to undermine the meritocratic model held up by French republican ideals (Darchy-Koechlin and Draelants 2010).

By contrast, students who have the opportunity to interact with a range of local people, who develop some long-term relationships, especially in unsupervised settings and unfiltered conditions, tend to have better overall experiences. Atkinson (2014) shows this is true for midcareer foreign military officers hosted at US military academies. Its programs actively encourage American hosts and foreign guests to build relationships to last a lifetime through interactions in class and in outside field trips. US military elite schools divide students into seminar groups of fewer than twenty who train and study together for a semester at a time, unlike students at civilian universities, who have different classmates in each class. Within a primary seminar group, students are likely to remain friends for life. Foreign military officers are fully integrated into these seminar groups. Special for foreign students, however, are the required field studies that take them into American communities to observe life off-campus and outside the military. Foreign military officers come to the United States with their families, and they are paired with sponsor families to integrate them into community life. The officers experience the United States not only through their own lives but also through the eyes of their family members (Atkinson 2014).

Walton's (2005) study of American and French students similarly emphasizes the importance not only of the curriculum but also of the opportunity to develop friendships and integrate with the local community as an essential aspect of a positive overall experience, even when close contact increased cultural frictions and personal conflict. Close, personal interaction with locals gives foreign students a different perspective on the host country's life and culture, reappraises any stereotypes they might have held earlier, and offers the opportunity to reexamine the image of their own country (Walton 2005). In the case of Australians, those who traveled and studied abroad in Asia came back with a different worldview and new ideas of their own country's role in the world.

Avoiding the Trap of Treating Foreign Students as Pawns in Diplomacy

Not to be forgotten are warnings from education scholars to keep in mind the whole development of the student and to not turn education into a tool of international politics. Altbach recounts the history of the global university, now divided between prestigious research universities in prestigious countries with expert faculty, large libraries, and deep research funds at the center, and at the periphery most other universities in most other countries. The center develops and publishes knowledge; the periphery depends on them for innovation and direction (Altbach 2012; Altbach and Kelly 1984). Furthermore, Takayama (2018) shows that American attitudes of white racial superiority influence curricula to the degree that many Asian and African countries jettisoned their own language and intellectual traditions when influenced to establish a Western model of university education.

In a different context, but with similar warnings, Lomer (2016) raises flags that British political policy talk promoting higher education as a booster to the United Kingdom's diminishing international influence risks instrumentalizing foreign students as pawns in foreign policy, when instead they should be treated as agents of their own future and their individual development as the proper objective of their education. This concern is echoed in its own way among Australian policymakers. Byrne (2018) remarks in a blog post, "For the past decade, Canberra has remained resistant to the soft power concept. Indeed, for some, shining a spotlight on Australian soft power is a problem. 'Isn't soft power like Fight Club?' one policy official suggested to me recently. I was perplexed. They continued, 'And the first rule of Fight Club is that you don't talk about Fight Club.' Ah. Got it. There's the resistance." This echoes Chitty's (2023) view that soft [power] that is unintentional is as important or possibly more so than soft power with intention behind it.

How Travel Abroad and Hosting Foreign Students Transformed Australian Identity

Among the Soft Power Rubric elements, by volume the number of foreign students is tiny compared to the number of immigrants and foreign visitors who travel the world in a given year. Nevertheless, the quantitative research discussed in Chapter 3 shows that international education is one of the most potent opportunities for countries to develop soft power relationships. Research on student experience shows they form better views of their host country when they have frequent social interaction with local communities and the opportunity to develop sustained friendships. The example of Australia as an education destination reveals how several elements of the Soft Power Rubric interact. The Colombo Plan to influence neighboring Asian countries by hosting their young people as students at Australian universities undermined support for the White Australia policy that intended to maintain the European identity of Australia. Australians traveling to Asia—an increasingly fashionable trend in the 1960s onward—changed many Australians' minds about the value of personal relationships with Asians, which changed foreign policy relationships with Asian countries. Expansion of the domestic higher education system led to attracting more foreign students to the country, in the long term leading to greater soft power influence, or as Chitty would phrase it, soft [power]. While interethnic and interracial frictions in Australian society remain, as they do in all countries that are truly diverse, today, in a complete reversal from the days of White Australia, Australia is regarded as an Asian nation, the third largest destination for foreign students, a major leader in the region, and an important global player.

8

Indian Emigrants as Drivers of Soft Power

YEARS AGO, TRAVELING ON A HIGH ASIAN PLATEAU, I BOUGHT a yak jacket from a street market merchant. I still wear it today. We bargained, we settled a price, I paid, she made too much change, I returned the difference. Surprised, she asked me where I was from. Befuddled at outing myself as a foreigner, "America," I replied. In economics, the purchase connects directly to the calculation of the country's gross domestic product. The sum of all yak jacket prices is added to sums across other sectors and published as a yearly total. How about in international relations and politics? She left an impression of her country, and I of mine. Can that be entered into a calculus of soft power resources?[1]

Much has been written about India's soft power—how much it has, its sources and origins, and its deficits and applications. In this chapter I aim to place India's soft power in context of other nations like China and the United States, by applying the Soft Power Rubric, a model that harnesses quantitative data on ordinary human interactions—like foreign visitors appearing in local street markets—to understand the relationships among countries. In this examination of India's soft power, the focus is on the activity of ordinary people, not necessarily actions by the government. Up to this point, I have analyzed soft power by the flows of people into a country—for example, by emphasizing how many immigrants, students, and visitors went to France rather than examining the influence of French abroad. This chapter gives primacy not to the directionality of the flow or the geographic location of an interaction, but to the social interaction itself. Drawing on the insights from Chapter 2 on social interaction and trust, how is it that most people in the world have the opportunity to interact socially with Indians? Is it in India or elsewhere, and what implications does this have for understanding its soft power? (Wu 2021).

The international relations literature on soft power includes several significant volumes on India. Tharoor (2007) writes, "Mahatma Gandhi won us our independence through the use of soft power—because nonviolence and satyagraha were indeed classic uses of soft power before the term was even coined. Pandit Nehru was also a skilled exponent of soft power: he developed a role for India in the world based entirely on its civilizational history and its moral standing, making India the voice of the oppressed and the marginalized against the big power hegemons of the day." Nair (2020, 2023) writes that today's debates around India's secular identity, widely admired abroad but contested within India, have implications for its soft power abroad. Kugiel's book *India's Soft Power* (2017) also emphasizes India's moral authority. Kugiel identifies India's cultural diversity—racial, religious, ethnic, and linguistic—as a major source of soft power. He also emphasizes its democratic political values, diaspora, and economic potential as attractive to foreigners (Kugiel 2017). Chadda's *Why India Matters* (2014) focuses on India's civilization, democracy, and diaspora as its main soft power resources. She highlights the success of the Indian diaspora, especially in market economies abroad, as an important way for India to project soft power (Chadda 2014). Kumar and Biswas's edited volume *Modi's Cultural Diplomacy and Soft Power* (2016) covers this government's heightened interest in cultural and diasporic connections with other countries along with special essays on movies, religion, diaspora, and cuisine. Finally, Schaefer and Karan's edited volume *Bollywood and Globalization* (2012) provides a historical and social analysis of the Indian movie industry's growing global influence, including the effects of political change in India on the type of movies exported abroad.

There are several soft power indices. The Soft Power 30 index identifies annually the leading countries with quantitative data on culture, digital diplomacy, education, engagement, enterprise, and government. In recent years, India does not appear among the global top thirty, but in the 2018 report, which included an Asia Index, India ranks eighth (McClory 2021). India also appears in the cultural influence section of the Lowy Asia Power Index, ranked third in 2018 and fourth in 2019 (Lowy Institute 2021). These indices' simplicity keeps soft power on the radar of policymaking and business elites, although the confidentiality of their algorithms reduces their academic rigor.

In contrast, the Soft Power Rubric centers on understanding in which foreign countries are people attracted to India and, vice versa, which foreign countries attract Indians to go abroad. The sum of this activity paints a picture of cultural affinity and social interaction unlike any other analysis of soft power.

Exploring India with the Soft Power Rubric

The quantitative data of the Soft Power Rubric are indicators that suggest which lines of qualitative inquiry might prove fruitful. From movies to migration, scholars of India's soft power highlight its strengths and weaknesses; the quantitative data can place India in global context and also unearth changes over time. Throughout this analysis India is compared with other countries. Indian government reports and other research on soft power often highlight China (Singh et al. 2010), which also has an active soft power strategy; therefore, China is included in several instances. Further, India aspires to join groups like the G7, membership in which is determined as much by a country's soft power as its economic power; therefore, India is compared to G7 members like France and Italy.

Foreign Audiences for Indian Movies

Indian movies are the most popular image of the country in many regions of the world. In the 1970s, in several countries ranging from Indonesia to Nigeria, Indian movies had a virtual monopoly since few were locally made. In the Soviet Union, they were very popular, until American movies were allowed (Roy 2012). With greater economic liberalization in the early 1990s, Indian movies took a more popular turn, shifting from the mainly classical styles to more Western-style, hybridized productions (Schaefer and Karan 2012). While there is substantial qualitative work on the popularity of Indian films, quantitative data on the number of foreigners who watch Indian movies is difficult to come by and, therefore, is an opportunity for further research.

In qualitative studies and compelling personal stories, India's movie industry is often held up as an example of its soft power, but no quantitative studies have been able to link empirically its movies to influence in foreign policy. The trend is that more countries are producing and coproducing movies that reach a global audience. It is reasonable to expect that there will be more diversity of movies in the global market, as has happened in other media markets like television and radio. Straubhaar, an expert on Brazil's media industry, argued in the 1990s that the United States was not as dominant in the world media market as it once was, and that this was part of a predictable cycle of technology and structural change. If the United States was an early entrant into an industry, like the movies, then it has a first mover advantage, especially when the costs of production and distribution are high. However, as production and distribution costs decline, other countries' producers will grow (Straubhaar 1991). The UNESCO data show that while US-produced movies continue to sell tickets, the number of coproductions among investors from different countries is also rising. Given that India is already among the small number of countries with movies appearing regularly in the UNESCO top ten lists, as discussed in Chapter 6 on movies, the prospects for growing prominence are good.

Foreign Visitors, Students, and Immigrants in India

For the other three elements of the Soft Power Rubric, there are excellent data on India. There has been a steady increase in foreign visitors and students to India in recent years, reflecting India's pull on people in other parts of the world. Tourists come to see the sites and businesspeople to explore opportunities. Foreigners enrolling in an Indian university shows an even greater commitment to learn about the country. It also reflects the students' confidence that India offers opportunities for intellectual and technical learning that are better than at home.

To put India's soft power influence into context, it helps to compare India with China's pull on foreign visitors and foreign students as shown in Figure 8.1.

As the bars in Figure 8.1 show, while in 1980 and 1990 there were more foreign students in India (solid bar) than in China (dotted bar), around

Figure 8.1 Foreign Visitors and Foreign Students in India and China, 1980–2020

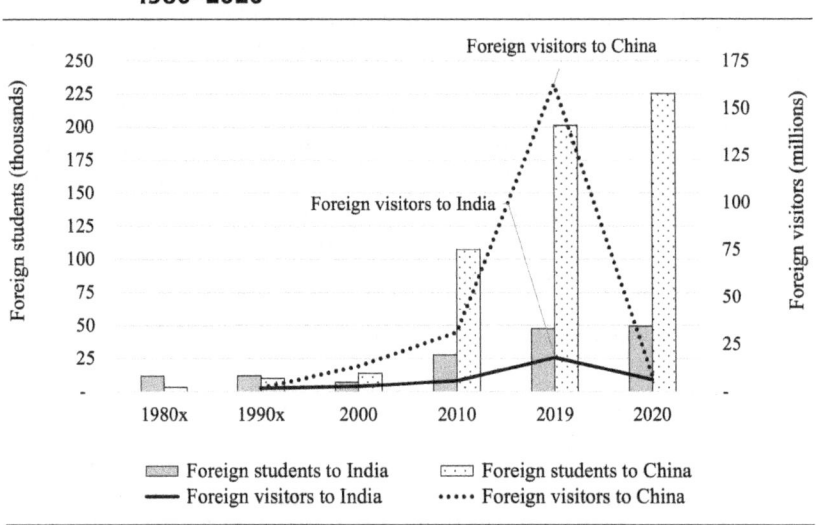

Sources: UN World Tourism Organization and UNESCO Institute of Statistics.
Notes: Reporting years vary: 1980x = 1981 (China) and 1978 (India); 1990x = 1989 (China) and 1986 (India).

2000 China overtook India. Similarly, in foreign visitors, represented by lines in Figure 8.1, India (solid line) and China (dotted line) were at comparable levels in the 1990s, but foreign visitors to China have grown faster than to India. In 2020 at the beginning of the global Covid-19 pandemic, foreign visitors to both India and China dropped dramatically; however, foreign student numbers remained steady. Hosting foreign visitors is a short-term and hosting foreign students is a long-term opportunity to build soft power with people from other nations. Even though India's numbers have grown rapidly, China began to overtake it in 2000, also reflecting a shift in soft power influence.

Where India far exceeds China is as host for foreign immigrants, and through these immigrants India has deeper soft power relationships with their home countries that China lacks. Figure 8.2 shows the number of foreigners who lived in both countries from 1990 to 2020.

In 2020, India is home to over 4.9 million immigrants; China just over 1 million. Historically, there were two large waves of refugees that came to India, first after Partition in 1947 and the second from Bangladesh after the 1971 war. The decline in total immigrants in India since 1990 is due to these now elderly refugees passing away (Shrinivasan 2012). China hosts more immigrants than it did before, more than doubling between 1990 and 2015. However, the government's concerns about foreigners is reflected in

Figure 8.2   India and China Immigrants (millions), 1990–2020

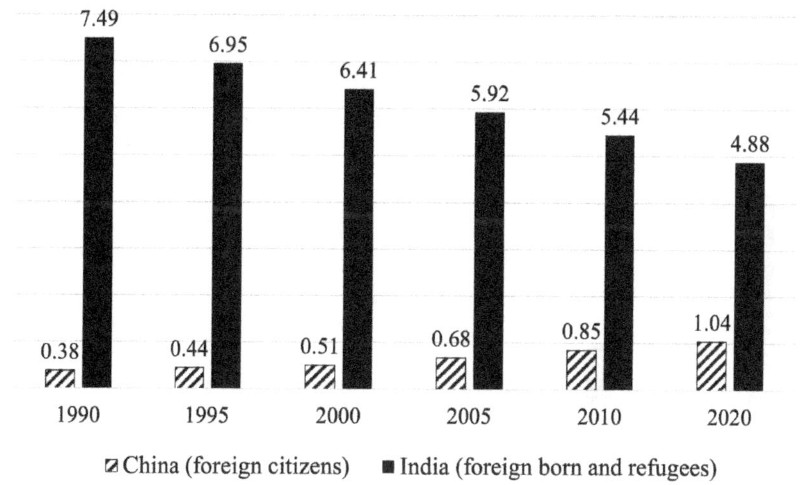

Year	China (foreign citizens)	India (foreign born and refugees)
1990	0.38	7.49
1995	0.44	6.95
2000	0.51	6.41
2005	0.68	5.92
2010	0.85	5.44
2020	1.04	4.88

Source: UN Population Division.

its immigration policy (He and Ye 2017). Especially compared to India, China's restrictive approach is a missed opportunity in terms of extending its soft power influence.[2]

When emigrants move to India, that is evidence that foreigners are attracted to the country, an indicator that there is a soft power relationship between the two countries. When immigrants come for a better life, they hold India in high esteem. When refugees arrive to escape troubles at home, at minimum India is a safer haven than before. Figure 8.3 shows which countries sent immigrants to India as of 2020.

Of all the immigrants in India, 3 million were from in Bangladesh, 1 million from Pakistan, and over half a million from Nepal. These are the countries where India's soft power influence is likely to be the greatest.

Indians Abroad Building Soft Power Relationships

Indian Students Abroad

Another important aspect of the Soft Power Rubric is how many Indian students go abroad, serving as unofficial cultural ambassadors. For a few years, these students are part of these foreign communities, building friendships and relationships that leave a lasting impression of India (Wu 2020). Figure 8.4 shows the remarkable movement of Indian students to study at foreign universities for a degree.

By 2010, with annual figures approaching 200,000 students abroad a year, India is second only to China with the largest movement of young people to foreign universities. Kapur (2010), in his book on the Indian diaspora, argues that the government was able to undertake reforms that

Figure 8.3 Indian Immigrants: Top Ten Countries of Origin, 2020

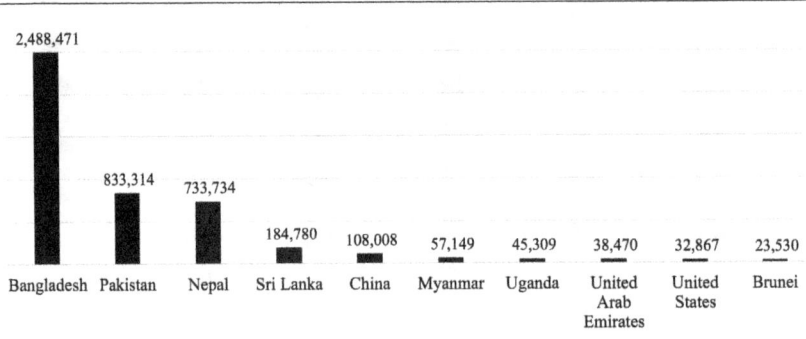

Source: UN Population Division.

Figure 8.4   Indian Students Abroad, 1960–2020

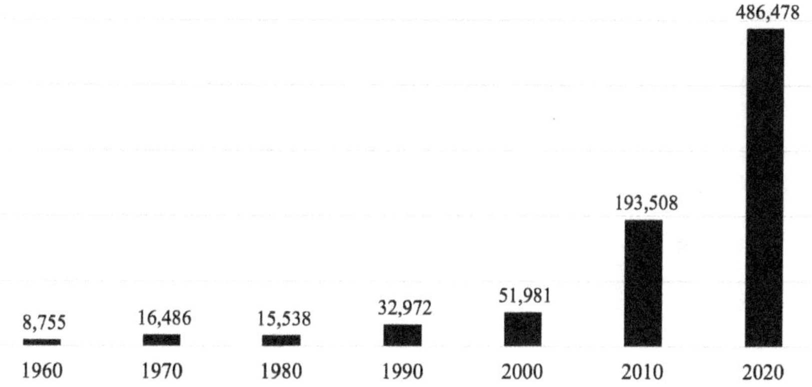

1960	1970	1980	1990	2000	2010	2020
8,755	16,486	15,538	32,972	51,981	193,508	486,478

Source: UNESCO Institute of Statistics.

rebalanced privilege from the elites to non-elites in part because dissatisfied elites always had the option of emigrating. In particular, as education policy made it easier for non-elites to gain seats at university, elite families sent their children abroad to foreign campuses. While this drains talent away, it increases India's profile abroad. India's diaspora has deep network power, a consequence of personal relationships and professional ties (Kapur 2010).

Figures 8.5 and 8.6 show the top country destinations of Indian students enrolled in foreign universities. In 1960, about one-third of the students went to the United States; in 2017, 42 percent to the United States and 15 percent to Australia.

In 1960, the top destinations for Indian students studying abroad were the United States, the United Kingdom, and Germany. In 2021, the top destinations were still the United States and the United Kingdom, but now also Canada and Australia. These figures also reflect the rise of English-speaking countries besides the United States and the United Kingdom that seek more foreign students—Canada, New Zealand, and Australia, especially.

Indian Emigrants Abroad

India has the largest emigrant community outside its borders of any other country—nearly 18 million people abroad. If counted as a country itself, this emigrant community would be the 66th largest of the over 200 countries in the world (see Table 8.1).

Figure 8.5 Indian Students Abroad by Country, 1960

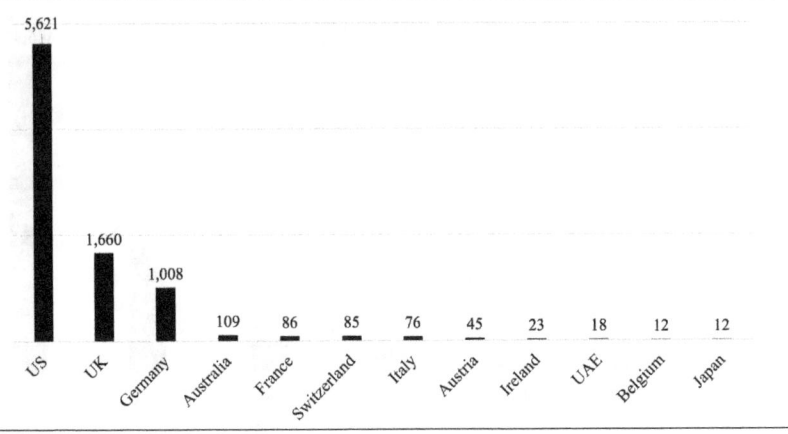

Source: UNESCO Institute of Statistics.

Figure 8.6 Indian Students Abroad by Country, 2021

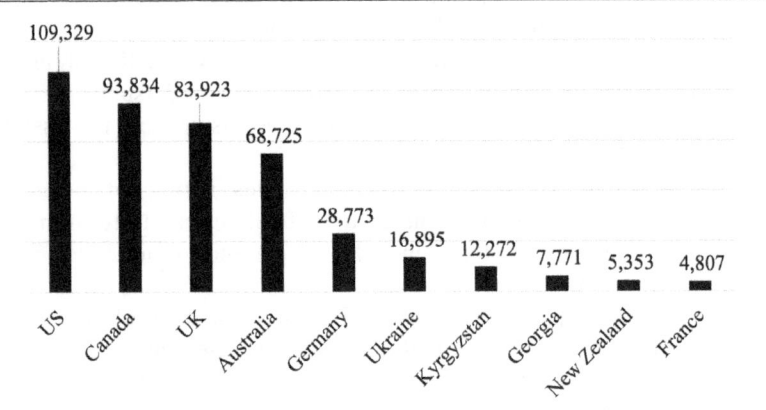

Source: UNESCO Institute of Statistics.

Countries that host immigrants report their citizenship or country of origin.[3] Therefore, these figures do not capture those in the diaspora who retain strong cultural ties to India but were born outside India and/or have non-Indian citizenship. If they are considered, the Indian diaspora community abroad is even larger than the 18 million.

Diaspora communities are inevitably linked to the ancestral country's soft power. The Indian diaspora is a particularly important one, and the

Table 8.1 India's Emigrant Community Compared to Other Countries' Total Population

World Rank	Country	Total Population 2020
61	Malawi	19,377,061
62	Chile	19,300,315
63	Romania	19,265,250
64	Zambia	18,927,715
65	Kazakhstan	18,755,666
	Indian emigrant community	*17,869,492*
66	Ecuador	17,588,595
67	Netherlands	17,441,500
68	Guatemala	16,858,333
69	Chad	16,644,701
70	Somalia	16,537,016

Source: World Bank.

Indian government publishes data regularly on how many there are and where they live (India, Government of 2001). Comparable data for the diaspora of other countries are not easily available; therefore, for the purposes of this chapter, I compare only immigration data. However, this would be a fruitful avenue for further research.

Kapur (2010) explains some of the historic, political drivers behind this migration. When India introduced universal franchise soon after independence, the political hegemony of upper castes evaporated. Later in the 1950s, the upper castes of South India were squeezed out of government jobs and universities; they migrated to other parts of India and into central government jobs. In the late 1960s, they exited from the public to the private sector, and then out of the country. In 1990, the government increased affirmative action. Migration was an effective outlet for elites who found their status ebbing; within ten years the political controversy over affirmative action faded (Kapur 2010).

Since 1990 India has been among the top five countries with the largest emigrant communities abroad, as shown in Table 8.2. India's emigrant community was the third largest in the world in 1990 and 2000, and first largest in 2010 and 2019. Figure 8.7 shows the top ten host countries for Indians living abroad as of 2020. Again, as with Figure 8.2, these figures represent a snapshot of the total size of the Indian emigrant community living there in a given year, not the number of new Indian immigrants who crossed the border that year.

In 2020, there were nearly 3.5 million Indian emigrants in the United Arab Emirates (UAE), 2.7 million in the United States, and 2.5 million in

Table 8.2 Top Five Countries with the Largest Emigrant Communities Abroad

	1990		2000		2010		2020
Total World	152,542,373	Total World	172,604,257	Total World	220,019,266	Total World	280,598,105
Russia	12,664,537	Russia	10,734,963	*India*	13,321,332	*India*	17,869,492
Afghanistan	6,724,681	Mexico	9,562,278	Mexico	12,413,085	Mexico	11,185,737
India	6,718,862	*India*	7,978,365	Russia	10,213,313	China	10,756,697
Ukraine	5,549,477	China	5,786,954	China	8,648,885	Russia	10,461,170
Bangladesh	5,451,546	Ukraine	5,596,463	Bangladesh	6,742,845	Syria	8,457,214

Source: UN Population Division.

Notes: In South Asia, the Partition is an example of borders shifting, making "immigrants" of some people who had not moved. Sometimes, immigration data reveal moving borders, not moving people. While the UN data released in 2017 list Russia in 1990, the Soviet Union did not officially dissolve until 1991. The UN data reflect the political boundaries after the collapse of the Soviet Union. The number of Russians abroad declined. In Central Asia, in 1990 there were 4.6 million, but in 2015 there were 3.6 million; in Eastern Europe, in 1990 there were 6.2 million Russians, but in 2015 there were 1.1 million.

Figure 8.7 Top Ten Host Countries of Indian Emigrants Abroad, 2020

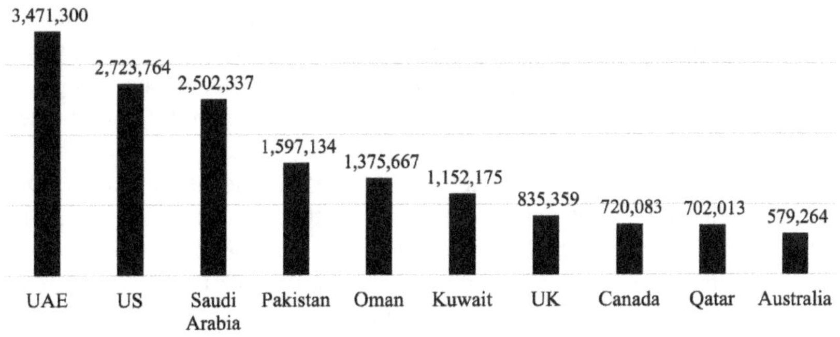

UAE	US	Saudi Arabia	Pakistan	Oman	Kuwait	UK	Canada	Qatar	Australia
3,471,300	2,723,764	2,502,337	1,597,134	1,375,667	1,152,175	835,359	720,083	702,013	579,264

Source: UN Population Division.

Saudi Arabia. Using the lens of the Soft Power Rubric, India outranks most other countries in terms of the number of students and emigrants abroad. These are the major sources of India's soft power relationships with other countries. While typically a country's ability to attract foreigners would be the measure of its soft power influence, through inward visitors, students, and migrants, India is a special case. For most countries, their best chance of interacting with foreigners is when foreigners visit. For India, however, its community abroad is as large as many countries and represents the main opportunity for foreigners to enjoy social interactions with Indians and Indian culture. Beyond the Soft Power Rubric, there are innumerable areas for transnational social interaction ranging from music to cuisine, and fashion to literature. While for the moment they lend themselves less to quantitative cross-national comparisons, there is ample room for further work.

Soft Power Success: The G20

India's membership in the leading global leadership group, the G20, is an example of its soft power. Perhaps it is overlooked in the India soft power literature because bigger diplomatic prizes—such as a seat on the UN Security Council—still elude it. Nevertheless, a closer inspection of how G20 countries were selected shows that being included is less a matter of economic size and more a matter of political importance, underpinned by soft power.

India aspires to be part of not just the G20, perhaps, but also of the leading G8 (with Russia's expulsion, now G7). Consequently, for India, getting into the G20 may seem like second best. Parthasarathi Shome in one of two volumes on the G20 development agenda says, "In the new multipolar world, India enjoys considerable attention reflective of its integration with the global economy through the current and capital accounts of its balance of payments. However, its growing economic advances are not fully reflected in the prevailing global governance arrangements, beginning with the above-mentioned G8+O5 outreach programme, which did not represent India's interests adequately" (Shome 2014).

Shome refers to an effort that began in 2005 for the G8 to include "Outreach 5" countries, India among them. A vignette captures the reality: At the 2005 meeting in Gleneagles, Scotland, though in principle the O5 were welcome guests, in reality G8 leaders held a summit lunch to discuss outreach while O5 leaders were kept waiting outside the room (Naylor 2019). Around this time India and others also sought to reform the United Nations and gain a seat on the Security Council, reforms that today have yet to take place. These frustrations for India may loom larger than the successes—getting into the G20.

G-groups are responses to financial crises. Table 8.3 identifies the stages of G-group meetings at the leadership and finance minister level (Bradford and Linn 2012). The smaller G7 and G8 leader meetings are more prestigious. The larger G20 began as a lower-level meeting, a gathering of finance ministers in the wake of the 1998 financial crisis. In 2005, concerned it was losing relevance, the G8 created an outreach program to include Mexico, China, India, Brazil, and South Africa (O5). However, G8 countries continued to set the agenda with O5 in secondary roles. Not until the global financial crisis of 2007 was the broad G20 group elevated from finance minister to leader level.

In 1998, the formal decisions on creating the ministerial-level G20 were made by US Treasury Secretary Lawrence Summers and Canadian Finance Minister Paul Martin (Naylor 2019). A more informal accounting of events suggests that they were selected by US Treasury official Timothy Geithner and his German Finance Ministry counterpart Caio Koch-Weser (Wade 2009). The incumbent members of the G8 were all included, and the group expanded to encompass systematically significant countries that subscribed to a liberal economic agenda with a domestic standard of good governance (Naylor 2019). However, this definition is more honored in the breach, as Tristen Naylor argues.

> Despite original club members no longer being undisputedly larger economies than others, they remain in the top-tier group. G7 members have not maintained the relative economic power that they enjoyed in 1975. Within only five years both China and Brazil had displaced Italy to make it ranked eighth in 1980. By the time the G20 was established at the ministerial level in 1999, India had achieved the rank of being the seventh largest economy. Despite club members' declining rank, their status was unaffected. This

Table 8.3 Brief History of G-Group Meetings

Stage	Leader Level	Finance Minister Level
Building to G8	1973: After the collapse of the Bretton Woods foreign exchange regime andthe onset of a global oil crisis, a group met as the "Library" group, and included the US, UK, France and Germany. Japan joined later in 1973, Italy in 1975, Canada in 1976, making it the G7. The European Community in 1977; Russia joined in 1997, now it was the G8.	
G20 created		1999: The 1998 financial crisis triggered in Southeast Asia led to the creation of the first G20 finance ministerial-level meeting—a lower level meeting compared to the leaders meetings.
G8+O5	2005: G8 added the Outreach 5 (O5), Mexico, China, India, Brazil, and South Africa.	
G20 elevated	2008: After the global financial crisis of 2007, the G20 was elevated from finance minister to leader level in 2008.	
G8 becomes G7	2014: Russia cast out of G8 after its invasion of Crimea. Back to G7.	

was particularly so for Italy and Canada. Indeed, Canada has never ranked as a top-seven economy and Italy has not been worthy of the distinction since 1980. They were able to maintain their spots because of precedence. As a result, having gained inclusion they could not lose it. (Naylor 2019)

José Antonio Campo and Joseph Stiglitz (2012) also raise concerns that the G20 membership is limited. Countries with large populations and GDP like Nigeria have been excluded; the Arab members fall short in meeting the criteria; the Europeans are overrepresented; and least-developed countries are unrepresented (Ocampo and Stiglitz 2012). In short, there is widespread agreement in the scholarly literature that inclusion in the G20 has less to do with the size of a country's economy and the democratic and good governance values of its political system than with customary diplomatic influence, a version of soft power.

At the time of the G20's formation in 1998, India was the thirteenth largest economy.[4] In Table 8.4, the italicized countries were not included despite their large economies. In particular, several of the smaller European economies in the top twenty were excluded. Countries like South Africa and Indonesia were included in an effort to be more representative, but Spain, the Netherlands, Switzerland, and Sweden were excluded even though at the time they were among the top twenty largest economies. In addition, there are thirteen excluded economies larger than Indonesia, which was included.

Table 8.4 Top Countries by GDP, 1998

Rank	Country	1998 GDP (current US$)
1	United States	9,062,818,202,000
2	Japan	4,032,509,760,873
3	Germany	2,238,990,774,703
4	United Kingdom	1,650,172,242,464
5	France	1,503,108,739,159
6	Italy	1,270,052,525,928
7	China	1,029,043,097,554
8	Brazil	863,723,411,633
9	Canada	631,813,279,407
10	*Spain*	*619,214,834,614*
11	Mexico	526,502,129,378
12	*Netherlands*	*438,008,220,395*
13	India	421,351,477,505
14	Australia	398,899,138,574
15	Korea, Rep.	383,330,931,042
16	Argentina	298,948,250,000
17	*Switzerland*	*295,045,151,745*
18	Türkiye	275,967,393,985
19	Russian Federation	270,955,486,862
20	*Sweden*	*270,809,066,781*
21	*Belgium*	*258,528,339,631*
22	*Austria*	*218,259,904,402*
23	*Denmark*	*176,991,934,993*
24	Poland	174,685,791,564
25	Hong Kong SAR, China	168,886,163,222
26	Norway	154,163,364,303
27	Saudi Arabia	146,775,498,093
28	Greece	144,428,172,489
29	South Africa	137,774,755,609
30	Finland	134,038,718,291
31	Portugal	123,946,327,916
32	Israel	115,932,846,767
33	Thailand	113,675,561,057
34	Iran, Islamic Rep.	110,276,913,363
35	Colombia	98,443,739,941
36	Indonesia	95,445,547,873

Source: World Bank.

The language used by various country scholars in Hofmeister's (2011) collected volume on perceptions of the G20 reflects their knowledge of how precarious their membership is. Türkiye is aware it might have been excluded, following a pattern that it is often isolated in the international community, say Huseyin Bagci and Ilan Turan. Indonesia is grateful to be included, especially as a representative of Southeast Asia and ASEAN in particular, writes Zamroni Salim. South Africa is willing to be a responsible stakeholder, but also notes that the job of representing all of Africa in its diversity is an onerous responsibility, writes Laurence Bourelle. All these scholars note that membership in the G20 is affirmation of a country's political importance—not just its economic significance—an opportunity to take part in setting the rules of global governance rather than simply being subjected to them (Hofmeister 2011).

Economic size alone does not determine membership in the G20 or G7. Therefore, India's successful membership in the G20 reflects the soft power it exercises, in addition to its growing economic influence. A summary of India's Soft Power Rubric data shows that in the period leading up to the late 1990s when the G20 was formed, India became more outward facing. Figure 8.8 below shows an increase in nearly every metric of Indians' social interactions with foreigners. Foreign visitors and Indian visitors going abroad rise sharply from 1960 forward, except for 2020 when the Covid-19 pandemic reduced travel worldwide. Foreign visitors to India dropped from 18 million in 2019 to 6.3 million in 2020; Indian visitors abroad dropped from 26.7 million in 2019 to 7.1 million in 2020. Indian emigrants and Indian students abroad grow tremendously from 1980 forward. From 2010 the number of foreign students attracted to India also rises. The only indicator that declines is the number of foreign immigrants in India, explained earlier as the advancing age of immigrants who arrived during Partition.

Figure 8.8 shows that the period 1980 to 2000 marks the start of more Indians going abroad and foreigners coming into the country.[5] For people across the globe, at a personal level, global awareness of India grew significantly, and this would be one factor influencing India's inclusion in the G20 at the finance minister level in 1998 and again at the leader level in 2008.

Should India seek membership in a refashioned G7, another set of data lays out the challenges ahead. Figure 8.9 compares India's Soft Power Rubric data to France and Italy, both G7 members. Whereas in terms of GDP size, in 2020, India is already at a level comparable to France and Italy, in the other arenas of hosting foreign immigrants, foreign students, and foreign visitors, it is evident how much more foreigners are attracted to French and Italian culture and society than to India's.

In 2020, India's GDP is larger than that of both Italy and France. However, in terms of hosting foreign immigrants, India is 1.5 million people

Figure 8.8 More Indians Abroad Than Foreigners in India: Migrants, Visitors, Students, 1960–2020

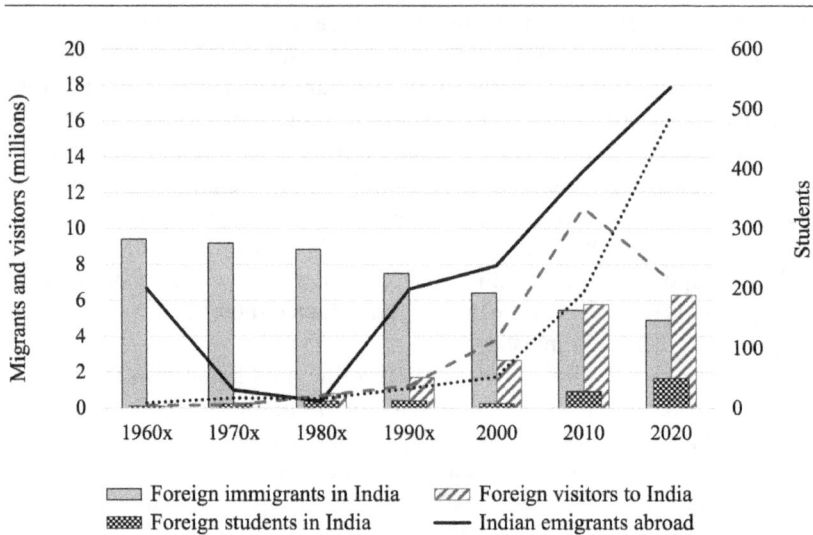

Sources: UN Population Division, UNESCO, and UN World Tourism Organization.
Note: When data for specific years are missing, I pulled data for nearby years.

Figure 8.9 India's Soft Power Rubric Data Compared with France and Italy

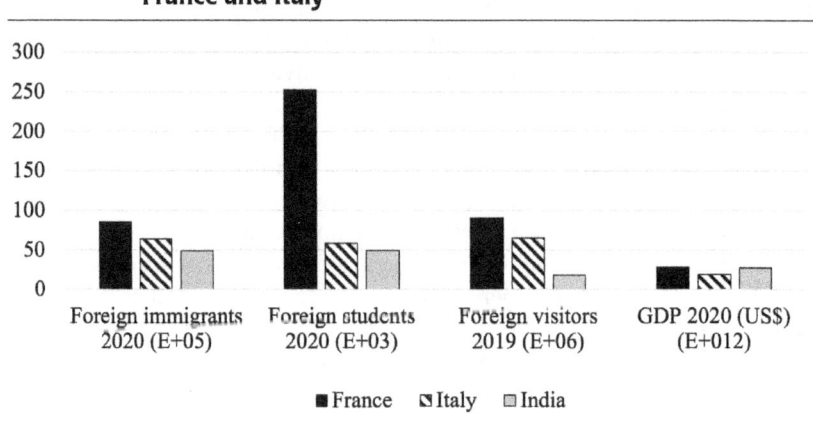

Sources: UNESCO Institute of Statistics, UN Population Division, and UN World Tourism Organization.
Note: Each data series is followed by scientific notation in order for all four series to fit on a single y-axis. For example, India hosts 5.2 million or 52 x 10^5 noted as E+05 immigrants and 42,000 or 42 x 10^3 noted as E+03 foreign students.

behind Italy and 3.7 million people behind France. In terms of hosting foreign students, France hosts five times more students than India. In terms of attracting foreign visitors in 2019 before the Covid-19 pandemic, France and Italy each host over three times more than India. The Soft Power Rubric is one way to capture the intangible attraction that foreigners have for a particular country and is a useful tool for measuring a country's cultural influence.

Emigrants and Students Abroad as a Soft Power Resource

The Soft Power Rubric builds a picture of a country's relationships with the rest of the world by examining data on its people-to-people interactions with foreigners—from what foreign movies are watched and from where foreign visitors, students, and immigrants come. Seen through the prism of the Soft Power Rubric, India has exceptional soft power resources. Ordinarily, soft power is understood as foreigners' interest in a country, which would make foreign visitors, students, and immigrants coming into India the natural place to look for influence. For example, the best chance for a foreigner to meet a Dane is in Denmark; a chance encounter outside of Denmark is less likely. In the case of India, however, its large population abroad is an outstanding soft power asset. The most likely opportunity today for foreigners to interact with Indians is to meet an Indian who is abroad—as an immigrant, student, or visitor. This underscores the main insight of the Soft Power Rubric—that social interaction builds soft power relationships, not necessarily the directionality of the interaction or its geographic location, as discussed in Chapter 10.

When compared to China, in the 1980s Indians had more social interactions with foreigners—whether as visitors, students, or immigrants—than China, but by 2000 China had opened up more to the outside world than India. When compared to G7 nations, India's economy is already of similar size. However, countries like France and Italy have deeper people-to-people relationships with a wider array of countries.

What would increase India's soft power in the future? On the movie front, India is certainly one in a very small set of countries that has a successful export industry, which is a major achievement, as discussed in Chapter 6. However, compared to the US industry's level of foreign policy impact, India's is still a distance away. Keep in mind the studies that show foreigners have the most accurate impression of a country when they have multiple and different social interactions with people from that country. When foreigners both watch Indian movies *and* have opportunities to meet Indian people, that is the most potent formula for growing soft power relationships. In other arenas, initiatives that would bring more foreigners to

India—as visitors, students, and immigrants—would also help build its soft power relationships with other countries. These, of course, are primarily domestic policies and not usually undertaken as foreign policy initiatives. However, should domestic political conditions align to make India easier for foreigners to access, there should be a foreign policy payoff—a soft power bonus.

Notes

1. An earlier version of this chapter appeared in *India Review* 20(4) in 2021. Used with permission of Taylor and Francis.

2. As Figure 8.2 indicates, the definition of migrant varies from country to country. In the case of China, migrant refers only to those living in China who are foreign citizens. In India, migrant refers to those living in India who are foreign born or are refugees. In both cases, these data are stock, not flow. They capture the total number of immigrants living in a country, not the number that crossed the border that year.

3. When using the UN data on Indians abroad, the definition of the host country applies. For example, for Indian immigrants in the United States, the US migrant definition will apply; whereas for Indian immigrants in Germany, the German migrant definition will apply. In the UN data the three major categories used by most countries to count migrants are foreign born and/or foreign citizens; further, some countries include refugees.

4. India's rank as thirteenth largest economy in 1998 is based on GDP (current US$) as reported by the World Bank in November 2019, which reflects, among other things, data as routinely revised by governments to provide the most accurate economic data possible.

5. Figure 8.8. When data for specific years are missing, I pulled data for nearby years.

	Source	1960x	1970x	1980x	1990x
Foreign students	UNESCO			1978	1986
Foreign visitors	UN World Tourism Organization	1961			
Foreign immigrants	UN Demographic Yearbook and UN Population Division	no data	1971	1981	
Indian visitors abroad	UN World Tourism Organization	1961		1979–1980	1989–1990
Indian students abroad	UNESCO	1961–1962		1980–1981	1988–1991
Indian emigrants abroad	UN Demographic Yearbook and UN Population Division	1955–1961	1970–1973 only a few countries reporting	1980–1986 only a few countries reporting	

9

Russia's and China's Soft Power Competition

IN RECENT YEARS, BOTH RUSSIAN AND CHINESE LEADERS have taken the cultivation and application of soft power seriously; however, scholars assessing their efforts from outside these countries generally agree they have not been very successful. One challenge is that if the foundation of soft power is its civil society, in both China and Russia, the authoritarian regimes promote a state-led civil society that is hard to distinguish from the government. The Soft Power Rubric approach underscores the importance of openness to foreigners as a lynchpin to building influence. The Russian and Chinese regimes' pattern of resisting foreign influence and pointing toward foreign values as weakening national strength make this kind of openness difficult. However, by applying the Rubric to China and Russia and examining the basic quantitative data available, it is possible to see important, fundamental differences between these two countries and divergent trends over time. These data, combined with an understanding of historical events, ideological trends, and political objectives, suggest which kinds of activities and investments may build or undermine these countries' future soft power influence.

China's State-Led Soft Power Campaign

Starting in 2006 President Hu Jintao identified soft power development as a foreign policy priority (Li 2009a, 2009b). Repnikova's (2022) book on Chinese soft power identifies four main areas of work: (1) Confucius Institutes, (2) global media, (3) education, and (4) public diplomacy spectacles. The Confucius Institutes are a network of educational centers located around the world to teach Mandarin Chinese in its simplified form, as compared to the traditional form used in Taiwan (Gil 2017; Nguyen 2014). The government invests substantially in international media, expanding support for *Xinhua* news and developing the China Global Television Network, which broadcasts news in foreign languages (Kurlantzick 2007; Shambaugh 2013, 2015). Also, Chinese companies are significant players in the global movies market, including investing in foreign-produced movies that become worldwide blockbusters (Kokas 2017; Voci and Hui 2018). In education, China has welcomed students from around the world to its universities; Repnikova (2022) notes this is an understudied area of China's soft power, and the Soft Power Rubric in part addresses this gap. Finally, the public diplomacy spectacles include hosting major events from international expositions to the Olympics (Repnikova 2022). Other scholars include the economic aid China gives to other countries as part of its soft power strategy. As part of its foreign policy, the government now gives out significant economic aid and humanitarian assistance, including in the Belt and Road Initiative (Ashbee 2023).

Countervailing this soft power campaign is a major theme in China's foreign policy—respect for national sovereignty, whether it is other countries' respect for China's sovereignty or China's respect for other countries' sovereignty by not interfering in their domestic affairs. While China's economic growth potentially presents to the world an alternative development model to the "Washington Consensus" neoliberal model that emphasizes free markets and democracy, many observers suggest that China's first principle of respecting national sovereignty hinders it from promoting its development model (Pang 2009; Zhao 2009).

Russia's Soft Power Goal May Be National Security

Foreign Minister Sergei Lavrov is one proponent of soft power in the Russian government. A 2007 Foreign Ministry document calls for using nongovernmental organizations and cultural institutions in foreign policy programs. In 2012 Putin mentions soft power as a foreign policy tool, although he also indicates his concern that foreign countries are using soft power to destabilize Russia (Wilson 2015b). An important goal of Russia's soft power strategy is to recover its Soviet superpower status, especially in the near abroad, its neighboring countries, and, especially, the former Soviet states. Many scholars like Grigas (2016) call this a kind of imperial strategy, an effort to reconstitute a Russian sphere of influence. Others, such as Rotaru (2018), see this as a national security strategy, a bid to keep neighboring countries friendly to protect Russia itself. With neighboring states, Russian measures to build soft power include supporting a compatriot network through governmental and nongovernmental organizations like the Russia World Foundation; working closely with the Russian Orthodox Church; offering passports to residents of former Soviet republics; and using propaganda (Grigas 2016; Herpen 2016; Rutland and Kazantsev 2016).

Russia's soft power campaigns invest in cultural relationships and media policy to pave the way, not as a substitute, for hard power tactics. Ukrainians' rejection of Russia's invasion in 2014 and again in 2020 testifies that Russia's investment in near abroad soft relationships has failed (Wilson 2016). Graney in her 2019 book *Russia, the Former Soviet Republics, and Europe Since 1989* examines measures of Europeanization of the former Soviet states. While in the 1990s, in the immediate aftermath of the fall of the Berlin Wall, Russia was positioned as part of Europe, starting in the 2000s Russia began to present itself as an alternative to Europe. In terms of culture, in particular, Graney tracks the inclusion of former Soviet states in Europe-wide events such as Eurovision and the Union of European Football Associations as key indicators of interest in integration with Europe. She characterizes Ukraine as mixed in terms of its intrinsic Europeanness, measured by religion, imperial experience, geography, history, and the presence of a Russian or Soviet narrative. "Mixed" is less European than the Baltic states and more European than the Central Asian states (Graney 2019). Either the soft power relationship that Russia built with Ukraine failed, or Russia's hard power decision to invade undermined what soft power relationship existed.

Postcommunist Cultural Nationalism as a Bulwark Against Foreign Influence

As the relevance of Marxist-Leninist ideology evaporated for both China and Russia, these regimes have searched for a different set of values and ideals around which to build a national identity, Wilson reminds us in her series of comparisons of Russia's and China's soft power. While leaders in both countries find soft power appealing as an alternative to military and economic power to influence the world, the idea that civil society leads in soft power development contradicts these authoritarian regimes' state-led approach. From their perspective, the fact that the concept of soft power prioritizes civil society over the state is evidence of its neoliberal, American roots, an ideology both China and Russia resist (Wilson 2015a).

In their search for a relevant set of national values, both Russia and China have emphasized their unique civilizational identity and defined this identity in contrast to Western values. In the case of Russia, Putin emphasizes Russia's role as upholder of conservative social values, in alignment with the Russian Orthodox Church, for example, and as a bulwark against foreign, hedonistic values. In the case of China, Xi Jinping proclaims China's development path as unique and warns against the corrupting influences of outsiders and their ideas (Wilson 2015a, 2016). If soft power is built on interactions with foreigners, it is hard to reconcile being a bulwark against bad outside influences with a civil-society-led soft power campaign.

Although China and Russia are now highlighting their ancient civilizational history, less than a century ago during their respective communist revolutions, each eagerly discarded their feudal pasts. Things may change yet again. The next sections of this chapter look at the Soft Power Rubric data that show how open or closed Russia and China have been to foreigners in the last couple of decades. While the ideological discussion up to this point highlighted the similarities, the data show important differences.

Applying the Soft Power Rubric

Russia and China each have tremendous soft power in certain regions and relatively little in others, and there is variance over time. It puts into perspective the qualitative case studies—China and Russia may have relatively little soft power in the United States, but in their respective neighborhoods there are different stories.

Immigrants

Figure 9.1 compares the number of foreign immigrants living in Russia and China from 1990 to 2020. Russia's immigrant community is between 10

Figure 9.1 Immigrants to Russia and China, 1990–2020

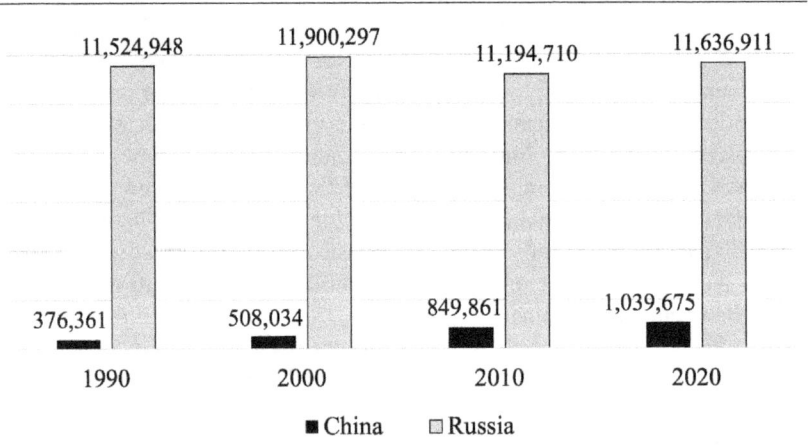

Source: UN Population Division.

and 12 million in this timeframe; in 2020 Russia's immigrant community was the fourth largest in the world, behind the United States, Germany, and Saudi Arabia (see Appendix 2, Table A2.b. Meanwhile China's immigrant community more than doubles from 1990 to 2020; at just above 1 million in 2020, it ranked fifty-fourth in the world.

Figures 9.2 and 9.3 show the countries of origin for Russia's and China's immigrants as of 2020. In essence, each map represents the country's social network of personal ties with foreign countries. Not surprisingly, Russia's social network is much more complex and diverse. China's network is concentrated in neighboring Asian countries. The data reflect government policy. Russia is relatively open to immigrants, especially from countries that previously were Soviet republics (Matveenko, Rumyantseva, and Rubtsova 2017). China has very strict immigration control. (Ding and Koslowski 2017; He and Ye 2017). China was closed to the outside world during the Mao era, only began reopening in the 1980s, and in terms of immigration is still not yet open. While from the Chinese perspective their country is much more open to foreigners now compared to the 1970s, compared to global soft power leaders, China is still isolated. For ordinary Chinese, for example, there may be too few foreigners around to build long-term relationships, and, therefore, they may lack insight into other people's worldviews and their views of China.

Both Russia and China have among the largest emigrant populations in the world. In 2020, Russia's emigrants were 10.8 million and China's 10.5 million, third and fourth largest in the world, respectively. Only India and Mexico have larger emigrant populations. In United Nations data, emigrants are foreign born. Therefore, Russian and Chinese diaspora communities, which may include emigrants' descendants, are even larger. On the whole, diaspora communities, as they engage with foreigners around the world, can be important ambassadors and an extension of their origin countries' soft power, as discussed in Chapter 8 on India. For Russian and Chinese emigrants, however, there may be more emigrant stories that are less about pursuing better life opportunities and more about leaving political or other constraints behind. In its near abroad, Russia will sometimes identify protection of its nationals abroad as a reason for military incursions into other countries, blurring even further whether its diaspora communities can be expected to add to its soft power influence.

Foreign Students

Both Russia and China are major hosts of international students; in 2020, Russia ranked fifth and China eleventh in the world (see Appendix 2, Table A2.7c). Figure 9.4 shows the change in the number of foreign students enrolling in Chinese and Russian universities for a degree. The line

Figure 9.2   Immigrants to Russia: Countries of Origin, 2020

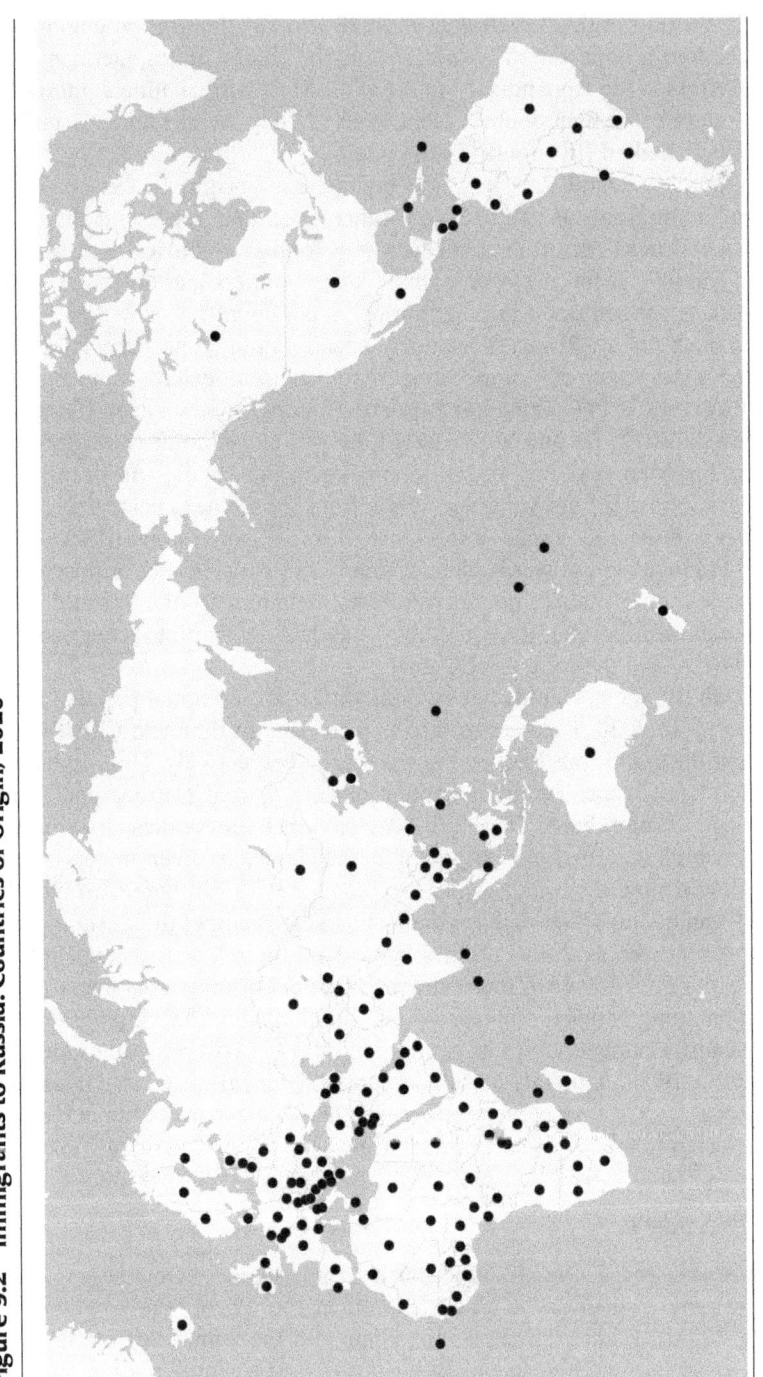

Source: UN Population Division.

Figure 9.3 Immigrants to China: Countries of Origin, 2020

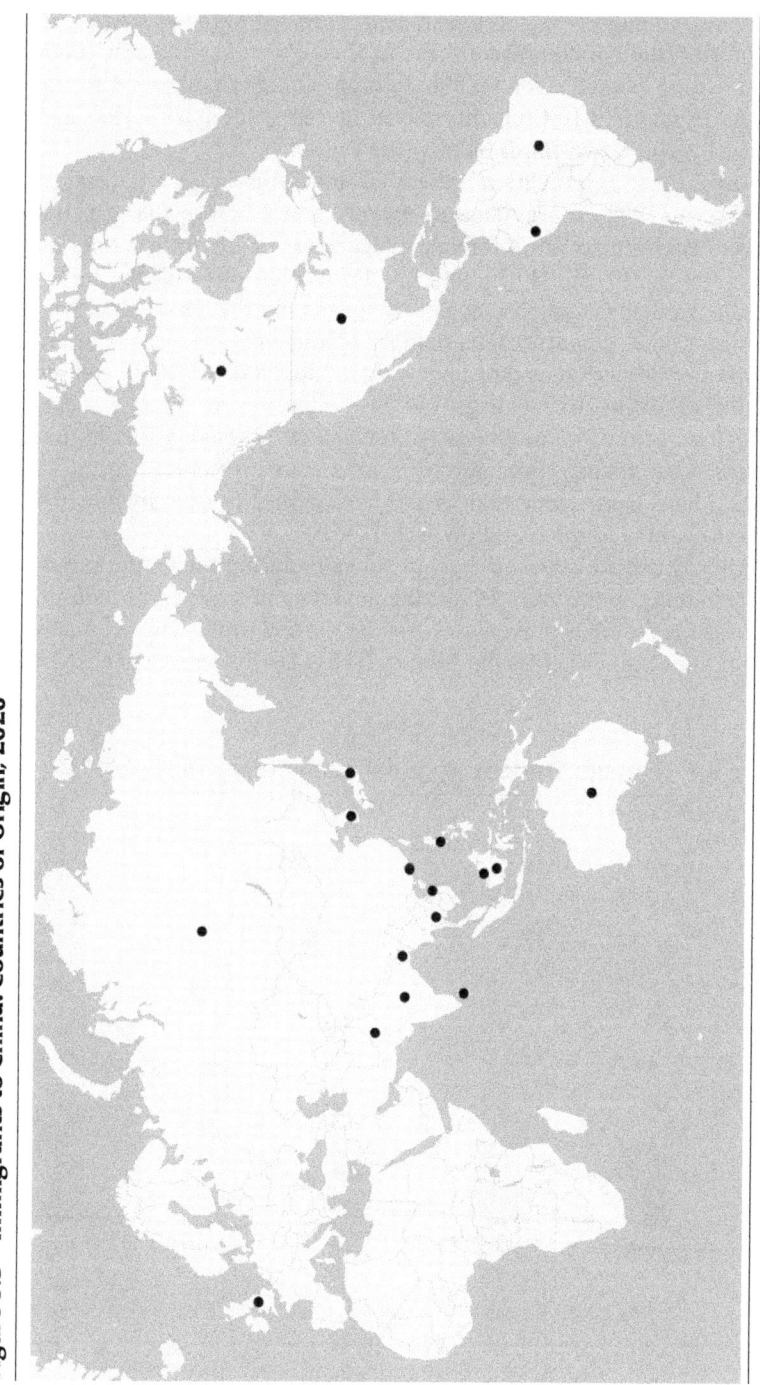

Source: UN Population Division.

represents the number of foreign students enrolled for a degree in Chinese universities; the bars represent those in Russian universities. In 1980, the Soviet Union hosted over 50,000 foreign students compared to almost none in China. In 2010 China hosted half as many foreign students as Russia, and by 2019, two-thirds as many as Russia.

After the Soviet Union separated into Russia and several other republics in 1991, it was another twenty years before the government renewed its efforts to enroll foreign students, especially from former Soviet states (Wilson 2015b). In Figure 9.4, from 2000 onward, the light bars show the students from former Soviet states, and the dark bars show students from other countries. The number of students to Russia who are not from former Soviet states dips below 50,000 in 2000 and 2010, and returns to above 50,000 in 2019. One goal of this policy was for foreign students to reach 10 percent of total university enrollment. In today's Russia, foreign students come mainly from former Soviet states, whereas during Soviet days, students came from a wider array of politically friendly countries in different regions of the world (Wilson 2015b).

After China's closure to foreign students during the Cultural Revolution, beginning in the early 1990s, the government made large investments in its most prestigious universities, and by the end of the decade, in a wider range of universities across the country. These institutions were encouraged

Figure 9.4 Foreign Students to Russia and China, 1980–2019

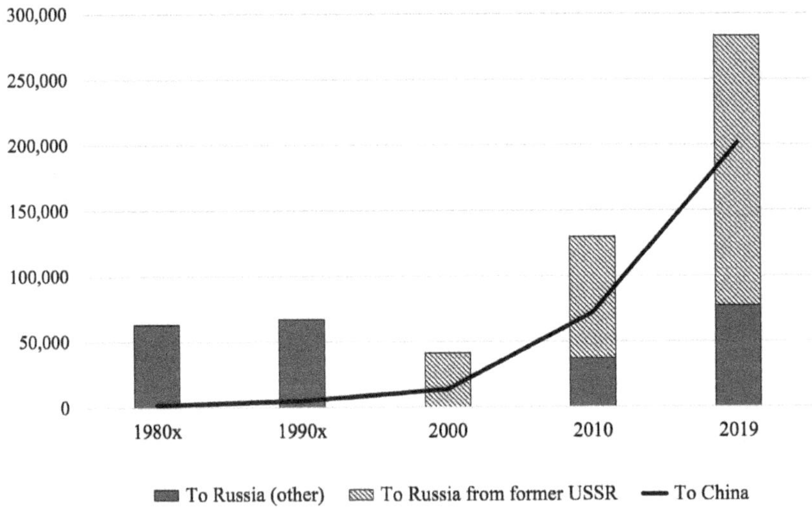

■ To Russia (other)   ▩ To Russia from former USSR   — To China

Sources: UNESCO, CAFSA.

by the government to welcome foreign students. Another incentive was that international standards evaluated universities partly on the enrollment of foreign students. Cheng (2009) also observes that in the 1990s and 2000s, the relatively strong economic growth in China as compared to Japan attracted to China those foreign students interested in Asia.

South Korea sends more students to enroll in Chinese universities than any other country by far, according to the periodic news releases by China's Ministry of Education and Chinese Association for International Education (CAFSA). These news releases sometimes report that most of the foreign students at Chinese universities are from neighboring countries.[1] The UNESCO data on foreign student mobility into China are limited to summary statistics and do not include breakdowns by country.

There is criticism of foreign students' experience in China and Russia. Russian universities attract many foreign students through distance learning programs, and Wilson notes that the quality of distance education may be poor. Distance learners are not included in the UNESCO data (Wilson 2015b). Similarly, Repnikova (2022) discusses both the positive and negative experiences of African students. While many fulfill their academic goals, admire China's development path, and take on its worldview, there are also complaints of racial discrimination and poor learning environments, with the two concerns possibly linked. While all these issues are serious, as long as foreign students are freely choosing to study in Russia and China, if demand continues to grow, then it is reasonable to think that on balance they find the education useful. We will be able to make these observations in the coming years as the education sector recovers from the pause imposed by the Covid-19 pandemic.

As for sending their own students abroad, in 2021, there were 880,000 Chinese students abroad and 57,000 Russian students. Among Chinese students, 34 percent were in the United States, and another 35 percent in the United Kingdom, Australia, and Canada. Among Russian students 20 percent were in Germany, 14 percent in the Czech Republic, and 8 percent in the United States. Another 20 percent were in other Western European countries.

Foreign Visitors

While Russia hosted more foreign visitors than China in 1990, as early as 1995 the trend reversed, as shown in Figure 9.5.[2] In 2019 China was the third largest host of visitors in the world; Russia was twenty-fourth. For China, visitors from Hong Kong and Macao are included as foreign visitors in the data. As the hatched bars show, there has been an enormous increase in visitors from Hong Kong and Macao to China since those two territories were returned from Great Britain and Portugal. Over time, these visitors may be considered domestic rather than foreign; currently, both students and workers commute daily across these borders. Even taking into account the ambiguity of the Hong Kong/Macao data, China would still be in the top dozen visitor destinations in the world, still surpassing Russia.

On the outbound side, China has a relatively unique system of "Approved Destination Status (ADS)." The government evaluates which countries offer attractive tourist destinations and amenities, free of discrimination against Chinese, and in countries that are politically aligned with China. Many Chinese tourists' travel plans are guided by ADS status. Chen and Duggan (2016) discuss how the Chinese government uses the granting of ADS status as one economic aid tool in its relationships with African governments, but many governments do not make achieving such status a priority. There is room for further research on how tourism relates to soft power and, especially, how and when government intervention bolsters or hinders relationships.

Figure 9.5 Foreign Visitors to China and Russia, 1995–2018

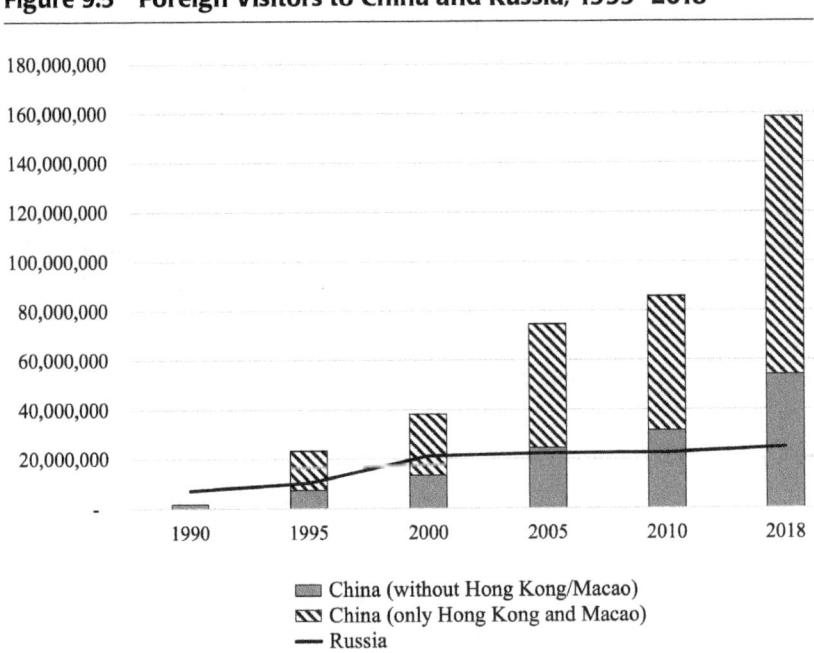

Source: UN World Tourism Organization.

Movies

UNESCO published data on movie admissions—or tickets sold—from 2005 to 2017. Figures 9.6 and 9.7 show admissions for Chinese- and Russian-produced movies when they were shown outside of China and Russia, respectively, and in the top ten films of the year, as reported by other countries. In other words, Figures 9.6 and 9.7 capture how many tickets foreigners purchased to see Chinese- and Russian-produced movies. The graph shows data from 2007 to 2017 on the number of tickets sold in foreign

Figure 9.6 Russian Productions: Movie Admissions Outside Russia, 2005–2017

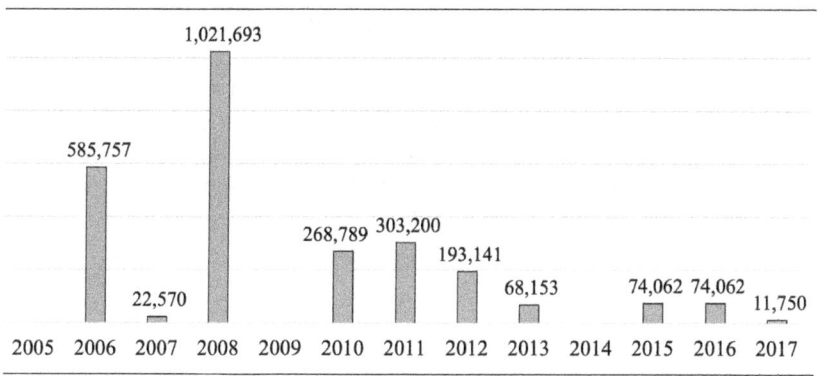

Source: UNESCO.

Figure 9.7 Chinese Productions: Movie Admissions Outside China, 2005–2017

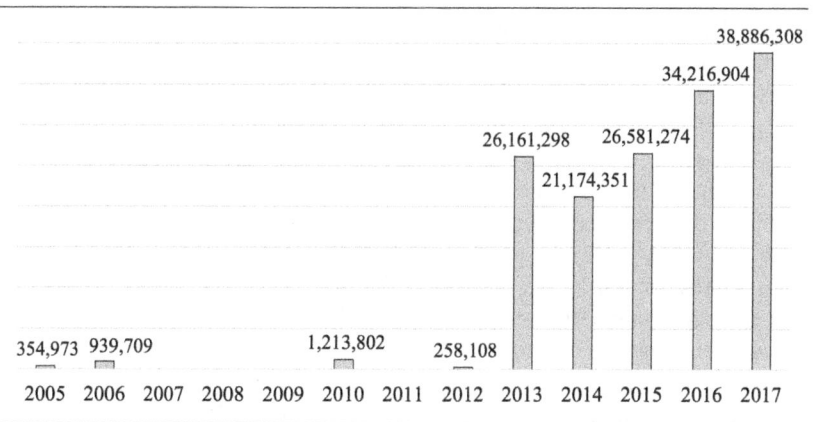

Source: UNESCO.

countries for showings of Chinese and Russian movies. This only includes data on admissions to movie theaters and does not include movies as broadcast on television or distributed online. These two charts show how variable the data are from year to year for Russia and China. In most years, but not every year, a China- or Russia-produced movie did make it to the top ten in other countries, Chinese-produced movies more than Russian movies.

Figure 9.6 includes Russia-coproduced movies, or movies that were produced by companies from more than one country. In 2008, when admissions topped 1 million, titles included *The Irony of Fate 2*; *Admiral*; *Wanted* (coproduced with United States and Germany); *The Best Movie*; and *Hitler's Kaput,* coproduced with Ukraine. *Wanted* is in English, the other four movies in Russian.

In Figure 9.7, which shows admissions to Chinese-produced movies, in 2017 the top three movies were *The Fast and the Furious*, coproduced with US and Japanese companies, *Wonder Woman*, coproduced with US and Hong Kong companies, and *Fifty Shades Darker,* coproduced with US companies. All three movies are in English. In 2010, the top two movies were *The Karate Kid,* coproduced with the United States, and *Ip Man 2,* coproduced with Hong Kong. *Karate Kid* is in English, *Ip Man 2* in Cantonese. The increase in foreign admissions to Chinese-produced movies follows growing Chinese investment in English-language movies (Kokas 2017).

Russia's Long-Term Relationships and China's Recent Momentum

What can this collection of data points say about China's and Russia's soft power? The immigration data show that a wider range of foreigners over time commit to integrating into Russian society; these are long-term personal relationships that Russia has with all these countries. Further, Russians are more likely to live in communities with foreigners, which likely influences their view of the outside world. China lacks these kinds of relationships. Furthermore, when China's attitude is that foreigners are a bad influence on society, this path to increasing soft power seems closed.

In education, the large number of students flocking to China suggests that the younger generation perceives its universities to be a path to skills and knowledge useful for the future. Both Russia and China draw students from nearby regions. This is perhaps the most potent path for further soft power development for both countries. The data show that for the time being, China has the momentum advantage over Russia.

In terms of foreign visitors, again China has the momentum advantage with nearly double the number of visitors in 2019 as Russia. Compared to immigration and education data, visitor data can quickly change from year to year as a result of changes in policy, which governments control, and external factors like public health and economics, which governments do not.

Even more volatile is the movie data. Russia has a steady audience for its mostly Russian-language movies, and China in some years reaches a much larger audience by investing in English-language movies. China is investing more heavily in this area, for commercial reasons as well as potential political reasons (Kokas 2017). What benefit to soft power relationships there is from this investment is worth exploring further.

This chapter began with knowledge gleaned from the many case studies written about China's and Russia's soft power influence, which mostly focus on the state's efforts to influence other countries. Wilson's direct comparisons of Chinese and Russian soft power also underscore the similar ideological conundrums these two governments face. First, bolstering soft power with government efforts, when soft power generally is believed to emanate from civil society, faces constraints in both Russia and China. Second, seeking to influence the societies of other countries is in tension with publicly proclaiming that foreigners have insidious influence in their own. While these broad similarities remain pertinent, the Soft Power Rubric data do unpack Russia's and China's different points of departure. China's extreme isolation under Mao's leadership, especially during the Cultural Revolution, means that while in arenas easier to open up to the world like movies, tourism, and education it has made a lot of progress, in immigration, which would allow more ordinary Chinese to have long-standing relationships with foreigners, China is still closed. For Russia, the quantitative data show that its international network of immigrants developed during the Soviet period still stands, but in the areas quicker to change—like education and tourism—its soft power relationships now are strongest in its near abroad.

Notes

1. In recent years, China does not report data to UNESCO on foreign students but annually releases (1) total students from top sending countries and (2) percentage of all foreign students who are enrolled in universities for a degree. See CAFSA (www.cafsa.org.cn) and Ministry of Education (www.moe.gov.cn).

2. As of September 15, 2023, visitor data for 2018 was the most recent available with Hong Kong/Macao breakdown.

10

Understanding Soft Power in Southeast Asia

IN THE COFFEE BREAK CULTURE OF WASHINGTON, DC, SOFT power talk centers first on movies and second on cuisine. In recent years Thailand is the leading star of gastrodiplomacy. As touted in the *Economist* in 2002, the government established a network of Thai restaurants around the world in an effort to build more connections with foreigners with a goal of attracting them to visit Thailand as tourists (*Economist* 2002). Further, they developed a "Thai Select" logo that identified restaurants of quality, that used ingredients from Thailand—especially the correct kind of rice— and presented cuisine prepared by skilled Thai chefs, neatly compressing cultural and social exchange with commerce and labor market creation. So marked is its success that several countries followed suit—Malaysia, Taiwan, Peru, and South Korea (Zhang 2015). The very success of Thai cuisine abroad—no doubt mostly due to the entrepreneurship of the restauranteurs themselves—is the backdrop to the striking difficulties of some Thai emigrants abroad. In the United States, Mark Padoongpatt (2017) chronicles the Thai American community in Los Angeles and its growing political consciousness and activism in local politics. The cuisine in its popularity became a stand-in for Thais in America. The incandescent success of the cuisine blinded the larger community to the problems that Thai Americans faced, especially workers subject to human trafficking (Padoongpatt 2017). Similarly, in Taiwan, geographers Chi and Jackson (2011) juxtapose the popularity of Thai cuisine in the island's restaurant scene with the scandalous exploitation of Thai guest workers building its railways.

Policymakers often are assigned a country or region to study, and for most countries and regions in the world, the work on soft power will be fragmented and multistranded, without a central theme and coherent debate, as there might be for a country like Russia or China. This chapter is an example of how several strands can be woven together, to provide a complex view of the soft power relationships in a region.

When reflecting on soft power and its relevance to Southeast Asia, the work to date is multistranded, rich in perspectives, but also still evolving in terms of coherence—kaleidoscopic rather than focused, but deserving of attention nonetheless. First, there is a cluster of work on soft power competition in the region that is related to the hard power concerns that are related to the broader balance of power in the global international system. A cluster of work examines the specific situation of individual countries. There is work on US-China competition, and also discussion of other countries like Japan, Taiwan, and India. The Soft Power Rubric data show where Southeast Asians go to emigrate, study abroad, and travel. The data place agency with the people of Southeast Asia and foreground their interests and preferences. Second, I turn to a question less often asked—What soft power does the Southeast Asia region have over other countries? For countries like Malaysia, attracting foreign students is a potentially fruitful path for developing deeper relationships with other countries. In other regions, other arenas of transnational engagement might be through sport, religion, or cultural pursuits like cuisine. Investigating the possible scope of Southeast Asia's soft power influence, other than as an object of larger power competition, is a novel, important, and understudied arena of research.

Southeast Asia as a Foreign Policy Priority

After observing the economic success of South Korea, Taiwan, Hong Kong, and Singapore in the 1960s and 1970s, other Southeast Asian countries were inclined to follow what became known as the Washington Consensus, a preference for free trade and democracy, recounts Wibowo (2009) in his discussion of Chinese soft power in the region. When China's insulation from foreign shocks protected it against the 1998 financial crisis, Southeast Asian countries reevaluated their views. As China's economy continued to rise, Wibowo argues, Southeast Asian countries were more skeptical of the Western model. Still, the Philippines, Indonesia, and Thailand continue to be democracies, while the other pursues a more authoritarian path (Wibowo 2009).

Wibowo's views are reflected in the Asia Barometer polling data, regular public opinion polls run by scholars that began in 2001. The first survey included Thailand and the Philippines. In 2005 they added Vietnam, Cambodia, Indonesia, Malaysia, and Singapore, and Myanmar in 2014. Huang and Welsh (2017) use the Asia Barometer polling series to assess views of the United States and China. On the whole, they argue that US soft power is in decline and China is actively cultivating soft power. Among those polled, those who prioritize economic freedom and live in countries with good economic conditions prefer the US economic model; the China economic model is more attractive to those who live in countries with poor economic conditions (Huang and Welsh 2017). Also working with Asia Barometer data, Chu, Chang, and Huang (2016) find that US influence in Asia is declining; however, people in Southeast Asia have more faith in the United States than those in Northeast Asia. If the poll respondent believes their own country's democracy to be more advanced than China's, then they see China negatively. In general, the United States is more welcome in Asia than China, except in Thailand and in Muslim countries (Chu, Chang, and Huang 2016).

Southeast Asian nations are the target of diplomatic initiatives and public diplomacy programs, and some scholars perceive a competitive quality about their establishment. When China established its Public Diplomacy Division in its Foreign Ministry in 2004, its neighbors quickly followed suit—India, Japan, Malaysia, South Korea, and Myanmar (Hall and Smith 2013). Taiwan's Go South policy toward South and Southeast Asia under Tsai Ing-wen includes promoting mutual investment and trade, promoting Taiwan's science and technology achievements, and supporting more people-to-people interaction such as scholarships for South and Southeast Asian students to study in Taiwan (Bing 2017). India's "Act East" under Modi sought to increase cultural diplomacy, highlight cultural traditions such as yoga and Nalanda University, and improve military cooperation (Bajpaee 2017). The Indian government's diaspora policies to date have focused on the professional classes that have migrated to the West and less on the older diaspora in Southeast Asia who migrated as workers under the British and Dutch colonial rule; Kumar (2021) argues reconnecting with this older diaspora is a way forward for India in the region.

Several outside powers use foreign aid to build partnerships in Southeast Asia. Japan's aid to Southeast Asia began as reparations after World War II, over time developing into an aid model that supported both Southeast Asian country development and Japanese exports (Araki 2007). China's programs include railroad construction in Thailand and Indonesia as part of Beijing's soft power diplomacy strategy (Wu and Chong 2018). South Korea's official development assistance to Myanmar as part of its "contribution diplomacy" was an effort to increase its political influence in the recipient country (Kim 2018). These and the broader research on aid suggest that while such assistance can build positive relationships, it is not guaranteed.

Southeast Asian Students Go Abroad

In Southeast Asia, soft power relationships built through higher education exchanges are very prominent. International education and immigration, argues Sutter (2009), transformed the US relationship with Asia, including Southeast Asia. The end of legal discrimination against Asian immigrants to the United States in 1965, which enabled foreign students from Asia to stay in the United States after graduation, had a huge impact (Sutter 2009). Particularly in Indonesia, Murphy (2010) and Suryodiningrat (2010) show that educational exchange contributed the most to building US-Indonesia ties, implying that today these relationships are not as close as they once were. In past years, they argue that these exchanges influenced all sectors of society, including Indonesia's Islamic scholars, who now run their universities on an American model. Suryodiningrat notes that grassroots linkages with China were not as strong because of the lack of personal exchange between elites, but that now in Indonesia those exchanges are growing (Murphy 2010; Suryodiningrat 2010).

New Zealand's soft power assets include the historical Colombo Plan that sponsored foreign students from Southeast Asia to study in New Zealand (Butcher 2012). Australia's Colombo Plan from the same period is discussed in Chapter 7 on education. Another reminder that soft power relationships are rooted in history is Bukh's (2016) examination of Russia's soft power in Laos, Thailand, and Vietnam. He finds that historical memory shapes current perceptions of young, educated elites. Vietnam and Laos, which had stronger relationships with the Soviet Union, still view Russia as having influence today, even though their view of its image is somewhat dissonant with Russians' self-image today. The Thai students have positive views of Russia but are less affirmative about its influences in the region (Bukh 2016).

Japan in recent years has seen a huge increase in students from Southeast Asia. From the ASEAN 10 countries, total students to Japan grew from 14,000 in 2013 to 61,000 in 2020, a fourfold increase in seven years. Two-thirds of the ASEAN 10 students in Japan in 2020 were from Vietnam (UNESCO 2024). Taiwan when launching its New South Policy in 2016 reoriented its international education policy from targeting overseas Chinese to attract a broader range of students (Lee 2023). In 2023, of its 49,000 foreign students, 33 percent were from Vietnam, 10 percent from Indonesia, and 5 percent from Malaysia (Taiwan, Ministry of Education, Department of Statistics 2024). A growing number of students from ASEAN are studying in Chinese universities, especially in nearby Guangxi and Yunnan province (Rui 2012). Chinese universities have established foreign campuses in Laos, Malaysia, and Thailand, where programs are attractive in part because the language of instruction is Chinese (He and Wilkins 2019).

Prior work on soft power in Southeast Asia underscores education, but there is less work on migration and travel. On movies, media, and popular culture in general, there is far less scholarly research and quantitative data, and much opportunity for further work. Many scholarly accounts examine flourishing music, television programs, animation, and movies out of Japan and South Korea, and also from mainland China, Hong Kong, and Taiwan, but there is room for making more connection to Southeast Asia and to study Southeast Asian culture's appeal abroad. The next section presents the available Soft Power Rubric data, both in terms of other countries' interest in Southeast Asia and Southeast Asians' interest in other countries.

People of Southeast Asia: Their Attraction to the United States and China, 2000–present

The Soft Power Rubric data in Figures 10.1a, 10.1b, and 10.1c show how many people from Southeast Asian countries emigrated, studied abroad, and visited the United States and China since 2000. While both the United States and China are major destinations in all these categories, their relative position shifts over time. Also, other countries beyond the United States and China are major magnets for people from Southeast Asia. These data provide an empirical foundation for understanding which countries have soft power influence in the Southeast Asia region, but from the perspective of actions taken by Southeast Asians themselves, not the initiatives of outside foreign governments.

Immigration

The three graphs in Figure 10.1a show the top destinations for people from Southeast Asians who emigrate abroad. The United States is the overwhelming leader in 2000 to 2020, the most recent data for this series. In 1990, there were about 2 million Southeast Asian emigrants in the United States; in 2000, 3 million and by 2020, 4.5 million. In 2020, the United States was home to 2 million immigrants from the Philippines and 1.4 million from Vietnam. China is among the top destinations for Southeast Asian people emigrating abroad, but behind the United States. In 2000 there were 117,000 Southeast Asian immigrants and China ranked the thirteenth most popular destination; in 2020, there were 408,000 Southeast Asian immigrants and China ranked the ninth most popular destination.

Education

Worldwide, there is a growing number of students who enroll in foreign universities for a degree, including students from Southeast Asian countries. The three graphs in Figure 10.1b show the top destinations for Southeast Asian students. China rises from 1,300 students in 2000 and the tenth most popular destination to an estimated 41,000 students in 2018.[1] For China, country-level data for 2020 inbound students from ASEAN is not available; 41,000 students would place China after the United States and before the United Kingdom in 2020 data. The United States attracts more Southeast Asian students than China, but its relative position declines.

Figure 10.1a   ASEAN Emigrants Abroad, 2000–2020

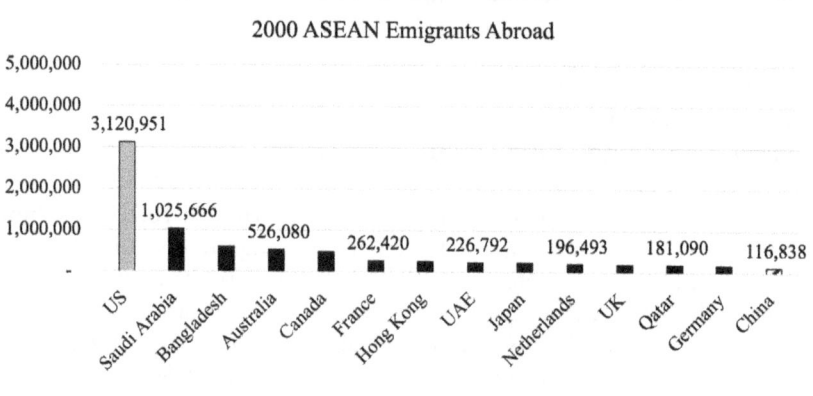

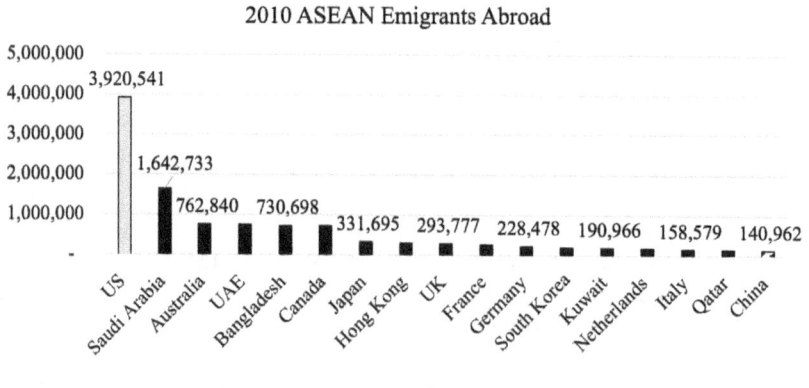

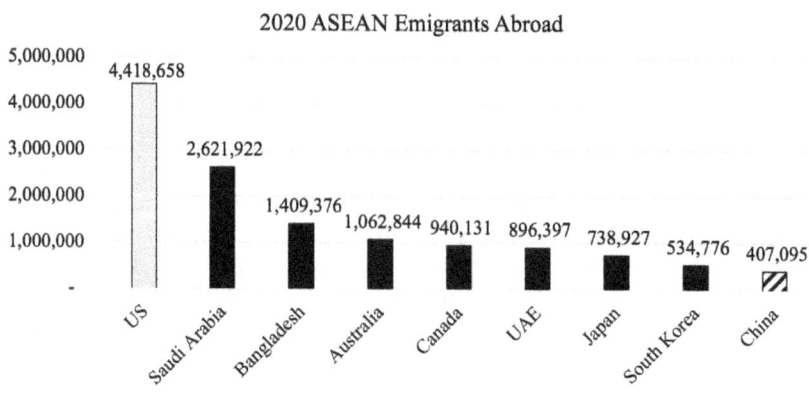

Figure 10.1b ASEAN Students Abroad, 2000–2020

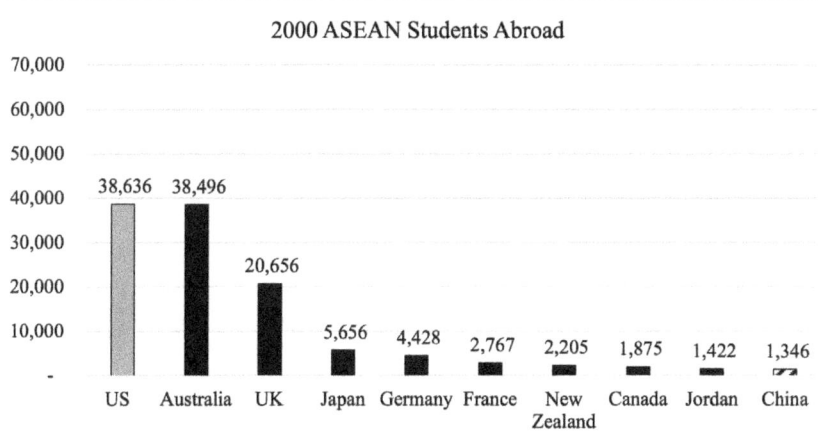

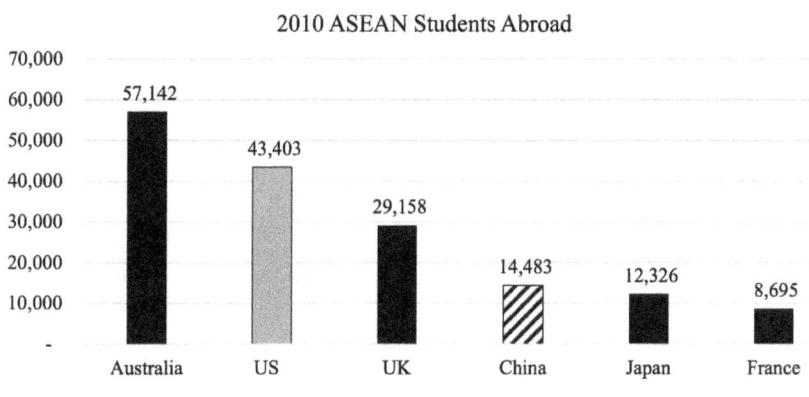

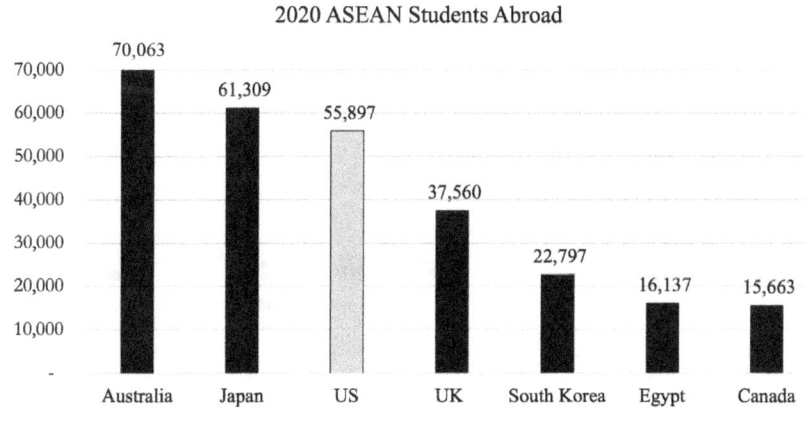

Figure 10.1c ASEAN Visitors Abroad, 2000–2020

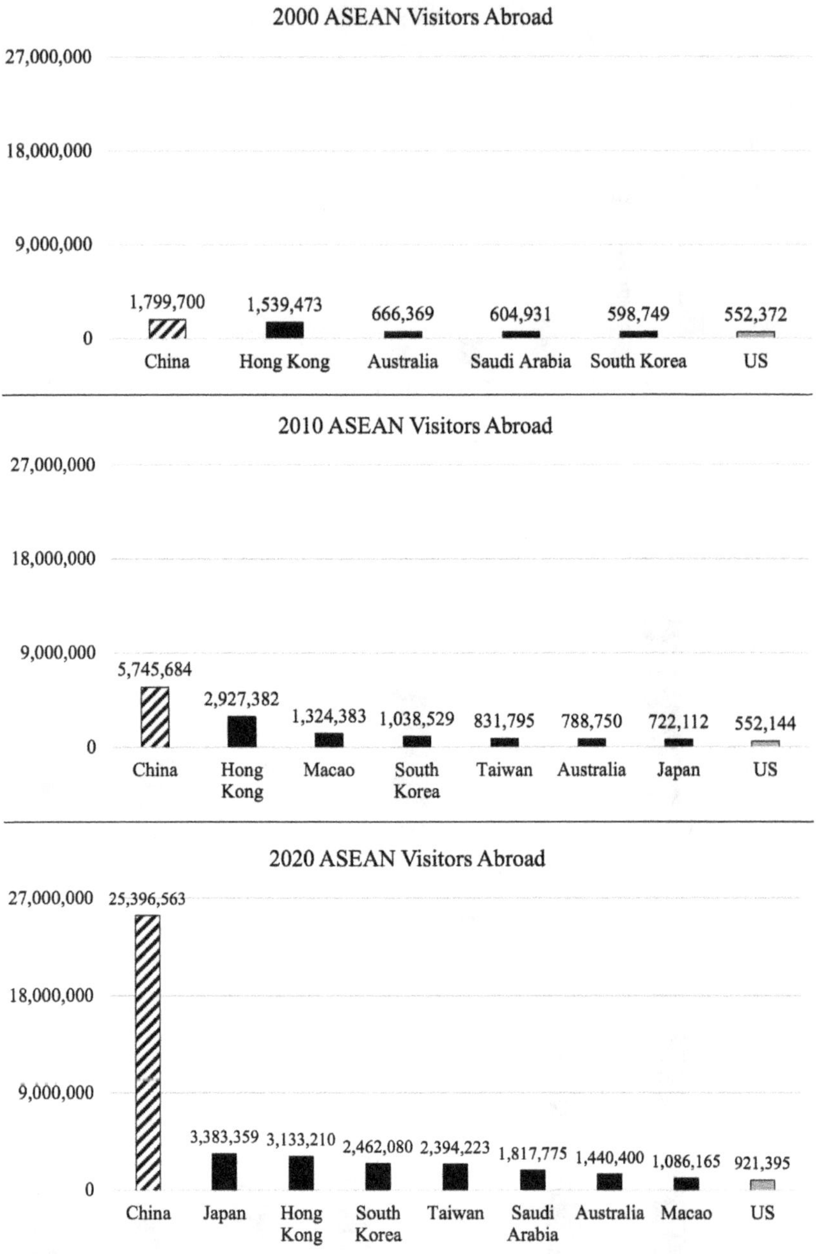

2000 ASEAN Visitors Abroad

China	Hong Kong	Australia	Saudi Arabia	South Korea	US
1,799,700	1,539,473	666,369	604,931	598,749	552,372

2010 ASEAN Visitors Abroad

China	Hong Kong	Macao	South Korea	Taiwan	Australia	Japan	US
5,745,684	2,927,382	1,324,383	1,038,529	831,795	788,750	722,112	552,144

2020 ASEAN Visitors Abroad

China	Japan	Hong Kong	South Korea	Taiwan	Saudi Arabia	Australia	Macao	US
25,396,563	3,383,359	3,133,210	2,462,080	2,394,223	1,817,775	1,440,400	1,086,165	921,395

Sources: UN Population Division, UNESCO Institute of Statistics, and UN World Tourism Organization.

In 2000, the United States hosted 39,000 students and was the top destination; in 2020, it hosted 56,000 students and was third after Australia and Japan as the most popular destination.

Travel

The number of people traveling worldwide has also increased dramatically, including people from Southeast Asian countries, as seen in Figure 10.1c. In 2000, China was top destination, hosting 1.8 million Southeast Asian travelers; in 2018, China was still the top destination, hosting 25.4 million visitors, about half of whom are from Myanmar. The United States is also a major destination. In 2000, it was the sixth most popular destination, hosting 550,000 Southeast Asian visitors; in 2018 it dropped to ninth most popular destination, hosting 920,000 Southeast Asian visitors.[2]

Movies

Finally, with the exception of Singapore, Southeast Asian members do not regularly report their movie data to UNESCO. For example, in Singapore in 2017, of the top ten movies in terms of box office revenue, all ten were US coproductions and three were China coproductions.

Other Leading Countries

Figures 10.1a, 10.1b, and 10.1c also reveal the deep connections that ASEAN people have with other foreign countries. For Southeast Asian emigrants, Saudi Arabia is the second and Bangladesh the third most popular destination, highlighting Southeast Asia's cultural connections to South Asia and to Muslim countries. In education, Australia, the United Kingdom, and more recently Japan are major destinations for students from Southeast Asia. Australia in particular surpassed the United States in popularity in the early 2000s. In travel, Hong Kong is a major destination for Southeast Asian travelers. In the last decade, Japan has grown into one of the more popular destinations as well.

Southeast Asian Countries' Soft Power Influence: Foreigners Traveling to ASEAN

A rarely asked question about soft power in Southeast Asia is: Where do Southeast Asian countries have soft power influence? The Soft Power Rubric data shown in Figures 10.2a, 10.2b, and 10.2c provide an empirical basis for assessing this as well. Data show a dramatic increase in foreigners

Figure 10.2a Immigrants to ASEAN, 2000–2020

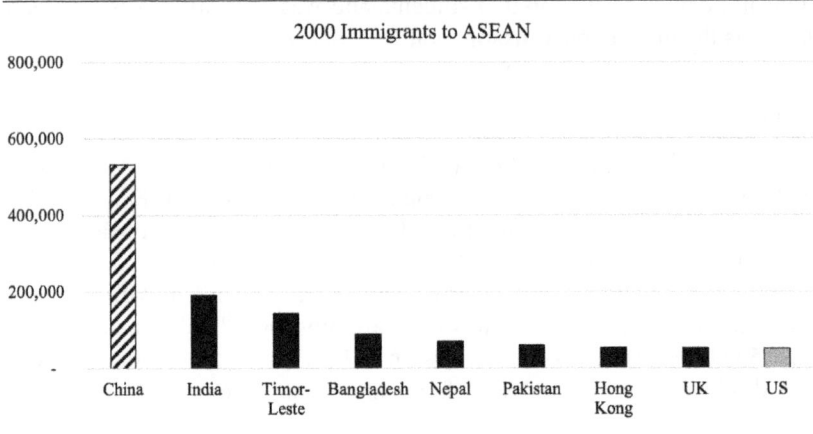

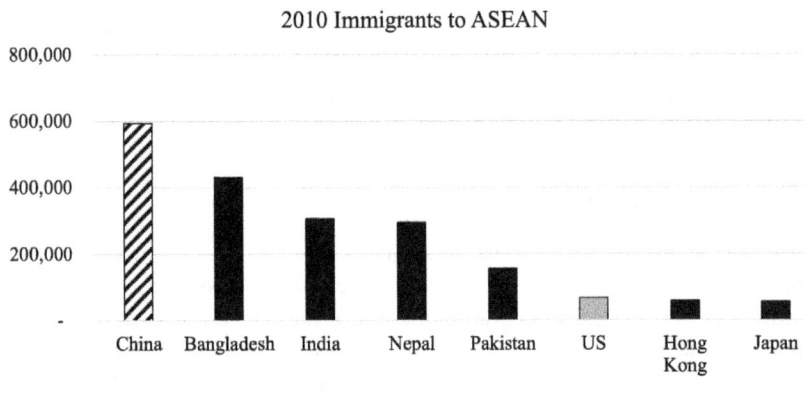

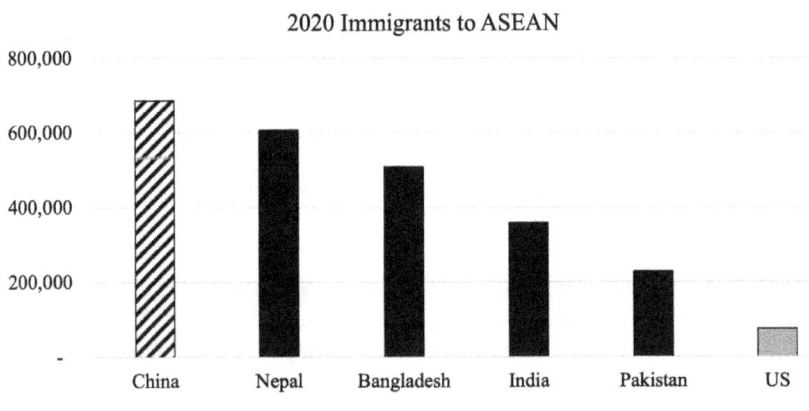

133

Figure 10.2b Foreign Students to ASEAN, 2000–2020

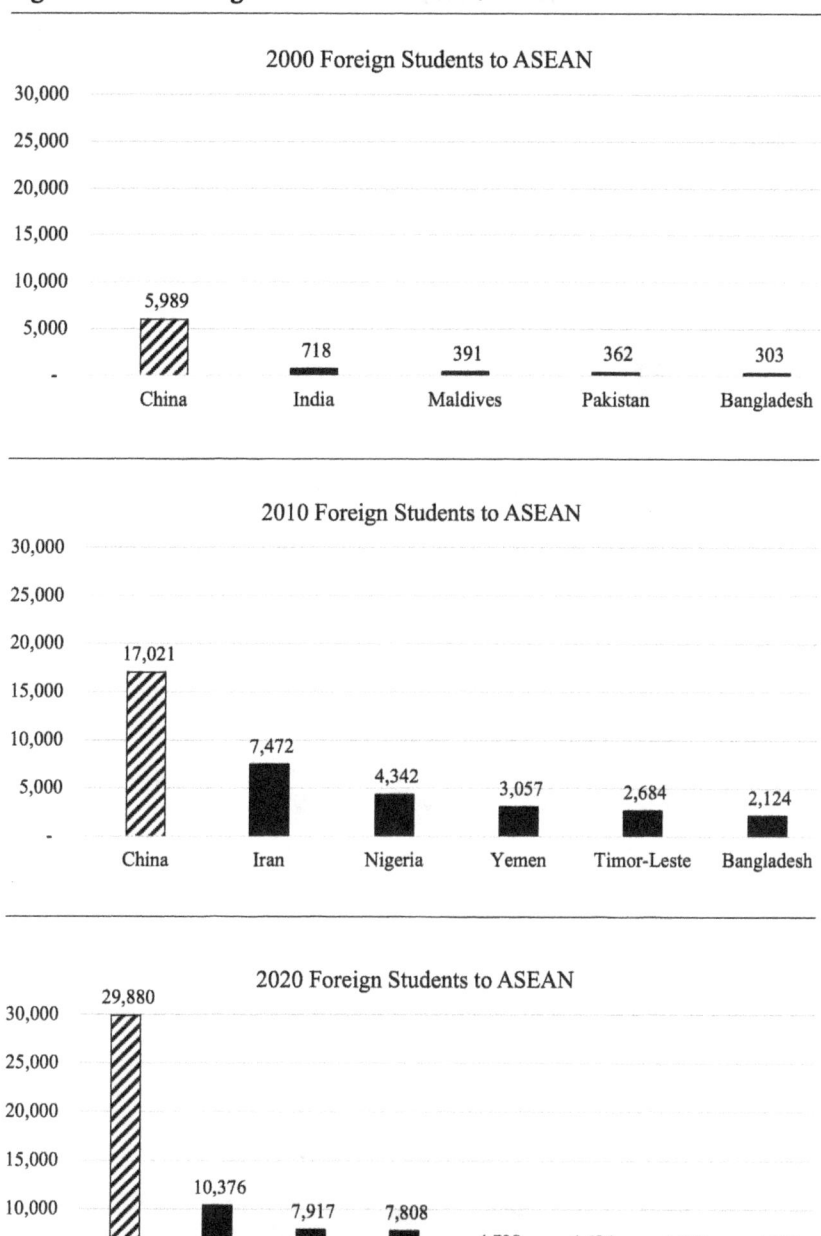

Figure 10.2c Foreign Visitors to ASEAN, 2000–2020

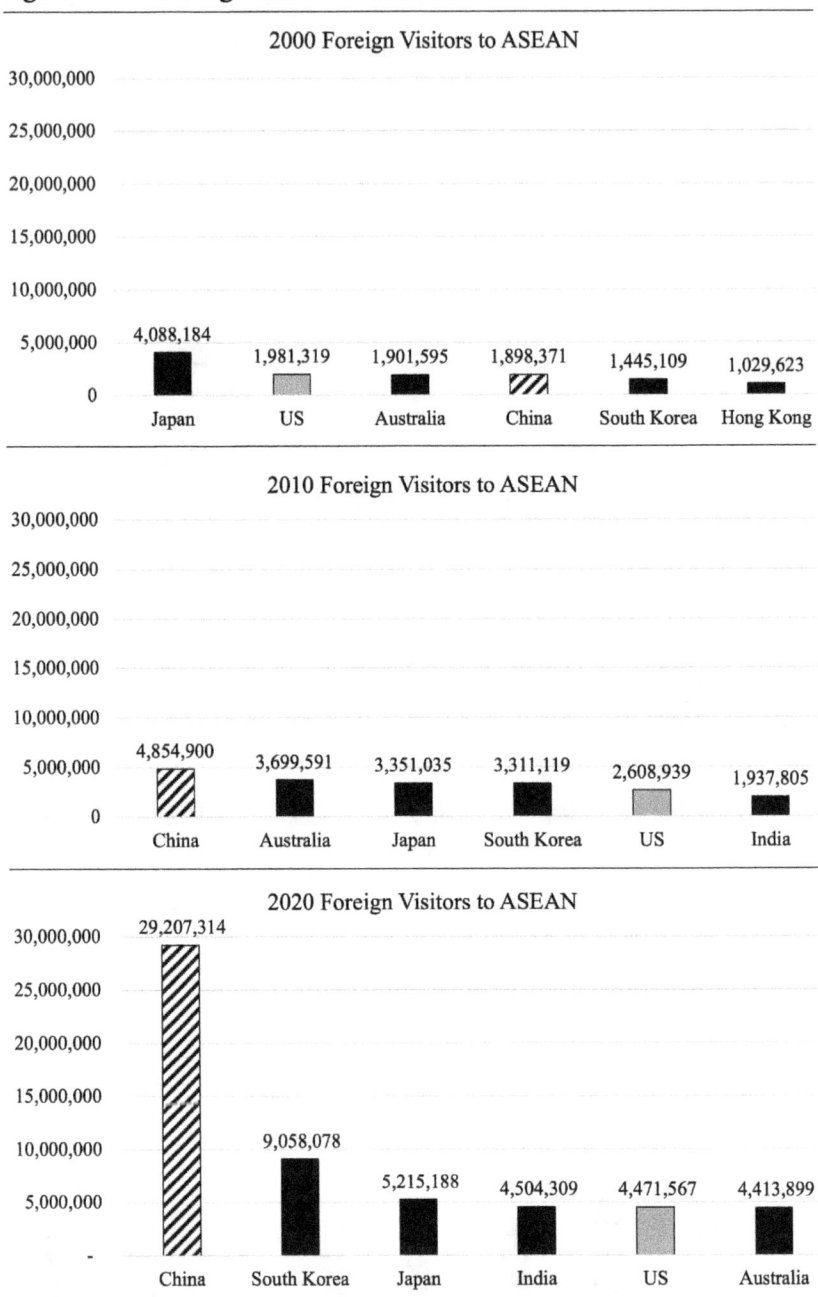

Sources: UN Population Division, UNESCO Institute of Statistics, and UN World Tourism Organization.

immigrating to, studying in, and traveling to Southeast Asia since 2000. Both China and the United States are in the top ranks of sending immigrants and visitors to Southeast Asia, and China also sends a large number of students to Southeast Asian universities.

Immigration

The largest community of immigrants in Southeast Asia are from China, as shown in Figure 10.2a. In 2000, there were 530,000, in 2020, 687,000. In 2000 the United States was the ninth largest immigrant community in Southeast Asia at 50,000 people; in 2020 the United States ranked sixth at 75,000 people. Note that in these data, immigrants are foreign-born residents; diaspora communities are larger, as they include the children of immigrants.

Education

Only a few Southeast Asian countries report the number of foreign students they host, as Figure 10.2b shows.[3] Of the countries that report, Malaysia and Thailand host the largest number of foreign students. Malaysia's work will be discussed in the next section. China sends the most students to Southeast Asia in 2000, 2010, and 2020. The United States sends only a few students to enroll in ASEAN universities for a degree, although the number has grown from 38 in 2000 to 470 in 2020.

Travel

Both China and the United States are major senders of visitors to Southeast Asia, as shown in Figure 10.2c. In 2000, the United States ranked second at 2 million visitors, while China ranked fourth at 1.9 million visitors. By 2010, China ranked first at 4.9 million and the United States ranked fifth at 2.6 million. By 2017, visitors from China to Southeast Asia soared to 30 million, about half from Myanmar; the United States continued to rank fifth at 4.5 million.[4]

Other Leading Countries

The immigration flows to Southeast Asia also reveal deep connections to South Asia. India, Bangladesh, Pakistan, and Nepal send large numbers of immigrants to Southeast Asia. In the realm of education, Malaysia attracts a major flow of students from Bangladesh and Nigeria.

Southeast Asia is a magnet for immigrants, students, and visitors from China; Americans are present as a significant community of immigrants and visitors. In addition, South Asian immigrants, students, and visitors are attracted to Southeast Asia. Southeast Asia attracts a growing number of foreigners. Foreign visitors from outside the region more than tripled from 19 million in 2000 to 76 million in 2018. Even with limited data on education, the reported number increases fivefold from 19,000 in 2000 to 130,000 in 2020.

Southeast Asians take action to cultivate relationships with other parts of the world. The intensity and volume of the region's interactions with the United States are greater than China's, especially in terms of committed, long-term connections, as the immigration data show. However, China's attraction for Southeast Asian students means that a new generation of leaders will have more intimate knowledge of China's culture and society than previously. In terms of travel, many more people from Southeast Asia have opportunities to visit China than the United States. While more and more people from Southeast Asia emigrate to, study in, and travel to the United States, the growth rate of similar interactions with China is greater. This is the empirical backdrop that animates the foreign policy discussion of China's rising influence in recent years in a context where personal, professional, and political ties to the United States once prevailed. The Soft Power Rubric data confirm Wibowo's narrative of US and China influence in the region and the Asia Barometer studies of public opinion.

Southeast Asia also attracts many foreigners—immigrants, students, and visitors. In addition, to people from China, South Asian immigrants, students, and visitors are among the largest communities of foreigners. Southeast Asia's Muslim societies also have important soft power relationships with other Muslim societies in South Asia and the Middle East. Each of these trends would be fruitful areas for further research. The biases of the international relations policy and research community mainly consider Southeast Asia the policy object of outside powers, overlooking how Southeast Asian countries are agents of their own relationships in the international system. In this case, one contribution of the Soft Power Rubric is that an objective framework reveals the arenas where the stories have not yet been told.

Southeast Asian countries feature in some international soft power indices and rankings. In the Soft Power 30 series of publications, Singapore is the only ASEAN country that appears on the main list. In 2017, it ranked 20th in 2017, 21st in 2018, and 21st again in 2019. In 2017, Thailand was identified as "one to watch," ranked number 36. When Soft Power 30 has a regional focus, then ASEAN countries appear. In 2019, there was an Asia region ranking. Singapore ranked 3rd; Thailand, 6th; Malaysia, 7th; Indonesia, 9th; and the Philippines, 10th. Soft Power 30 rankings are developed in part based on a survey of international elites. Of the ten ASEAN countries, elites in Indonesia, Malaysia, and Vietnam are included. The Lowy Asia Power Index covers twenty-five countries in Asia, all ten ASEAN members included. In terms of cultural influence, in 2018, Malaysia, Thailand, and Singapore ranked 6th, 7th, and 8th. While from a scholarly perspective the indices are limited in their usefulness, because their calculations are partly hidden, they serve an important purpose in publicly reminding governments that persuasion as a foreign policy tool is as legitimate as coercion. The Soft Power Rubric, an alternative to these indices, is built on stronger scholarly foundations while still enabling clear and simple empirical comparisons.

Spotlight on Malaysia as an Educational Hub

In 2020, Malaysia was the fifteenth largest destination in the world for students enrolled in foreign universities for a degree. Malaysia promotes itself as a value-for-money education hotspot (Arachi 2006). Malaysians' education ministry aims to improve the ranking of Malaysian universities in global lists and to make Malaysia an educational hub, a concerted effort to build Malaysia's destination image in the eyes of foreign students. To meet surging domestic demand for university education, the government's 1996 reforms established alongside the public universities a private higher education sector that could also attract foreign students (Kassim 2014). According to UNESCO data, the number of foreign students in Malaysia grew from around 40,000 in 2005 to over 100,000 in 2022.

In parallel with its 1996 educational reforms, the government has encouraged foreign universities to organize branch campuses in Malaysia. Monash University from Australia and University of Nottingham from Great Britain, for example, issue Australian and British degrees taught in English from their Malaysian branch campuses (Arachi 2006). While Malaysia is not a primarily English-speaking country, many universities offer instruction primarily in English. At the end of the Cold War, English became the global language of politics and commerce. Throughout Eastern Europe, English replaced Russian as the major second language to learn. Universities in English-speaking countries successfully attract the lion's share of foreign students. Universities in non-English-speaking countries with aspirations to global prestige seriously weigh how much curricula to offer in English to attract foreign students. At the graduate level, for example, German universities are increasing the number of master's and doctoral programs taught in English (Schaefer-Wilke 2018). Between 2011 and 2017, the number of English-language master's programs in Germany increased by 11 percent (Gonzalez 2017). Similarly, Malaysia's decision to allow and encourage university instruction in English makes it an attractive destination for a larger pool of foreign students. Figure 10.3 shows the top ten countries that sent foreign students to Malaysia in 2015.

Figure 10.3 shows Malaysia as an educational hub with potential for fostering linkages with South Asia, Africa, and the Middle East at a moment in time when these countries have talented young people eager to go abroad for training. Surveys of foreign students show they are drawn to Malaysia because of the relatively low cost of enrolling in a reputable academic program with

Figure 10.3 Foreign Students in Malaysia, Top 10 Countries of Origin, 2022

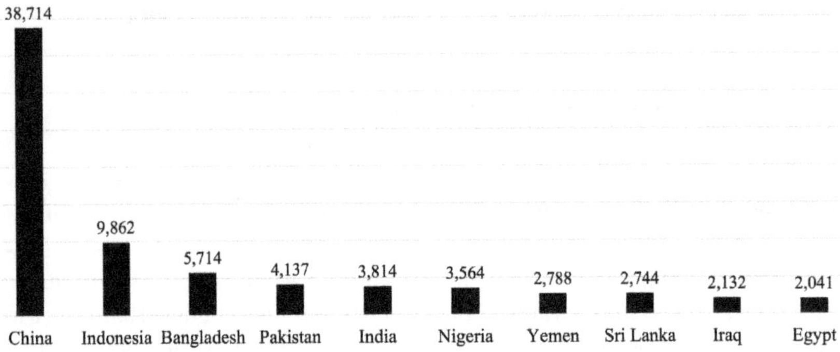

China	Indonesia	Bangladesh	Pakistan	India	Nigeria	Yemen	Sri Lanka	Iraq	Egypt
38,714	9,862	5,714	4,137	3,814	3,564	2,788	2,744	2,132	2,041

Source: UNESCO Institute of Statistics.

good teachers and good facilities (Migin et al. 2015; Zeeshan et al. 2013). Many also look forward to opportunities to work and build careers in Malaysia after graduating. Attracting human capital is an explicit goal of Malaysia's education policy reforms (Kassim 2014). In addition, after the 9/11 attacks on the United States, students from Asia and the Middle East faced increasingly restricted visa and university admissions and began to search for other educational centers. Malaysia's place identity is as a majority Muslim country, making it particularly attractive to Muslim students (Zeeshan et al. 2013).

Returning to the Culinary Scene

Padoongpatt's (2017) account of the Thai American community provides a sidelong glance into the concerns of the Thai government. On the one hand, the success of Thai cuisine and community in Los Angeles likely contributed to the development of the Thai gastrodiplomacy campaign. On the other hand, the Thai government's willingness to support the Thai American community was mixed. When Thai businesses were destroyed in 1992 riots, the Thai consul general did work to help them rebuild. However, in 1995 when the El Monte factory exposed that Thai women garment workers were exploited like slaves, the Thai government was anxious to avoid attention, as it confirmed an ugly image of Thailand as a center of sex tourism and exploited labor. The tensions of transnational identity are on full display here. To whom should Thai Americans turn for justice? In international labor exploitation, both governments bear responsibility. Padoongpatt describes this event as one of the turning points that mobilized Thais in Los Angeles to create their own civil society organization, the Thai Community Development Center, to advocate for their own causes (Padoongpatt 2017).

In Taiwan, the complexity of the Thai government's gastrodiplomacy work is also on view. Chi and Jackson (2011) describe the Thai restaurant scene as bookended by upscale Thai restaurants serving affluent Taiwanese customers, on one hand, and inexpensive restaurants catering to Thai workers, mostly at the railroad stations in Taoyuan, with a range of shops in between. The Thai Select campaign in Taiwan awarded recognition to several restaurants—all of the upscale type and none to the worker type. The scholars interviewed several of the upscale restauranteurs, and all were comfortable discussing the degree to which they modified their cuisines to Taiwanese tastes, even putting on the menu dishes that were popularly considered Thai in Taiwan but were really from Yunnan or Myanmar, the native regions of many of Thai restauranteurs. This is somewhat ironic, given that Thai Select recognition is in part recognizing the authenticity of the cultural and culinary experience offered by the restaurant (Chi and Jackson 2011). By this reckoning, gastrodiplomacy is an effort to create a destination image in the minds of potential tourists to Thailand, in which authenticity is malleable.

In terms of volume, the Thai restaurant industry globally is a big success. In the United States, if taking the ratio of a community's population, there are ten times more Thai than Mexican restaurants. The chef training, export of Thai ingredients, and advice on setting menus suitable for foreign tastes has helped the proliferation of restaurants (Lam 2019). The Thai gastrodiplomacy campaign is viewed around the world as a model and has been emulated by countries as diverse as South Korea and Peru.

However, the unfortunate flip side of gastrodiplomacy is the problem of gastronationalism. From the Ozyegin University Department of Gastronomy and Culinary Arts in Istanbul, Tettner and Kalyoncu (2016) discuss cuisine's rising role in promoting tourism. As countries gained independence, they note, culinary nationalism in Latin America, Asia, and Africa was part of the creation of new national identities in opposition to former imperial powers and to other newly formed nations. Unfortunately, the nationalization of cuisine tends to result in a monolithic image, which both ignores the interrelatedness of many culinary traditions and suppresses other traditions altogether (Tettner and Kalyoncu 2016).

> The logic of nation-states pushes them to a narrow, simplistic and self-serving framing of culinary cultures. This thinking leads to a kind of "ontological politics" where the question of whether the Dolma, the stuffed grape leaf, is a Turkish, Armenian or Azerbaijani dish constitutes a legitimate point of contestation between these countries. This state of being is precisely the one we want to move away from, . . . and [instead we should move toward] food being a source of cooperation rather than competition between countries. (Tettner and Kalyoncu 2016)

Tettner and Kalyoncu argue for a more regional approach to promoting culinary tourism. Padoongpatt actually provides an example in Los Angeles. When the Thai Community Development Center succeeded in establishing a Thai Town location in East Hollywood, an area targeted for urban development by the city, few Thais lived there any longer. Instead, among other groups were Armenians. The Thai and Armenian community worked together to promote Thai Town and Little Armenia as a tourist destination in Los Angeles (Padoongpatt 2017). Surely, dolmas were served.

The Soft Power Rubric provides an aerial overview of the people-to-people relationships among countries. The data form a big picture of the connections between people and nations. In this picture it is possible to see the ambitions of Malaysia to improve the skills of its workforce and play a role in Asia and in the global Muslim community. In Thailand, the soft power story is about Thai cuisine and gastrodiplomacy, the realpolitik status of Thailand's destination image in the world, and most importantly the transnational flourishing of Thai people at home and as immigrants abroad. In the study of soft power, beyond the research on the great power countries of the moment, the literature becomes more scattered and a coherent view more difficult to piece together. Rather than narrow the focus of the chapter, presented here is a multistranded, kaleidoscopic perspective, tied together by the several elements of the Soft Power Rubric and the major themes that intersect them all—a different sense of who is at the core and who is at the periphery, the dual push and pull of which countries attract Southeast Asians abroad and which foreigners are attracted to the region, the making of destination images and place identities, and the evolution of transnational identities.

Notes

1. The most recent country-level data available for foreign students in China are from 2018. Data on all foreign students in China collected from the Ministry of Education (www.moe.gov.cn) and Chinese Association for International Education (www.cafsa.org.cn). Country-level data on the number of foreign students enrolled at Chinese universities for a degree are estimated.

2. Post-2018 updated travel data at the country level are still being processed.

3. Notably, while Singapore promotes itself as an education hub, it does not publish how many foreign students are enrolled in its universities. For example, for the 2018/2020 graph, the UNESCO data on foreign students enrolled in Southeast Asian universities for a degree include data from Brunei (2020), Cambodia (2021), Indonesia (2018), Laos (2020), Malaysia (2020), Myanmar (2018), Thailand (2020), and Vietnam (2020).

4. Again, travel data after 2018 are still in process and not yet published by the UN World Tourism Organization.

11

The Soft Power Leaders: Global Rankings

France becomes the world no. 1 for soft power.
World Economic Forum, Switzerland (Gray 2017)

The UK is on top of the world—at least when it comes to soft power. We analyse the latest global soft power ranking.
British Council (MacDonald 2018)

Japan: it's all about the soft sell—and Japan is finally getting it right.
"Monocle's Ranking of Soft Power in Asia,"
Nikkei Asian Review based in Tokyo (Hall 2017)

THE SOFT POWER RUBRIC, WITH ITS HISTORICAL QUANTITAtive dataset, is not immune to the jockeying. In my innumerable conversations about soft power, the most frequent question asked me is, Well, who is number one in soft power these days? In this chapter I seek to answer this question with a responsible, yet flexible approach. However, an important counter-question to keep in mind is, What does it mean to be a leading soft power country? With military power, does the number one seed always win? Military history would be thin on stories if this were true. Neither is it the case that the biggest economic power wins the trade dispute. Vulnerabilities as well as strengths are important factors. Nevertheless, the question remains. I compare the Soft Power Rubric to the most popular ranking, the Soft Power 30, and show the similarities and differences, and how the Rubric further provides insight well beyond current rankings.

The Soft Power 30 rankings were calculated almost every year between 2010 and 2019.[1] For the Soft Power Rubric data, I have calculated rankings every decade from 1960 to 2020, the latest year for which complete data are available. Table 11.1 shows Soft Power 30 and the Soft Power Rubric rankings for the top five countries in 2010 and 2020 (the latest Soft Power 30 ranking is for 2019). The two methods agree that France, Germany, the United Kingdom, and the United States are the top four soft power leaders. In 2010 the only difference is the Soft Power 30 includes Switzerland, while the Soft Power Rubric includes Russia. In 2019, the only difference is that Soft Power 30 includes Sweden, whereas the Soft Power Rubric includes Spain instead.

The Soft Power Rubric and the Soft Power 30 rankings look similar, with the same four countries in varying rankings within the top five: the United States, France, Germany, and the United Kingdom. Therefore, despite its vastly different methodology, the Soft Power Rubric successfully captures the soft power zeitgeist of the moment. Full details on how the Soft Power Rubric rankings were calculated from publicly available data are in the Appendixes.

Why Are Rankings Important, or Not?

Should we take international country rankings seriously, or do they just reflect the momentary fads? Status, Renshon (2017) argues, should be reckoned with: "While guns and tanks are easy to count, far more can be explained by things that we cannot see, hear, or hold. It is ultimately on *status*, not bullets, that the 'success or failure of all international policies' rests." Countries care most about status compared to their peers—the countries in their reference group. Examining country status relative to the appropriate reference group keeps comparisons relevant. One way Renshon identifies reference groups is through network diagrams of diplomatic exchanges between countries—the number of diplomats countries send to represent them in foreign countries. Among members of a status community, Renshon expects higher numbers of diplomatic exchanges (2017).

Table 11.1 Comparing Soft Power 30 and Soft Power Rubric Rankings, 2010 and 2019/2020

	SP30 (2010)	SP Rubric (2010)	SP30 (2019)	SP Rubric (2020)
1	*France*	*US*	*France*	*US*
2	*UK*	*France*	*UK*	*France*
3	*US*	*UK*	*Germany*	*Germany*
4	*Germany*	*Germany*	*Sweden*	*UK*
5	*Switzerland*	*Russia*	*US*	*Spain*

This principle mirrors closely the reasoning behind the Soft Power Rubric—countries that have greater numbers of social interactions have closer ties and greater soft power influence over each other.

International institutions like the World Bank use status competition to progress principles of economic development, in particular with the Ease of Doing Business Index. Beginning in the 1990s, the World Bank identified burdensome business regulation as a primary cause of underinvestment in developing countries. By publishing an index that rated countries on the Ease of Doing Business, the bank unleashed social pressure for states to deregulate. Rather than the World Bank exerting direct pressure on governments, the pressure instead is communicated through international and national media from the countries' domestic business sector and from political leaders who wish to be seen in the international community as open to foreign investment (Doshi, Kelley, and Simmons 2019). The Ease of Doing Business Index coincides with an acceleration of international index and rating development by governmental and nongovernmental organizations alike seeking to affect nation-states through social pressure (Doshi, Kelley, and Simmons 2019). The Soft Power 30 list published annually and often distributed and discussed at the World Economic Forum held annually in Davos, Switzerland, is also an example of such an index. The Soft Power Rubric is conceptually more in the tradition of national accounting and the calculation of the gross domestic product, but like GDP it is possible to use the Rubric to rank countries as well.

Comparing the Soft Power Rubric to the Soft Power 30 List

There are numerous international rankings relevant to soft power. They include the Pew Global Attitudes Poll, which regularly conducts an international survey that includes questions on how foreigners see a set of leading countries (Pew Research 2021). In addition, there is the Lowy Institute's Asia Power Index, which focuses on Asia specifically and power broadly—including soft, but also economic and military (Lowy Institute 2021). Further, there are a number of issue-specific indices such as Freedom House's Freedom in the World index on political and civil liberties (Freedom House 2021) and the Happiness Index published by the United Nations (Sustainable Development Solutions Network 2019). These are all interesting and useful indices.

However, in this chapter I focus on Portland's Soft Power 30 as substantively closest in subject and scope to the Soft Power Rubric. I show similarities and differences between the two when ranking soft power leaders. Further, I discuss the applications of the Soft Power Rubric that go beyond ranking: the transparency of the Rubric data makes it possible to analyze what's behind the rankings; the Rubric gives a longer historical perspective; and finally the Rubric can provide insight into soft power countries that are leaders but not always ranked in the top four or five powers.

As shown in Table 11.2, in the Soft Power 30 rankings, from 2010 to 2019, the top four countries were almost always France, Germany, the United Kingdom, and the United States. Ranked fourth through sixth were Switzerland, Australia, Sweden, Canada, and Japan.

The Soft Power 30 rankings are calculated based 70 percent on objective data and 30 percent on subjective data, every year with a revised combination of criteria. For the reports 2010 through 2012, there were five sub-indices of objective data: Business/Innovation, Culture, Diplomacy, Education, and Government. The subjective data relied on expert panels from culture magazines or outside survey data. The reports from 2015 to 2019 include six instead of five sub-indices of objective data: Culture, Digital, Education, Enterprise, Engagement, and Government. For subjective data, the analysts conducted their own survey. In 2015, 250–500 people were interviewed in twenty countries. In 2019, 500 people in twenty-five countries were interviewed, for a total of 12,500 individuals.

Examples of the data series are shown in Table 11.3. They include broad indicators like the number of tourists and students, symbolic achievements like medals and prizes, per capita socioeconomic indicators, and other indices from organizations like the OECD and World Bank.

While topics and data remain consistent over the report series, there are some variations in the specific series included from year to year. For example, under Digital, in 2015 the price of mobile broadband was included, whereas in 2018, the number of mobile phones per 100 people was included. Another is in Education: in 2012 and 2018 the OECD PISA test results of high schoolers' science and math knowledge were included, whereas in 2015 literacy rates were included.

Portland's Soft Power 30 encompasses a wide range of indicators and data that have an effect on foreigners' view of countries. Also, the simplicity of the final result—a single ranking from one to thirty—is part of its successful effort to bring more public attention to soft power in the international system. The diverse indicators are in some respects part of its strength, although many will have datasets limited to only a fraction of all countries in the world. Thus, the need to focus on the top thirty countries only.

Soft Power Rubric–Using It to Rank Countries

By contrast, the Soft Power Rubric relies on nearly global datasets; the top-ranked countries included in the Appendixes are only a fraction of the

Table 11.2 Soft Power 30 Results, 2010–2019, Available Years

Rank	2010	2011	2012	2015	2016	2017	2018	2019
1	France	US	UK	UK	US	France	UK	France
2	UK	UK	USA	Germany	UK	UK	France	UK
3	US	France	Germany	US	Germany	US	Germany	Germany
4	Germany	Germany	France	France	Canada	Germany	US	Sweden
5	Switzerland	Australia	Sweden	Canada	France	Canada	Japan	US
6	Sweden	Sweden	Japan	Australia	Australia	Japan	Canada	Switzerland
7	Denmark	Japan	Denmark	Switzerland	Japan	Switzerland	Switzerland	Canada
8	Australia	Switzerland	Switzerland	Japan	Switzerland	Australia	Sweden	Japan
9	Finland	Canada	Australia	Sweden	Sweden	Sweden	Netherlands	Australia
10	Netherlands	Netherlands	Canada	Netherlands	Netherlands	Netherlands	Australia	Netherlands

Table 11.3 Soft Power 30: Selected Indicators

Soft Power 30 Sub-index	Included Metrics
Culture	Number of tourists, Olympic medals
Digital	Facebook followers for head of state, mobile phones per 100 people
Education	OECD PISA science and math test scores, number of international students in the country
Engagement	Total overseas development aid, asylum seekers per 1000 people
Business/Innovation or Enterprise	Number of global patents filed/GDP, World Bank Ease of Doing Business Report
Government	UNDP Gender Equality Index Score, Press Freedom Index Score

Source: Soft Power 30 (2018).

countries available for analysis. Also, the Soft Power Rubric is extremely parsimonious in the type of indicator included—only those series that quantify transnational social interactions, either in person or mediated through communications technology. Thus, the Soft Power Rubric can be the basis of not just one index but diverse rankings depending on the research question at hand.

While ranking is not how the Soft Power Rubric is primarily useful, it is possible to construct. These rankings are constructed based on how many immigrants live in a country, how many foreign students are enrolled in its universities for a degree, and how many foreigners visit. For movies, the number of foreigners who buy tickets is available for a much smaller set of countries, which makes country-to-country comparisons possible but not global rankings.

To arrive at a global ranking, I compiled the data for the three series for all countries reporting. The next step is to rank countries in each of the series. For example, in 2020 Russia is the fourth largest destination for immigrants, Canada is eighth largest, and Türkiye is twelfth largest. Then, for each country, I take the sum of the three ranks. For Germany, in 2019 it ranks second in the world in immigrants, fourth in the world in foreign students, and fourteenth in the world for foreign visitors; the sum of ranks for Germany equals twenty. The final step is to rank the "sum of ranks." Only those countries reporting data for all three series are included. When these countries were sorted by "sum of ranks," the result is the order shown in Table 11.4. The first four are the United States, France, Germany, and the United Kingdom. This method is simple, replicable, and open to challenge; more details are in the Appendixes. The Soft Power Rubric's foundational principle is that regular cross-border interactions build trust. There may be other different but also reasonable ways to weight the elements against each other. More details on the method and data for ranking top countries from 1960 onward are in the Appendixes.

Beyond Rankings—Historical Application of the Soft Power Rubric

The Soft Power Rubric differs from the Soft Power 30 list in that the Rubric is less an answer and more a pathway to further questions. For example, the Rubric enables a longer historical lens. Also, the Rubric allows for direct comparison among France, Germany, and the United Kingdom. Finally, the Rubric can be used to assess and ask questions about those countries that are not typically in the highest ranks but are known as leaders based more on their soft power than their economic or military might. The rest of this chapter covers these three usages of the Rubric.

Well beyond the scope of the Soft Power 30 is a historical perspective. This is one of the advantages of the Soft Power Rubric; it is based on data collections that were made publicly available beginning in the 1960s. The following table shows the results of the Soft Power Rubric data for a nearly sixty-year span from 1960 to around 2020. For each decade, Table 11.4 shows leaders in terms of attracting immigrants, foreign students, and foreign travelers. Note that in the 2020 rankings, foreign visitor data are for 2019, the most recent year with a comprehensive set of countries reporting.

Based on the Soft Power Rubric data, the United States and France have been consistent soft power leaders with the United Kingdom close behind from the 1960s to today. Germany arrived and remained in the top ranks from 2000, after reunification in the 1990s. The strength of the Soft Power Rubric is not so much in pinpointing the exact rank of a country but rather providing in broad strokes a wider view of how countries are changing. Across the seven decades, Australia appears in every list except 2020. Italy appears in every list except 1970. Spain appears in every list except 1970 and 2000. Austria appears, but not after 2000. Russia appears in 1990 and every list thereafter.

Unpacking the Data for the United States, France, Germany, and the United Kingdom

The US Share of Immigrants, Foreign Students, and Foreign Visitors

The United States tops the Soft Power Rubric rankings in every decade from 1960 to the present. Figures 11.1, 11.2, and 11.3 show the US share of the world's immigrants, foreign students, and foreign visitors from 1990 to the most recent year available.

Table 11.4 Soft Power Rubric Global Rankings, 1960–2020

Rank	1960x	1970x	1980x	1990	2000	2010	2020
1	US	US	US	US	US	US	US
2	France	France	France	France	France	France	France
3	UK	Canada	UK	Canada	Germany	UK	Germany[a]
4	Switzerland	UK	Italy	Russia	Russia	Germany	UK[a]
5	Austria	Switzerland	Canada	UK	UK	Russia	Spain
6	Italy	Australia	Switzerland	Italy	Canada	Italy	Russia
7	Belgium	Spain	Austria	Australia	Italy	Canada	Canada
8	Australia	Israel	Poland	Spain	Spain	Spain	Türkiye
9	Japan	Lebanon	Spain	Saudi Arabia	Australia	Ukraine	UAE
10		Singapore	Australia	Japan	Switzerland	Australia	Italy

Notes: As of July 2023, the most recent United Nations immigration data for most countries are from 2020; for international visitors 2019. For some detailed data, the most recent are still from 2018. In normal circumstances, data take two years to be published. During the Covid-19 pandemic, which began in early 2020 and may be said to have subsided in March 2023, data collection and processing were disrupted and publication is still delayed.

a. In 2020, Germany and the United Kingdom tied in rank.

Figure 11.1a Immigrants: US Fraction of World Total

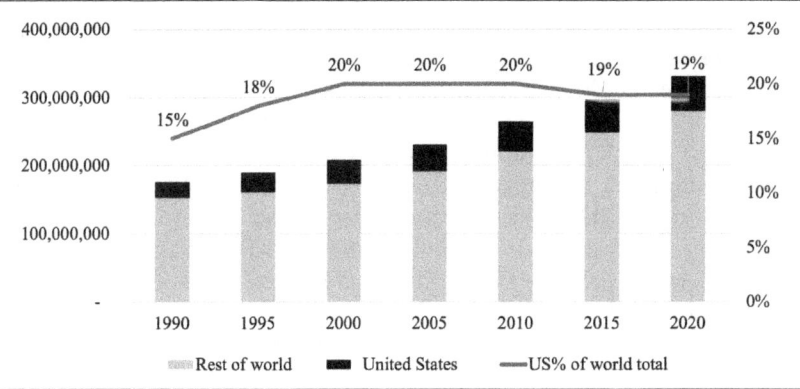

Source: UN Population Division.

Figure 11.1b Foreign Students: US Fraction of World Total

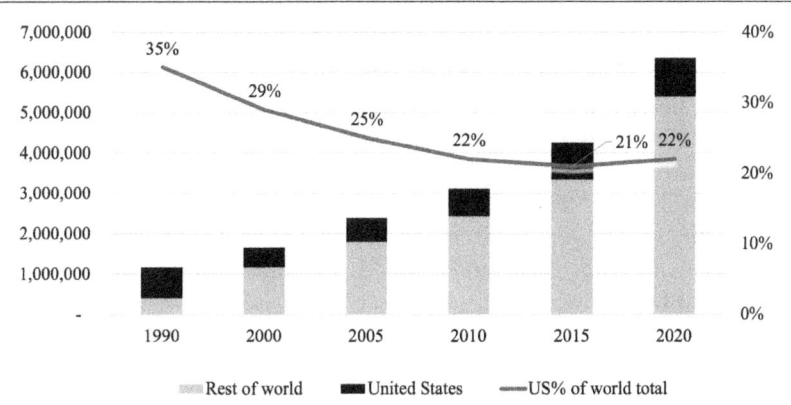

Source: UNESCO Institute of Statistics.

Figure 11.1c Foreign Visitors: US Fraction of World Total

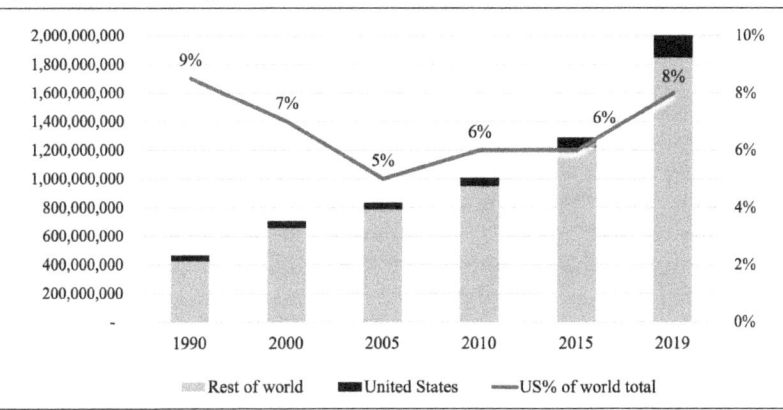

Source: UN World Tourism Organization.

In terms of immigration, the US share has grown from 15 percent in 1990 to 19 percent in 2020 of all immigrants in the world, as shown in Figures 11a, 11b, and 11c. This is a growing share of a growing category. In 1990 there were 153 million immigrants worldwide; in 2020 there were over 280 million. US immigration totals increased from 23 million in 1990 to 51 million in 2020. The largest immigrant communities in the United States are from China, India, and the Philippines. Fourth is Puerto Rico, a US territory. The next largest are El Salvador, Vietnam, and Cuba.

In terms of education, the US share declined significantly from 35 percent in 1990 to 22 percent in 2020 of all foreign students in the world, as shown in Figure 11.1b. The global total number of students enrolled in foreign universities for a degree grew from 1.2 million in 1990 to 5 million in 2018—a fourfold increase. Meanwhile, the number in the United States doubled from 475,000 in 1990 to 957,000 in 2020. The countries sending the most students to the United States include China, South Korea, and Saudi Arabia.

In terms of foreign visitors, the US share declined from 9 percent in 1990 to 8 percent in 2019, as shown in Figure 11.1c. The total number of visitors abroad grew from 430 million in 1990 to 2 billion in 2019, a fourfold increase. The number of foreign visitors to the United States increased from 40 million in 1990 to 165 million in 2019. The countries sending the most visitors to the United States are Canada at 21 million and Mexico at 18 million in 2018. They are followed by Japan, China, South Korea, Brazil, and Germany.

On the whole, the United States hosts a growing number of immigrants, foreign students, and visitors. In terms of students and visitors, US growth is outpaced by the even more rapid rate of growth worldwide. Especially of note is the decline in the US share of foreign students worldwide; as discussed in Chapter 3, the quantitative research on soft power identifies education as the kind of activity most apt to increase a country's soft power resources. However, the US share of immigrants is up, suggesting the United States is successfully competing for global talent and remains a positive destination in the minds of those migrating.

As discussed in Chapters 2 and 3, most of the research on soft power centers on the United States. Since Nye formulated the soft power concept in 1990, the main debate is whether the United States is declining in its world leadership, and can its considerable soft power resources make up the difference? Nye argued this was the case, in light of Japan's economic rise in the 1980s. The end of the Cold War and the simultaneous explosion of American popular culture driven by the internet and communications technology generated a backlash against US cultural influence. The US invasion of Iraq in 2003 undermined its credibility in global leadership. In more recent years, US soft power discussions are now turned toward

China's rise (Nye 1990a, 1990b; Ellwood 2012; Shambaugh 2013; Védrine and Moïsi 2001; Wilson 2008). Further, the quantitative analysis of soft power builds on the US literature and concludes that when foreign public opinion of the United States is high, then it is easier for it to achieve high-profile foreign policy goals (Goldsmith and Horiuchi 2009, 2012). Also, when foreign students study in democratic countries, that promotes democratic values at home (Atkinson 2014; Spilimbergo 2009).

Comparing France, Germany, and the United Kingdom

The three other countries that in recent years consistently top the list of both the Soft Power 30 and the Soft Power Rubric are France, Germany, and the United Kingdom. Figures 11.2a, 11.2b, and 11.2c compare the number of foreigners who interact with the three countries along three elements of the Rubric—immigrants, foreign students, and foreign visitors.

Immigration. All three countries welcome an increasing number of immigrants, with Germany and the United Kingdom nearly doubling in total between 1990 and 2020, as shown in Figure 11.2a. Germany is among the world's largest host countries for immigrants. The top countries sending immigrants to Germany are from its east—Poland, Türkiye, Russia,

Figure 11.2a Immigrants in France, Germany, and the United Kingdom, 1990–2020

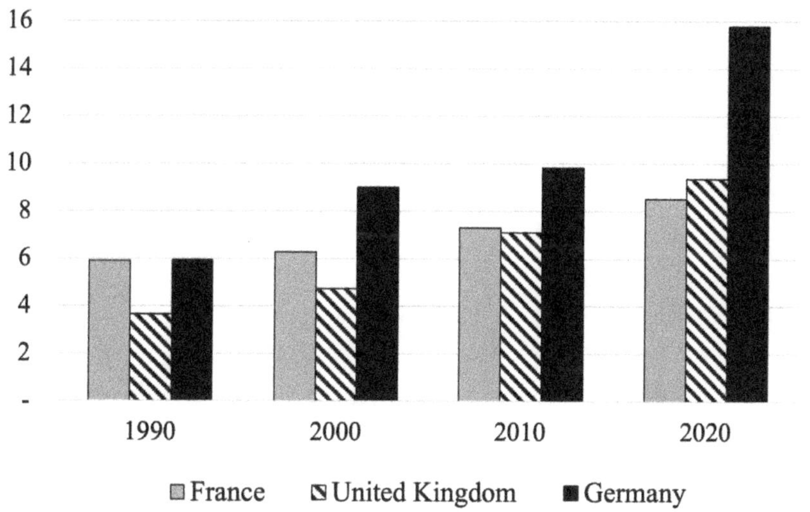

Source: UN Population Division.

Figure 11.2b Foreign Students in France, Germany, and the United Kingdom, 2000–2019

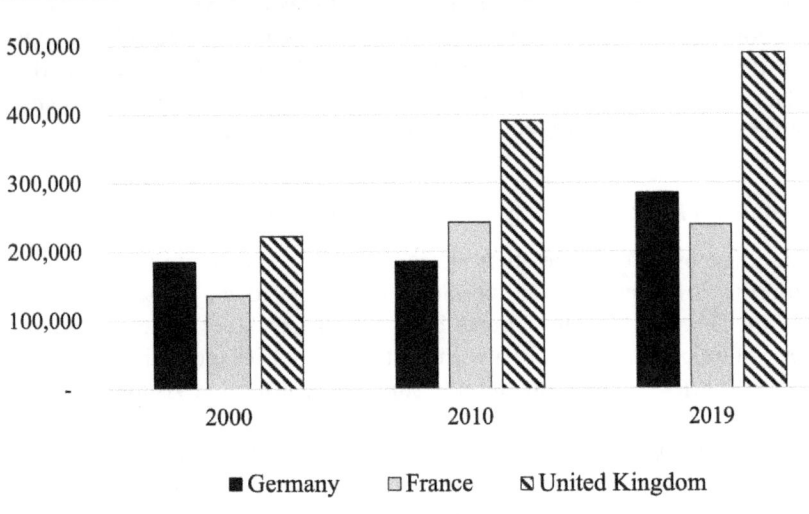

Source: UNESCO.

Figure 11.2c Foreign Visitors to France, Germany, and the United Kingdom, 2000–2019 (millions)

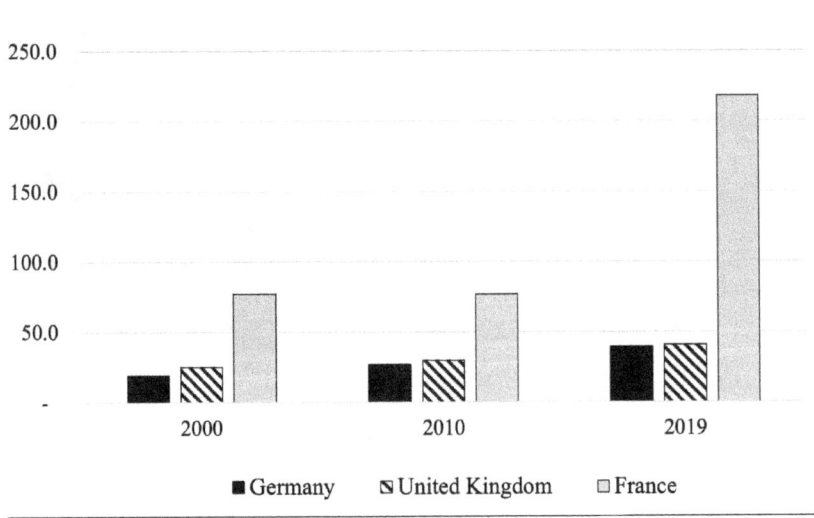

Source: UN World Tourism Organization.

Kazakhstan, and Syria. For France, three out of the top five sending countries are former colonies—Algeria, Morocco, and Tunisia, as well as Portugal and Italy. For the United Kingdom, former colonies are also top sending countries—India, Pakistan, and Ireland, as well as Poland and Germany.

Education. Foreign students in all three countries grew between 2000 and 2019, as shown in Figure 11.2b. For Germany, the top sending countries include China, India, the United Kingdom, and Austria. For the United Kingdom, one of the world's largest hosts for foreign students, the number doubled; its top sending countries include former colonies—Hong Kong, India, Malaysia, the United States—as well as China. For France, the top sending countries again include former colonies—Morocco, Algeria, Tunisia—as well as China.

Visitors. France is the top host country for foreign visitors in the world. All three countries increase tourists between 2000 and 2019, as shown in Figure 11.2c. For France, Germany, and the United Kingdom, the top sending countries are all neighboring European countries and the United States.

The qualitative soft power literature provides further insights. For France, the research discusses primarily France's interest in maintaining Francophonie, its relationships with its former colonies, symbolized by the promotion of the French language (Soba 2015). Particularly in the areas of immigration and international education, these ties are evident. Taking a historical perspective, in France, students from its colonies were 65 percent of its foreign student population in 1960, which fell to 54 percent in 2017. This, however, is much higher than for the United Kingdom where students from its colonies were 84 percent of its foreign student population in 1961 but only 36 percent in 2017 (Wu 2020). The research on British soft power emphasizes the interest in trade; indeed, historically, its acquisition of colonies followed the activities of the British East India Company around the world (Bell 2016).

In contrast, the research on Germany's soft power emphasizes its primary focus on overcoming the legacy of National Socialism in perpetrating the tragedies of World War II, and several scholars point to Germany's hosting the World Cup in 2006 as a major turning point (Grix and Houlihan 2014) in its own and foreign countries' perception of Germany's hospitality toward outsiders (Hein 2016). Germans not only host many foreigners but also themselves often go abroad. For example, in 2018, Germany had over 120,000 students enrolled in foreign universities for a degree, the French fewer than 100,000, and the United Kingdom fewer than 40,000. Also, there are more German emigrants living abroad, although the number of British are rising fast.

Which specific countries British, French, and Germans go to opens up another perspective on their relationships with foreigners. Figure 11.3 shows

Figure 11.3 French, German, and British Immigrants to China, Japan, and Russia, 2020

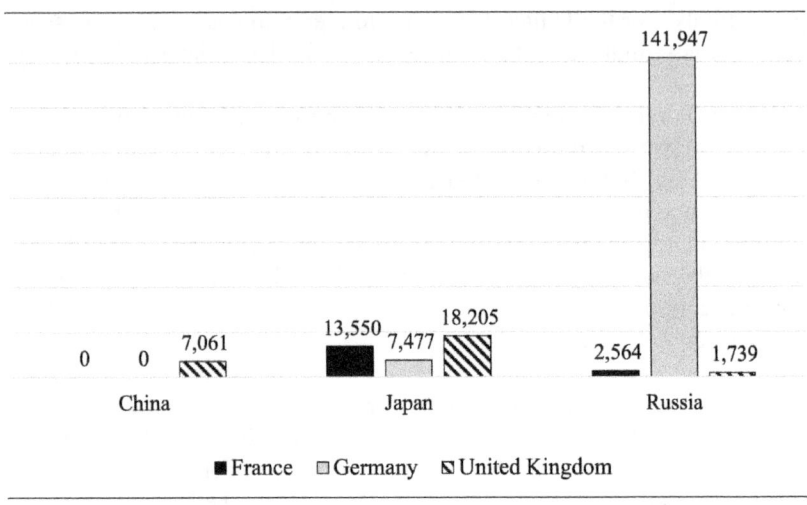

Source: UN Population Division.

how many emigrants each country has in China, Japan, and Russia in 2020. Of the three destinations, Japan is the most popular for French emigres. There are more British emigres in China and Japan than either French or German. Germany has the most emigrants in Russia.

Another contrast is in Figure 11.4 on British, French, and Germans going to the United States. In all three categories, the British go to the United States more than the French or Germans.[2]

For those familiar with British, French, and German societies, these observations may appear obvious. In a way, they are so apparent that they are rarely stated, which means for those who are not specialists, these relationships are invisible. If the Soft Power Rubric can make these relationships visible for highly studied countries like these three, it is even more helpful for the range of other countries that are far less frequently at the center of political science research.

South Africa: More Soft Power Than Their Hard Power Might Predict

Yet another segment of the soft power literature comprises case studies of countries with more soft power than their economic or military significance would predict. South Africa became an international model for delivering

Figure 11.4 French, German, and British Going to the United States, 2018 and 2020

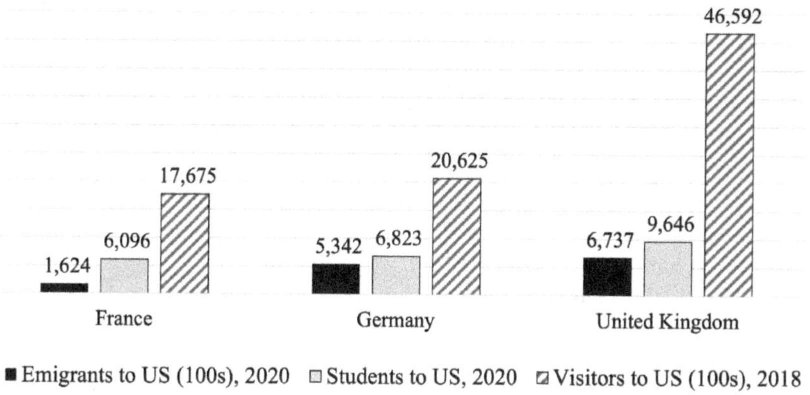

	France	Germany	United Kingdom
Emigrants to US (100s), 2020	1,624	5,342	6,737
Students to US, 2020	6,096	6,823	9,646
Visitors to US (100s), 2018	17,675	20,625	46,592

■ Emigrants to US (100s), 2020   □ Students to US, 2020   ▨ Visitors to US (100s), 2018

Sources: UN Population Division, UNESCO, and UNWTO.

social justice after a long history of racist exploitation. There is a cluster of studies of South Africa's soft power in the Africa region, especially as it transformed from international pariah to a moral authority on peace and reconciliation after apartheid ended. It is now the only African country in the G20. Building on its moral standing, South Africa relaxed immigration policies, and hosting of international events augments its soft power (Ogunnubi and Isike 2015). In *Superpower or Neocolonialist? South Africa in Africa,* Louw-Vaudran argues that twenty years after the end of apartheid, other African countries still acknowledge its leadership based on its democracy and values. Even neighbors' disappointment and resentment at changes in South Africa's foreign policy and immigration policy reflect their high expectations of it (Louw-Vaudran 2016).

Using the Soft Power Rubric, South Africa is the leading soft power country in Africa, from 2000 through 2019. Table 11.6 compares South Africa's Soft Power Rubric rank to two other measures—total armed forces personnel and GDP. Total armed forces personnel is one measure of the size of the nation's military. Although it certainly is not definitive in terms of identifying overall military power, it does reflect the nation's commitment to military force. GDP is widely accepted as an indicator of the size of an economy, although in fact it only captures production that has financial value. Much economically important production, such as family care, volunteer work, and even aspects of innovation, are not captured in GDP figures.

Nevertheless, the advantage of the Soft Power Rubric, the armed forces personnel, and GDP data are that they are available for a large set of countries over time. In the case of South Africa, the numbers show that its soft power influence exceeds rough indicators of its military and economic importance. Its soft power rank is 23rd, while its GDP is ranked 39th, and its armed forces personnel figures an even more distant 56th (see Table 11.5).

In the Soft Power 30, South Africa is not ranked. The data the Soft Power 30 relies on for its assessments are not comprehensively available for regional soft power leaders. By contrast, the Soft Power Rubric includes all these countries while remaining largely consistent with expert qualitative assessments—identifying it as a country that leads more by soft power than hard.

The Soft Power Rubric can be used to identify nations that have more or less soft power than economic or military power. Table 11.6 identifies a few prominent countries. Spain, like South Africa, has more soft power than military or economic power; the Soft Power Rubric ranks Spain 5th, while by GDP it ranks 14th, and by armed forces personnel it ranks 33rd.

China and India have more economic and military force than soft power influence. China's armed forces personnel ranks 2nd and its GDP 2nd, but its Soft Power Rubric rank is 16th. India's armed forces personnel ranks 1st and its GDP is ranked 6th, but its Soft Power Rubric rank is 19th.

Table 11.5 South Africa: Indicators of Soft, Military, and Economic Power

Country	Soft Power Rubric 2020—Rank	Armed Forces Personel, Total 2019—Rank	GDP (current $US) 2020—Rank
South Africa	23	56	39

Table 11.6 Spain, India, and China: Indicators of Soft, Military, and Economic Power

Country	Soft Power Rubric 2019/2020—Rank	Armed Forces Personel, Total 2019—Rank	GDP (current $US) 2020—Rank
Spain	5	33	14
India	19	1	6
China	16	2	2

Sources: Global Firepower and World Bank.

China is discussed in more detail in Chapter 9, which compares China with Russia. India is discussed in more detail in Chapter 8.

Toward a More Objective Ranking of Soft Power Relationships

International relations is not a competitive sport, and simple rankings oversimplify the subtleties of influence and the complexity of relationships. At the same time, Renshon's (2017) work shows that governments are sensitive to how they compare to other countries they consider worthy reference points and may change their behavior accordingly. Doshi, Kelley, and Simmons (2019) demonstrate this behavior does occur in their careful investigation of the effects of the World Bank Ease of Doing Business Index on individual government economic policy.

In the realm of soft power, the most influential index today is the Soft Power 30 sponsored by Portland and the Center for Public Diplomacy at the University of Southern California, and it is an important tool that regularly reminds governments that economic and military power are not the only ones important to cultivate. However, the Soft Power Rubric offers a method that includes a larger number of countries within its scope, provides a historical timeframe with data going back to 1960, with public data and a transparent calculation model that is adaptable to changing research questions. Details on method and data are in the Appendixes.

I began this chapter by showing the Soft Power Rubric produces rankings that are consistent with Soft Power 30 at the highest levels, diverging in lower ranks primarily by including countries outside the Soft Power 30's scope. Further, the Rubric analysis extends to 1960, fifty years further back than the Soft Power 30. In this historical perspective, the United States remains the leader—increasing its welcome to immigrants in recent years, but declining in its share of foreign students and foreign visitors. The Soft Power Rubric allows direct comparison among France, Germany, and the United Kingdom and each country's relationships with foreign countries. Finally, the soft power research qualitative literature identifies South Africa as one country that relies more on soft rather than hard power to lead.

For those readers frustrated with current soft power rankings that maintain proprietary data and algorithms, the Soft Power Rubric is an alternative that produces similar results with public data and an open model. For those readers skeptical that studying social and cultural influence, heretofore the primary domain of fieldwork scholars and historians, can benefit from the cold quantitative calculation, the Soft Power Rubric is a flexible tool grounded in the same theories of social capital and collective action that undergird qualitative research with results to match.

Notes

1. As of July 20, 2023, the most recent Soft Power 30 rankings are from 2019.
2. As of July 2023, 2018 is the most recent available data on specific visitor travel routes.

12

Implications of the Soft Power Rubric

SOFT POWER RELATIONSHIPS EXIST WHEN OTHERS INCLUDE us as part of their community, when we become friends of their nation. People express interest in foreign countries by engaging in activities like watching foreign movies, traveling, studying, and migrating abroad. The Soft Power Rubric brings together relevant, observable, and measurable activity that captures a country's potential scope for soft power—the number of cross-border interactions its people have with foreign countries. The Soft Power Rubric is a framework to track changes in the volume and direction of interactions people have with foreigners. Three elements are direct people-to-people interactions: emigration, study abroad, and travel abroad; the fourth is a mediated interaction: watching foreign movies. Emigration reflects a person's ultimate integration in a foreign society, permanently moving family and home to another country. Study abroad reflects a person's serious interest and commitment to understanding another society by spending substantial financial resources and formative time in a foreign country. Visiting a foreign country reflects a short-term interest in a foreign society. Watching a movie expresses an interest or curiosity about another country. For each of these series, government international institutions collect and publish quantitative data for many countries.

The Soft Power Rubric measures soft power *resources*, the *potential* for a country to have a soft power relationship with another. GDP, a measure of economic power resources, sums the financial value of goods and services produced by an economy. For military power, the number of military bases, aircraft carrier, or personnel are measures of military power resources (Global Firepower 2023). More resources likely mean more success, but there is no guarantee. A bigger GDP does not guarantee the upper hand in a trade negotiation. More military bases do not ensure victory in war. However, more resources make success more likely, and the depletion of resources heightens the risk of failure. Similarly, the Rubric reveals the volume and intensity of people-to-people interactions that form the basis of many individuals' views of foreign countries and the foundation of a country's soft power resources. More soft power resources no more predict greater political cooperation than more military resources predict victory in war. However, it is reasonable to expect that the presence of major soft power resources itself alters behavior.

This book establishes the conceptual foundation for the Soft Power Rubric, linking it to several arenas of work in social science research. Part One lifts the study of soft power out of the confines of international relations and takes advantage of many other aspects of political science research and other allied fields. In Part Two case studies show how the Soft Power Rubric can be applied, ranging from simple one- and two-country comparisons, to more complex regional and multistranded analyses.

Conceptual Foundations for the Soft Power Rubric

Nye's conception of power is rooted in a particular view of the international system, with soft and hard power on a spectrum, and international politics like a three-level chess-board—military, economic, and soft power levels. Wilson, and Nye himself, later advances the idea of smart power, referred to by Gallarotti as cosmopolitan power—an outlook that takes the application of hard and soft power together. Especially useful are Gallarotti's concepts of soft empowerment, the idea that choosing a soft power approach empowers the actor and possibly others, and hard disempowerment, the idea that choosing a hard power approach can at times undermine the actor's influence.

Nye describes power as having three faces: (1) threats and rewards, (2) agenda setting, and (3) shaping beliefs and preferences. Nye's work focuses primarily on the governments as actors, specifically in the area of public diplomacy and generally in his support for international engagement. Other scholars' work shows one path is to consider in more detail the agents behind the three faces. If we enlarge the cast of actors to include civil society—both organizations like business and nongovernmental institutions and individuals like scientists, artists, educators, and travelers—then we also expand the possible levers of soft power influence. The social science research on norms, institutions, trust, and collective action show there are some arenas where shared beliefs—for example, in human rights—can spur nations to action in ways not well-explained by military or economic interests. Fundamental to translating values into collective action is the process of people joining groups and building trust relationships within those communities, and with that social capital, groups are able to take political action that benefits the group, sometimes at the expense of the individual.

Nye separates power resources—things that potentially could be converted to power but in and of themselves do not predict success or failure—and relational power—the actual behavior of one country influencing another. Bringing these two together highlights the most complex problem in the study of soft power—converting soft power resources to soft power behavior. Gallarotti's idea of metapower, which situates understanding of soft power within a network of relationships, emphasizes its social aspect.

To get beyond Nye's problem of soft power conversion, many soft power scholars point out that the success of soft power depends not only on the state seeking to influence, but also on the states that are to be influenced, the audience of the soft power producer. Rather than thinking of the problem as one of power conversion, instead the challenge is whether there is soft power acceptance or rejection. Grant's work on ethics and power adds another dimension to this understanding, reminding us that the same use of force can be seen either as tyrannical or just, depending on context. The country's virtue and virtuosity as perceived by the audience are a major determinant of its soft power influence, argues Chitty. The emotional reaction to the soft power producer—whether it inspires endearment and emulation—is Gallarotti's measure of whether influence is successful. In all these discussions, Bially Mattern reminds us, the idea of attraction is central to soft power, and implied in attraction is some type of communication.

Empirical, quantitative researchers show that countries with soft power win more cooperation from and increased trade with other countries. Furthermore, countries with soft power attract more students, tourists, and foreign direct investment. Some scholars measure soft power with foreign public opinion data; others use indicators of democratic freedoms, per capita wealth, and cultural development. Soft power "success" includes political cooperation at the UN or other situations, attracting tourists and students, and bringing in trade and investment. Also, foreign public opinion about the United States is influenced by factors such as foreign policy credibility, effective and visible foreign aid, and direct social interaction with foreigners.

On education, a robust set of empirical studies show that when students train in foreign democracies, their sending countries experience an improvement in democratic institutions in later years. Spilimbergo's study using global data on international education from 1960 to 2005 shows that the effect on sending country political institutions is observable within a few years of sending students abroad. Leaders educated in Western countries are more likely to be democratic. Atkinson finds that foreign military officers, even those from authoritarian countries, bring back democratic norms when the training includes extensive interaction with Americans. Still under-researched from a quantitative perspective, however, is whether other kinds of political regimes also extend their influence by educating foreign students.

When democratic countries attract migrants, there may be several channels through which the migrants' origin countries also develop stronger democratic norms, suggests a growing area of research. They build a picture of how migration can affect political attitudes and behavior in the home country. While migration definitely has an effect, important variables include the politics of the destination as compared to the home country and the closeness and communication between the individuals with migrant experience and their community in the home country.

Soft power thinkers comfortable with broad-brush policy discussions are often uneasy with the sharply defined and narrowly focused quantitative studies that establish a measure for every intangible factor and use numbers to rank the success and failure of policies and programs. The range of the quantitative studies is indeed very narrow. So far, they focus primarily on the effect of democratic countries on others, and mostly on the United States and European countries on the rest of the world. Necessarily, the studies are limited to a few policy initiatives in specific timeframes. However, there has been substantial progress, and within these narrow constraints, there is positive evidence on a global scale over a significant timeframe that democracies influence other countries through training students and receiving immigrants. Nye's initial soft power writings were published in 1990; the earliest of the quantitative studies referenced here is in 2006. With more time, no doubt the quantitative research will expand and complicate our understanding of soft power.

There is a wealth of scholarship on political communications, trust, and social capital that provides both ideas and empirical strategies that could inform how people in one country develop and change their views of another with consequences for international cooperation and conflict. Several scholarly traditions suggest observing people-to-people interactions is likely to shed light on country-to-country politics. Two insights from political communications apply. The first is conceptual. When studying media broadcasting, political communications scholars are as interested in the reaction of the audience as the intent of the producer. Instead of approaching the study of soft power from the perspective of the government influencing foreign countries, suppose we flip the dynamic and define soft power as present when ordinary foreigners think of us as *we*, not *they*. That is the ultimate form of foreigners accepting our point of view. The second insight from political communications is empirical. We can detect the level of social integration among communities, in other words the extent and depth of "we," in changes in the direction and volume of communication activity between people.

From the study of culture and trust, two additional insights connect social interaction to possible cooperation and influence. One is that culture is not a force external to society; on the contrary, it is a world of meaning that is performed and created as people interact with each other. Therefore, transnational interaction is a basis for creating transnational culture, reflecting influences from all societies participating. A second is that trust between people is not simply a matter of faith but rather an attitude that grows through repeated, reciprocal interactions. Furthermore, this practical form of trust is one foundation of social capital, an important basis for cooperation. These two insights suggest that a country does not so much have soft power *over* another country, but rather countries have soft power relationships *with* each other. Getting to *we* and *with* suggests these societies are integrated, in whole or in part.

In some respects, the Soft Power Rubric is conventional. It relies on indicators already collected by established international organizations. However, the Soft Power Rubric is radical in other ways. The Soft Power Rubric assumes that power embodied in human relationships is as important as power embodied in money or in a gun, and as worthy of quantitative and historical assessment. The Soft Power Rubric suggests that soft power is not primarily the domain of high art, elegant diplomats, and clever cultural outreach programs but rather the everyday, mundane interactions among ordinary people across national borders. Like the free market forces in economics, government policy has a major role in shaping conditions but does not ultimately control them. The Soft Power Rubric brings people's life experience into analysis of foreign policy.

The Soft Power Rubric identifies a simple set of elements that mark the outlines of the soft power relationships of countries. However, to fill in the contours of the relationship requires concepts that interrogate the details of these relationships. The study of migration, international education, travel, and movies each produce ideas that are relevant to the other fields. From education, the push-pull model encourages balanced investigation of both host and destination countries, whether of migrants, students, travelers, or moviegoers. Migration's study of transnationalism brings attention to the multiple, hybrid identities of individuals. Travel studies' ideas of destination image and place identity underscore the importance of how communities see themselves and are viewed by others. In movies, theories of dependence, business cycles, and technology change link individual cross-border interactions to broader social structures. These are just a few examples of how individuals relate to the world, how locales relate with each other, how international interactions shapes individual and community identities, and how broad social structures constrain individual and community interaction.

These ideas are brought out by the Japanese student expressing pain at discrimination, the London teenager grappling with her growing identification with Türkiye and Cyprus, the Puerto Rican host's frustration with how his community is often perceived. In these examples, we glimpse conflict, trauma, and historical tragedy. Soft power in international relations is usually in terms of one country overpowering another, promoting a better image, or projecting a vision of a happier way of life. However, if soft power is about bonds among people, then shared hurt and pain are also paths to seeing others as "we" rather than as "they." From a scholarly perspective, the research on international migration, international education, travel, and movies grapples directly with the richness of human experience and the forces that shape how we see each other. Exploring soft power from these perspectives will deepen our understanding of how countries connect and communicate with each other.

Case Studies Applying the Soft Power Rubric

To illustrate different applications of the Soft Power Rubric, this book includes a range of case studies ranging from single countries to regional groups.

Japan

Joseph Nye's initial formulation of soft power argued that the United States had plenty of soft power and, therefore, should not fear a decline in its global leadership, despite the ascendency of Japan's economic power in the 1980s. Chapter 2 includes the data on Japan's openness to immigrants, foreign students, and visitors. The size of Japan's economy peaked in the 1990s, but the Soft Power Rubric data show its openness to foreigners continues to grow. The Soft Power 30 ranking includes Japan in the top ten every year starting in 2017.

Russia and China

In Chapter 9, China's and Russia's soft power are compared using historical data. The immigration data show that a wider range of foreigners over time commit to integrating into Russian society. China has far fewer of these relationships. In education, the large number of students flocking to China suggests that the younger generation perceives its universities to be a path to skills and knowledge useful for the future; China has the momentum advantage over Russia. In terms of foreign visitors, again China has the momentum advantage with nearly double the number of visitors in 2019 as Russia. As for movies, keeping in mind the limits of the dataset—discussed in detail in the case study on movies—Russia has a steady audience for its movies, and China in some years reaches a much larger audience.

India's Soft Power and the G20 and G7

Seen through the prism of the Soft Power Rubric, India has exceptional soft power resources, as discussed in Chapter 8. Ordinarily, soft power is understood as foreigners' interest in a country, which would make foreign visitors, students, and immigrants coming into India the natural place to look for influence. For example, the best chance for a foreigner to meet a Dane is in Denmark; a chance encounter outside of Denmark is less likely. In the case of India, however, its large population abroad is an outstanding soft power asset. The most likely opportunity today for foreigners to interact with Indians is to meet an Indian who is abroad—as an immigrant, student, or visitor.

When compared to China, in the 1980s, Indians had more social interactions with foreigners—whether as visitors, students, or immigrants—than China, but by 2000 China had opened up more to foreign visitors and students than India. When compared to G7 nations, India's economy is already of similar size. However, countries like France and Italy have deeper people-to-people relationships with a wider array of countries.

What would increase India's soft power in the future? On the movie front, India is certainly one in a very small set of countries that has a successful export industry, which is a major achievement. Studies show that foreigners have the most accurate impression of a country when they have multiple and different social interactions with people from that country. When foreigners both watch Indian movies *and* have opportunities to meet Indian people, that is the most potent formula for growing soft power relationships. In other arenas, initiatives that would bring more foreigners to India—as visitors, students, and immigrants—would also help build its soft power relationships with other countries. These, of course, are classically domestic policies and not usually undertaken as foreign policy initiatives. However, should domestic political conditions align to make India easier for foreigners to access, there should be a foreign policy payoff, a soft power bonus.

Southeast Asia: Great Power Competition, Transnational Identities, and Destination Image

In the study of soft power, when looking beyond the great powers of the moment, the literature becomes more scattered and a coherent view more difficult to piece together. Rather than a narrowed focus, in Chapter 10 is a multistranded, kaleidoscopic perspective, tied together by the several elements of the Soft Power Rubric and the major themes that intersect them all: a different sense of who is at the core and who is at the periphery; the dual push and pull of which countries attract Southeast Asians abroad and which foreigners are attracted to the region; the making of destination images and place identities; and the evolution of transnational identities of the Thai communities in the United States, Taiwan, and elsewhere.

The Soft Power Rubric provides an aerial overview of the people-to-people relationships among countries. The data form a big picture of the connections between people and nations. In this picture it is possible to see the ambitions of Malaysia to improve the skills of its workforce and play a role in Asia and in the global Muslim community. In Thailand, the soft power story is about Thai cuisine and gastrodiplomacy, the realpolitik status of Thailand's destination image in the world, and, most importantly, the transnational flourishing of Thai people at home and as immigrants abroad.

Movies

Most soft power thinkers assume that movies are the critical cultural product that promotes a country's image abroad. This kind of thinking tends to focus on the large number of movies a country produces, whereas the Soft Power Rubric perspective centers on how many foreigners actually see a country's movies. In Chapter 6, examining the available data on movie ticket sales for foreign movies in a large set of countries, there are three tiers of production countries. The United States is in the top tier, by far producing the movies that sell the most tickets in foreign countries. In the next tier are France and the United Kingdom; and in the third tier are Australia, China, Germany, India, and Russia. Long-term trends in the movie industry suggest that more countries can become major producers. Among communications technologies, of course, films are the ancestors of television, on-demand video platforms, and social media. Seen in this context, there are many opportunities for more research on newer media, transnational social interactions, and their relationship to soft power.

International Education

Among the Soft Power Rubric elements, by volume the number of foreign students is tiny compared to the number of immigrants and foreign visitors who travel the world in a given year. As Chapter 3 discusses, however, international education may be the most powerful of the four Rubric elements in deepening understanding of foreign countries. The example of Australia as an education destination reveals how several elements of the Soft Power Rubric interact, discussed in Chapter 7. The Colombo Plan to influence neighboring Asian countries by hosting their young people as students at Australian universities undermined support for the White Australia policy that intended to maintain the European identity of Australia. Australians traveling to Asia—an increasingly fashionable trend in the 1960s onward—changed many Australians' minds about the value of personal relationships with Asians, which translated into changed foreign policy relationships with Asian countries. While interethnic and interracial frictions in Australian society remain, as they do in all countries that are truly diverse, today, in a complete reversal from the days of White Australia, Australia is regarded as an Asian nation, a major leader in the region and an important global player.

Ranking Soft Power Leaders

The Soft Power Rubric produces rankings that are consistent with Soft Power 30 at the highest levels, with more details in Chapter 11. Further, the Rubric analysis extends to 1960, fifty years further back than the Soft Power 30. In this historical perspective, the United States remains the leader—increasing its welcome to immigrants in recent years, but declining in its share of foreign students and foreign visitors. The Soft Power Rubric allows direct comparison among France, Germany, and the United Kingdom and each country's relationships with foreign countries. Finally, the soft power research qualitative literature identifies South Africa as an example of a country that relies more on soft rather than hard power to lead. The Soft Power Rubric's quantitative data do confirm these countries as stronger in their soft power rankings than in their economic or military size.

The argument that the Soft Power Rubric successfully measures soft power rests on two sets of evidence. The first set is that in the Soft Power Rubric global rankings for 2020 are roughly similar to the Soft Power 30 rankings, the most widely used soft power measurement today, even though they have markedly different methodologies. The advantage of the Rubric dataset is its much longer historical view and broader set of countries. The second set is the discussion in Chapter 3 that shows foreign public opinion does have an effect on foreign policy cooperation, and that in the absence of public opinion surveys, there is evidence that international education and travel are usable proxies. Further, there is evidence from the study of international education and international migration that people's experiences in other countries influence their values, and these are communicated to others around them.

Implications of the Soft Power Rubric for Foreign Policy

In most discussions of soft power there is an implicit assumption that because it is noncoercive and based on attraction, soft power is somehow morally or ethically better than hard power. Several soft power scholars point out this is not necessarily the case, and I agree with them. Nye (2017) summarizes the difference between soft and hard power as "twisting minds instead of twisting arms." Marlin-Bennett (2022) shows how deliberate misinformation campaigns, using communications strategies that attract people to certain ideas, can successfully persuade large groups of people, even to violence. Gallarotti (2010) shows that whether efforts to build soft power are successful depends a lot on context. The distinction could be an ad campaign that promotes a movie people want to see (soft empowerment) in contrast to a propaganda campaign for a movie people will be required to see (soft disempowerment). While the campaigns can be identical, the context and, therefore, the outcome, are opposite.

Studies of US soft power emphasize the popularity of its movies, its music, and other popular culture in foreign countries. For the United States, popular culture is an important part of its soft power resources. It is like an on-ramp for foreigners curious about the United States to seek to learn more, to possibly visit, pursue training in the United States, and even to immigrate. Note, however, the US government is not an important promoter of the most popular of American popular culture. The most popular stuff is commercial, seeking to make a profit and, therefore, responsive to the needs and tastes of the market, American and abroad. Further, much of the most popular American cultural products are antiestablishmentarian in origin. They challenge the authority of the government; they make fun of social norms and standards; they point out the foibles and more serious flaws of the elites. Policymakers from other countries who would like to cultivate soft power relationships with movies, media, and other popular culture products should be aware that it is likely the mass market products that make the most difference, not the elite ones. Japan finds that it is manga and anime that bring the most foreigners to its culture, not kabuki and sumo. Supporting elite interest in high culture has its place in public diplomacy, but the reasoning that undergirds the Soft Power Rubric suggests that expectations for outcomes should remain modest.

Beyond media, the Soft Power Rubric also demonstrates that movies and media are not the only way to cultivate soft power relationships. It is the communication embedded in movies and media that make it an important soft power resource, not the product itself. Other arenas like travel, which brings people together and gives them an opportunity to interact with each other, are also important. Travel and its relationship to soft power are still understudied. People travel for many reasons, alone and in groups, triggered by waves of fashion or particular individual curiosities. Tourism campaigns often promote a country's most popular stereotypes, like Australia's recent campaign featuring kangaroos (Cassidy 2022). If soft power relationship building is a significant aspect of travel and tourism policy, is promoting stereotypes the wisest strategy? Such questions can provoke community introspection—What destination image would we like others to have of our community, and what place identity does our community already have that can be expressed to visitors?

Also, another potentially fruitful area of study is the relationship between soft power and migration. Americans' view of foreign countries is shaped by their interaction and friendships with immigrants in their communities (Wu 2023). Decisions to emigrate relate to destination image and place identity. Also important are the range of conditions that push people to leave home. In this year 2024, the US discussion around migration is about keeping more out, or letting them in through more orderly and predictable procedures. Unspoken in these debates is the soft power that attracts people to come to the United States. The goodwill that attracts people has taken decades to build up (Migration Policy Institute 2013). The United States and other countries that experience influxes of immigrants should be aware that what is now the case may not always be. If tides turn and people no longer view our countries positively as good places to live and grow, if that attraction somehow turns sour, our relationships disintegrate, and our soft power evaporates into thin air, it could take a long time to rebuild. Migration policy is part of foreign policy.

How a Parsimonious Approach Opens New Vistas to Understanding Soft Power Relationships

The Soft Power Rubric asserts that social interaction between people across national borders is the key building block for relationships that potentially influence foreign policy and the international system. By narrowing the focus to a single category, the Soft Power Rubric opens new vistas for analysis and connects the research on soft power to research on domestic policy issues.

For those frustrated with current soft power rankings that maintain proprietary data and algorithms, the Soft Power Rubric is an alternative that produces similar results with public data and an open model. For those readers skeptical that studying social and cultural influence, heretofore the primary domain of fieldwork scholars and historians, can benefit from the cold quantitative calculation, the Soft Power Rubric is a flexible tool grounded in the same theories of social capital and collective action that undergird qualitative research with results to match. The Soft Power Rubric shows that the countries with the most influence in the world are those with the most intimate knowledge and understanding of foreigners and foreign countries—in part by sending their citizens abroad to engage, but primarily by welcoming foreigners into their homes. The countries with the most expansive "we" in foreign policy have the greatest soft power.

Appendix 1: Calculating the Rankings of Soft Power Leaders

THIS APPENDIX PROVIDES A GUIDE TO HOW I CALCULATED country rankings based on the Soft Power Rubric data for immigrants, students, and visitors. First, Table A1.1 shows for three Rubric elements—immigration (2020), foreign students (2020), and foreign visitors (2019)—the data for a set of selected countries. Movie data are not available for the complete set of countries.[1]

These tables show in which ways a particular country is open to foreigners. The United States hosts an exceptional number of immigrants; France and Germany are second and third. France, only a fraction the size of the United States, hosts far more foreign visitors. The United Kingdom is a leading host of foreign students.

Table A1.1 Soft Power Rubric Ranking, 2020

SP Rank	Country	Immigrants (2020)	Foreign Students (2020)	Foreign Visitors (2019)
1	US	50,632,836	957,475	165,478,000
2	France	8,524,876	246,378	217,877,000
3 and 4	Germany	15,762,457	333,233	39,563,000
3 and 4	UK	9,359,587	489,019	40,857,000
5	Spain	6,842,202	77,062	126,170,000
6	Russia	11,636,911	282,922	24,419,000
7	Canada	8,049,323	279,168	32,430,000
8	Türkiye	6,052,652	154,505	51,747,000
9	UAE	8,716,332	225,339	25,282,000
10	Italy	6,386,998	54,855	95,399,000

Sources: UN Population Division, UNESCO, and UN World Tourism Organization.

The second step is to rank countries in each of the series within the world dataset. Table A1.2 below shows in column (b) that Russia is the 4th largest destination in the world for immigrants, Canada is 8th largest, and Türkiye is 12th largest. Third, for each country, I take the sum of the three ranks (b + c + d), shown in column (e). For Germany, it ranks 2nd in the world in immigrants, 4th in the world in foreign students, and 14th in the world for foreign visitors; the sum of ranks for Germany equals 20. The fourth step is to rank the "sum of ranks," the data in column (e); the final list is shown in order in column (a). This method is simple, replicable, and open to challenge.

Other Ways to Handle the Data

The Soft Power Rubric is powerful in bringing together data series on transnational social interactions to assess countries' openness and interest in foreign countries. That is its main contribution. Other technical aspects, like this particular method of summing and ranking, depend on how a researcher decides to address a particular question. There are several obvious alternative approaches, and other scholars will no doubt think of more.

Relative Weight of the Different Series

My approach gives relatively similar weighting to each of the three elements: migration, education, and travel. There are a few issues to keep in mind, many of which would make interesting topics for future research.

Table A1.2 Soft Power Rubric Data for Top Ten Soft Power Leaders, 2020

(a) Final Rubric Rank	Country	(b) Immigrants (2020)	(c) Foreign Students (2019)	(d) Foreign Visitors (2019)	(e) Sum of Ranks—3 Rubric Elements
1	US	1	1	2	4
2	France	7	8	1	16
3 and 4	Germany	2	4	14	20
3 and 4	UK	5	3	12	20
5	Spain	10	17	4	31
6	Russia	4	5	24	33
7	Canada	8	7	19	34
8	Türkiye	12	12	11	35
9	UAE	6	9	23	38
10	Italy	11	23	6	40

Appendix 1   173

The number of visitors vastly outnumber the immigrants, which in turn outnumber the foreign students. The Soft Power Rubric's foundational principle is that regular cross-border interactions build trust. There may be other different but also reasonable ways to weight the elements against each other.

Measuring Foreigners Coming In, or People Going Abroad, or Both

These results are based on the top host countries, but how about those that send people abroad? While up to now, soft power is talked about as a country's ability to attract others to its purposes, which suggests attracting immigrants, students, and visitors, sending people abroad is also part of a country's soft power resources, as described in Chapter 10 on India. This principle drives many governments' foreign development assistance programs and underpins many religious missionary movements. These people abroad affect how foreigners view their countries of origin. In 2015, major leaders in sending people abroad were China, India, and Germany. In the Americas, the United States is the leader. In the Middle East, Saudi Arabia and Syria topped the list; in Africa, Morocco and Egypt.

Total Figures or Per Capita Figures

The leadership table ranks on absolute numbers. In some cases a more relevant approach would be to calculate the number of foreigners per host population. With its large population, the United States would rank lower and other countries would rise.

Incorporating Movie Data and Other Communications and Media Data

Finally, movie data are not included in the calculation. The UNESCO foreign audience data are much smaller both in timeframe and in the number of countries that submit data. More research is necessary to develop ways to collect and incorporate movie data into Soft Power Rubric calculations. Similar data on television, radio, social media, and other media technologies are also relevant to soft power. To date, global datasets like the one available from UNESCO on movies are not developed yet, but they could be.

Historical Soft Power Rubric Calculations

Note that not every country reports each of the three data series. The following graph shows how many countries reported all three—immigrants, foreign students, and foreign visitors. In the 1960s, nine countries reported all three. That explains why the 1960x global ranking only includes nine countries. By 2010, seventy-nine countries reported all three. As of writing in June 2023, the number for 2019/2020 is at ninety countries. Two-year lags in reporting are standard; longer lags and periodic revisions are common in this kind of data. The Covid-19 pandemic has also delayed data reporting. For the purposes of this global ranking, countries reporting fewer than three series were not included. Finally, from 1960 to 1980, as indicated in Figure A1.1 by 1960x, 1970x, and 1980x, where data were not available, data from the year prior or year after were included. In other words, if 1970 data were not available for a country then, if available, I would use 1971 or 1969 data.

Data Sources

International Migrant Stock: United Nations Population Division

- 1960, 1970, 1980: United Nations Demographic Yearbook. 1977 and 1989 yearbooks feature migration data. Digitally scanned yearbooks available for download at unstats.un.org/unsd/demographic-social/products/dyb/index.cshtml#overview
- 1990 onward available at www.un.org/development/desa/pd/content/international-migrant-stock

Figure A1.1 Total Number of Countries Reporting All Three Series: Immigrants, Foreign Students, and Foreign Visitors, 1960–2020

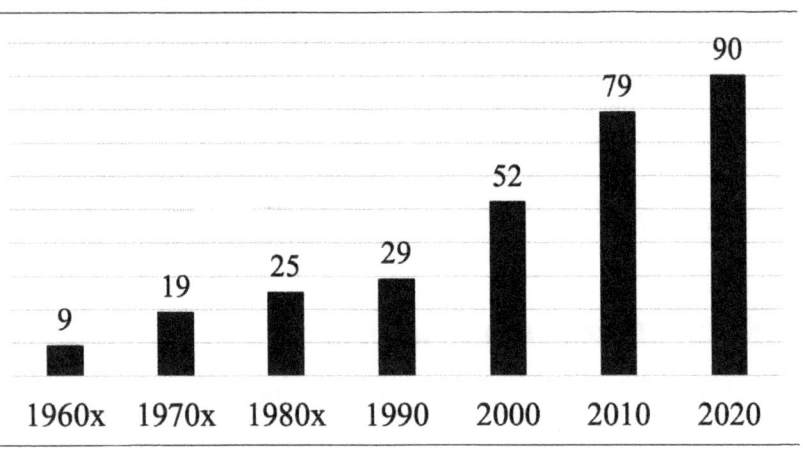

*International Education: United Nations Educational,
Scientific, and Cultural Organization (UNESCO)*

- 1963–1999. UNESCO Statistical Yearbooks. Bibliographic information available at unevoc.unesco.org/home/UNESCO+Publications
- 1999 onward. See number and rates of international mobile students, inbound internationally mobile students by country of origin. Database available at data.uis.unesco.org

*Foreign Visitor and Tourists: United Nations World Tourism
Organization (UNWTO)*

- 1960, 1970. International Travel Statistics, International Union of Official Travel Organisation.
- 1980. World Tourism Statistics, World Tourism Organization.
- 1990 onward. Data available to researchers on request.
- Also, see www.unwto.org/tourism-statistics/key-tourism-statistics and www.e-unwto.org

*Movies: United Nations Educational, Scientific,
and Cultural Organization (UNESCO)*

- 2005–2017, UNESCO, Culture, Feature Films, Top 10 movies viewed. data.uis.unesco.org

Note

1. As of publication, 2020 data for foreign visitors were not yet published.

Appendix 2: Soft Power Leaders: Data Tables, 1960–2020

Table A2.1a Top Countries Ranked by Soft Power Rubric, 1960

Country	Sum of Series 3 Ranks
United States	5
France	10
United Kingdom	23
Switzerland	33
Austria	37
Italy	43
Belgium	50
Australia	51
Japan	55

Note: Nine countries reporting data for immigration, students, and visitors.

Table A2.1b Number of Immigrants for Top 9 Countries, 1960

Country	1960x Immigrants	Series Rank
United States	10,825,599	1
France	3,507,213	4
Australia	1,698,085	9
United Kingdom	1,661,888	10
Austria	806,643	18
Switzerland	714,235	21
Japan	692,651	22
Italy	459,553	30
Belgium	441,555	32

Table A2.1c Number of Students for Top 9 Countries, 1960

Country	1960x Immigrants	Series Rank
United States	58,086	1
France	29,581	2
United Kingdom	13,385	4
Austria	10,655	5
Switzerland	8,200	7
Australia	6,400	8
Japan	4,934	9
Belgium	2,843	11
Italy	2,572	12

Table A2.1d Number of Visitors for Top 9 Countries, 1960

Country	1960x Immigrants	Series Rank
Italy	18,935,242	1
United States	6,215,706	3
France	5,800,000	4
Switzerland	5,367,270	5
Belgium	3,907,000	7
United Kingdom	1,823,755	9
Austria	524,088	14
Japan	178,130	24
Australia	99,296	34

Table A2.2a Top Countries Ranked by Soft Power Rubric, 1970

SP Rubric Rank 1970	Country	Sum of 3 Series Ranks
1	United States	6
2	France	8
3	Canada	11
4	United Kingdom	18
5	Switzerland	34
6	Australia	53
7	Spain	58
8	Israel	62
9	Lebanon	79
10	Singapore	83
11	Egypt	87
12	Mexico	99
13	Uganda	104
14	Greece	112
15	Philippines	115
16	Denmark	116
17	Portugal	132
18	Kenya	136
19	Bulgaria	178

Note: Nineteen countries reporting data for immigration, students, and visitors.

Table A2.2b Number of Immigrants for Top 15 Countries, 1970

Country	1970 Immigrants	Series Rank
United States	11,973,787	1
France	5,210,336	3
Canada	3,251,353	5
United Kingdom	2,945,896	6
Australia	2,456,522	7
Israel	1,408,744	12
Switzerland	1,091,990	16
Uganda	948,875	19
Singapore	530,873	28
Spain	355,727	39
Philippines	217,435	51
Egypt	203,514	52
Mexico	195,369	55
Lebanon	190,842	57
Greece	89,572	76

Table A2.2c Number of Students for Top 15 Countries, 1970

Country	1970 Students	Series Rank
United States	144,708	1
France	34,877	2
United Kingdom	24,606	4
Canada	22,263	5
Lebanon	20,857	6
Egypt	13,387	9
Switzerland	9,469	12
Spain	7,878	17
Australia	7,104	18
Greece	5,748	21
Israel	2,952	27
Philippines	2,724	29
Mexico	2,539	31
Singapore	1,975	34
Uganda	963	46

Table A2.2d Number of Visitors for Top 15 Countries, 1970

Country	1970 Visitors	Series Rank
Canada	37,688,476	1
Spain	24,105,312	2
France	13,700,000	3

continues

Table A2.2d Continued

Country	1970 Visitors	Series Rank
United States	13,167,408	4
Switzerland	8,839,859	6
United Kingdom	6,730,000	8
Mexico	2,245,481	13
Greece	1,609,210	15
Lebanon	1,210,157	16
Singapore	521,654	16
Israel	436,892	23
Egypt	357,661	26
Australia	338,395	28
Philipppines	144,071	35
Uganda	80,363	39

Table A2.3a Top Countries Ranked by Soft Power Rubric, 1980

SP Rubric Rank 1980	Country	Sum of 3 Series Ranks
1	United States	5
2	France	7
3	United Kingdom	16
4	Italy	28
5	Canada	35
6	Switzerland	42
7	Austria	50
8	Poland	51
9	Spain	51
10	Australia	53
11	Türkiye	76
12	Singapore	84
13	Netherlands	85
14	Hungary	86
15	Greece	100
16	Ireland	112
17	Portugal	114
18	New Zealand	122
19	Philippines	128
20	Algeria	157
21	Togo	192
22	Morocco	195
23	Guatemala	197
24	Panema	203
25	Cuba	214

Note: Twenty-five countries reporting data for immigration, students, and visitors.

Table A2.3b Number of Immigrants for Top 15 Countries, 1980

Country	1980 Immigrants	Series Rank
United States	16,364,410	1
France	5,890,633	3
Canada	3,810,578	5
United Kingdom	3,356,904	6
Australia	2,896,444	7
Poland	1,544,789	12
Italy	1,108,852	18
Switzerland	1,065,788	19
Türkiye	784,193	28
Austria	719,958	30
Spain	609,354	36
Singapore	527,453	40
Netherlands	490,976	42
Hungary	369,039	48
Greece	171,755	67

Table A2.3c Number of Students for Top 15 Countries, 1980

Country	1980 Students	Series Rank
United States	325,628	1
France	114,181	2
United Kingdom	56,003	4
Canada	32,303	5
Italy	27,784	6
Australia	17,694	9
Switzerland	15,515	10
Austria	12,885	12
Spain	10,997	14
Greece	8,304	17
Türkiye	6,378	20
Netherlands	4,228	22
Poland	2,813	28
Hungary	2,712	29
Singapore	1,709	34

Table A2.3d Number of Visitors for Top 15 Countries, 1980

Country	1980 Visitors	Series Rank
Spain	36,517,299	1
France	30,100,000	2
United States	22,500,000	3
Italy	14,581,731	4
United Kingdom	12,391,000	6

continues

Table A2.3d Continued

Country	1980 Visitors	Series Rank
Austria	9,684,581	8
Hungary	9,413,000	9
Singapore	7,562,009	10
Poland	7,079,893	11
Switzerland	6,661,098	13
Greece	4,795,400	16
Netherlands	2,279,305	21
Canada	1,625,500	25
Türkiye	1,288,060	28
Australia	904,558	37

Table A2.4a Top Countries Ranked by Soft Power Rubric, 1990

SP Rubric Rank 1990	Country	Sum of 3 Series Ranks
1	United States	6
2	France	11
3	Canada	20
4	Russia	21
5	United Kingdom	26
6	Italy	31
7	Australia	49
8	Spain	52
9	Saudi Arabia	55
10	Japan	63
11	Türkiye	65
12	Poland	68
13	Jordan	93
14	Portugal	101
15	Hungary	113
16	China	128
17	New Zealand	132
18	Romania	139
19	Egypt	141
20	Ireland	144
21	Algeria	157
22	Philippines	168
23	Morocco	186
24	Honduras	188
25	Bulgaria	195
26	South Korea	204
27	Cyprus	218
28	Cuba	242
29	Myanmar	286

Note: Twenty-nine countries reporting data for immigration, students, and visitors.

Table A2.4b   Number of Immigrants for Top 15 Countries, 1990

Country	1990 Immigrants	Series Rank
United States	23,251,026	1
Russia	11,524,948	2
France	5,897,267	7
Saudi Arabia	4,998,445	8
Canada	4,333,318	9
Australia	3,955,213	11
United Kingdom	3,650,286	12
Italy	1,428,219	19
Türkiye	1,163,686	26
Jordan	1,146,349	28
Poland	1,127,771	29
Japan	1,075,626	31
Spain	821,605	26
Portugal	435,782	61
Hungary	347,510	113

Table A2.4c   Number of Students for Top 15 Countries, 1990

Country	1990 Students	Series Rank
United States	407,529	1
France	136,015	2
United Kingdom	70,717	4
Russia	66,806	5
Canada	35,187	6
Australia	28,993	8
Japan	23,816	9
Italy	21,416	11
Spain	13,839	13
Saudi Arabia	12,408	15
Türkiye	7,661	21
Poland	4,259	30
Portugal	3,608	32
Hungary	2,538	36
Jordan	2,498	37

Table A2.4d   Number of Visitors for Top 15 Countries, 1990

Country	1990 Visitors	Series Rank
Italy	60,295,921	1
France	53,157,000	2
Spain	52,044,056	3
United States	39,772,000	4

continues

Table A2.4d Continued

Country	1990 Visitors	Series Rank
Canada	37,990,400	5
Hungary	37,632,174	6
Portugal	18,422,078	8
Poland	18,210,747	9
United Kingdom	18,021,000	10
Russia	7,203,635	14
Türkiye	5,389,308	18
Japan	3,235,860	23
Jordan	2,633,262	28
Australia	2,214,900	30
Saudi Arabia	1,982,149	32

Table A2.5a Top Countries Ranked by Soft Power Rubric, 2000

SP Rubric Rank 2000	Country	Sum of 3 Series Ranks
1	United States	7
2	France	12
3	Germany	17
4	Russia	18
5	United Kingdom	19
6	Canada	23
7	Italy	34
8	Spain	36
9	Australia	49
10	Switzerland	54
11	Saudi Arabia	55
12	Netherlands	57
13	Austria	59
14	Türkiye	59
15	Japan	63
16	Belgium	72
17	South Africa	72
18	Poland	73
19	China	82
20	India	83
21	Jordan	86
22	Portugal	100
23	Kazakhstan	105
24	Argentina	109
25	Mexico	111
26	Ireland	116
27	New Zealand	130
28	Denmark	134

continues

Table A2.5a Continued

SP Rubric Rank 2000	Country	Sum of 3 Series Ranks
29	Norway	144
30	Latvia	150
31	South Korea	151
32	Czech Republic	161
33	Romania	164
34	Finland	184
35	Chile	197
36	Bulgaria	202
37	Slovenia	216
38	Cyprus	218
39	Tunisia	224
40	Slovakia	229
41	Georgia	240
42	Lithuania	249
43	Tajikistan	264
44	Cuba	270
45	Albania	276
46	Jamaica	276
47	El Salvador	277
48	Macedonia	279
49	Malta	289
50	Gambia	293

Note: Fifty-four countries reporting data for immigration, students, and visitors.

Table A2.5b Number of Immigrants for Top 15 Countries, 2000

Country	2000 Immigrants	Series Rank
United States	34,814,053	1
Russia	11,900,297	2
Germany	8,992,631	3
France	6,278,718	5
Canada	5,511,914	7
Saudi Arabia	5,263,387	8
United Kingdom	4,730,165	9
Australia	4,386,250	10
Italy	2,121,688	16
Japan	1,686,567	20
Spain	1,657,285	21
Switzerland	1,570,756	22
Netherlands	1,556,337	23
Türkiye	1,280,963	27
Austria	996,547	36

Table A2.5c Number of Students for Top 15 Countries, 2000

Country	2000 Students	Series Rank
United States	475,169	1
United Kingdom	222,203	2
Germany	185,099	3
France	136,171	4
Australia	93,458	5
Japan	59,682	6
Russia	41,210	7
Spain	40,689	8
Canada	34,491	10
Austria	30,226	11
Switzerland	24,875	13
Italy	21,250	14
Türkiye	17,643	17
Netherlands	13,976	18
Saudi Arabia	7,561	25

Table A2.5d Number of Visitors for Top 15 Countries, 2000

Country	2000 Visitors	Series Rank
France	77,190,000	3
Italy	62,702,228	4
United States	51,237,701	5
Canada	48,637,000	6
Spain	46,402,926	7
United Kingdom	25,209,000	8
Russia	21,169,100	9
Germany	18,983,264	11
Austria	17,982,204	12
Türkiye	10,428,153	15
Netherlands	10,003,100	16
Switzerland	7,821,158	19
Saudi Arabia	6,585,326	22
Australia	4,931,336	34
Japan	4,757,146	37

Table A2.6a Top Countries Ranked by Soft Power Rubric, 2010

SP Rubric Rank 2010	Country	Sum of 3 Series Ranks
1	United States	6
2	France	13
3	United Kingdom	17
4	Germany	18

continues

Table A2.6a Continued

SP Rubric Rank 2010	Country	Sum of 3 Series Ranks
5	Russia	24
6	Italy	25
7	Canada	29
8	Spain	30
9	Ukraine	53
10	Australia	55
11	China	55
12	Saudi Arabia	57
13	Japan	59
14	Thailand	60
15	Austria	62
16	South Africa	62
17	Hong Kong	66
18	Türkiye	67
19	Switzerland	70
20	Netherlands	71
21	Jordan	72
22	Greece	78
23	South Korea	86
24	Poland	88
25	Belgium	102
26	Sweden	103
27	Hungary	105
28	Kazakhstan	106
29	New Zealand	117
30	Denmark	119
31	Ireland	123
32	Macao	124
33	Czech Republic	128
34	Iran	128
35	Portugal	128
36	Brazil	142
37	Israel	144
38	Qatar	159
39	Croatia	164
40	Finland	165
41	Indonesia	166
42	Chile	177
43	Romania	182
44	Latvia	190
45	Oman	190
46	Serbia	201
47	Zimbabwe	207
48	Azerbaijan	208
49	Bulgaria	210
50	Cyprus	212

Note: Eighty-one countries reporting data for immigration, students, and visitors.

Table A2.6b Number of Immigrants for Top 15 Countries, 2010

Country	2010 Immigrants	Series Rank
United States	44,183,643	1
Germany	11,605,690	2
Russia	11,194,710	3
Saudi Arabia	8,429,956	4
United Kingdom	7,604,583	5
France	7,196,481	7
Canada	7,011,226	8
Australia	5,882,980	10
Italy	5,787,893	11
Ukraine	4,818,767	13
Thailand	3,224,131	16
Japan	2,134,151	22
Sweden	1,384,929	32
Austria	1,275,992	36
China	849,861	46

Table A2.6c Number of Students for Top 15 Countries, 2010

Country	2010 Students	Series Rank
United States	684,517	1
United Kingdom	391,415	2
Australia	251,306	3
France	242,948	4
Germany	185,622	5
Russia	164,945	6
Japan	141,561	7
China	107,441	8
Canada	98,184	9
Austria	68,538	10
Italy	61,227	11
Spain	55,696	15
Ukraine	25,437	23
Thailand	19,049	26
Saudi Arabia	18,191	29

Table A2.6d Number of Visitors for Top 15 Countries, 2010

Country	2010 Visitors	Series Rank
China	133,762,239	1
France	76,647,003	2
Italy	73,225,219	3
United States	60,010,360	4

continues

Table A2.4d Continued

Country	2010 Visitors	Series Rank
Spain	52,676,972	6
United Kingdom	29,803,000	10
Germany	26,875,288	11
Canada	25,621,300	12
Russia	22,281,217	15
Austria	22,004,266	16
Ukraine	21,203,327	17
Thailand	15,936,400	18
Saudi Arabia	10,850,188	24
Japan	8,611,175	30
Australia	5,790,210	42

Table A2.7a Top Countries Ranked by Soft Power Rubric, 2020

SP Rubric Rank 2020	Country	Sum of 3 Series Ranks
1	United States	4
2	France	16
3	Germany	20
4	United Kingdom	20
5	Spain	31
6	Russia	33
7	Canada	34
8	Türkiye	35
9	United Arab Emirates	38
10	Italy	40
11	Saudi Arabia	47
12	Australia	54
13	Japan	55
14	Malaysia	55
15	Hong Kong SAR, China	60
16	China	68
17	Ukraine	68
18	Netherlands	69
19	India	70
20	Romania	74
21	Austria	75
22	South Korea	83
23	South Africa	85
24	Mexico	87
25	Switzerland	87
26	Poland	93
27	Argentina	99
28	Greece	99

continues

Table A2.7a Continued

29	Belgium	104
30	Kazakhstan	105
31	Hungary	112
32	Iran	114
33	Jordan	115
34	Portugal	118
35	Czech Republic	119
36	Denmark	120
37	Réunion	123
38	Sweden	124
39	Belarus	139
40	Ireland	140
41	New Zealand	146
42	Macao SAR, China	147
43	Qatar	150
44	Croatia	155
45	Brazil	156
46	Chile	163
47	Norway	178
48	Colombia	179
49	Lebanon	186
50	Oman	189

Note: Ninety-nine countries reporting data for immigration, students, and visitors.

Table A2.7b Number of Immigrants for Top 15 Countries, 2020

Country	2020 Immigrants	Series Rank
United States	50,632,836	1
Germany	15,762,457	2
Saudi Arabia	13,454,842	3
Russia	11,636,911	4
United Kingdom	9,359,587	5
United Arab Emirates	8,716,332	6
France	8,524,876	7
Canada	8,049,323	8
Australia	7,685,860	9
Spain	6,842,202	10
Italy	6,386,998	11
Türkiye	6,052,652	12
Malaysia	3,476,560	17
Hong Kong SAR, China	2,962,492	21
Japan	2,770,996	24

Table A2.7c Number of Students for Top 15 Countries, 2020

Country	2020 Students	Series Rank
United States	957,475	1
Australia	509,160	2
United Kingdom	489,019	3
Germany	333,233	4
Russia	282,922	5
Canada	279,168	7
France	246,378	8
United Arab Emirates	225,339	9
Japan	202,907	10
Türkiye	154,505	12
Malaysia	81,953	16
Spain	77,062	17
Saudi Arabia	73,216	19
Italy	54,855	23
Hong Kong SAR, China	42,641	29

Table A2.7d Number of Visitors for Top 15 Countries, 2020

Country	2020 Visitors	Series Rank
France	217,877,000	1
United States	165,478,000	2
Spain	126,170,000	4
Italy	95,399,000	6
Hong Kong SAR, China	55,913,000	10
Türkiye	51,747,000	11
United Kingdom	40,857,000	12
Germany	39,563,000	14
Canada	32,430,000	19
Japan	31,881,000	21
Malaysia	26,101,000	22
United Arab Emirates	25,282,000	23
Russia	24,419,000	24
Saudi Arabia	20,292,000	25
Australia	9,466,000	43

Note: As of 2023, 2020 data for foreign visitors were not yet published.

Bibliography

Adam, Thomas, and Charlotte A. Lerg. 2015. "Diplomacy on Campus: The Political Dimensions of Academic Exchange in the North Atlantic." *Journal of Transatlantic Studies* 13(4): 299–310.
Allen, Michael A., Michael E. Flynn, Carla Martinez Machain, and Andrew Stravers. 2020. "Outside the Wire: U.S. Military Deployments and Public Opinion in Host States." *American Political Science Review* 114(2): 326–341.
Almeida Santos, Carla, and Christine Buzinde. 2007. "Politics of Identity and Space: Representational Dynamics." *Journal of Travel Research* 45(3): 322–332.
Altbach, Philip G. 2012. "The Globalization of College and University Rankings." *Change: The Magazine of Higher Learning* 44(1): 26–31.
Altbach, Philip G., and Gail Paradise Kelly. 1984. *Education and the Colonial Experience*. 2nd ed. New Brunswick, NJ: Transaction Books.
Anderson, Benedict R. O'G. 1983. *Imagined Communities: Reflections on the Origin and Spread of Nationalism*. London: Verso.
Ang, Ien. 1985. *Watching Dallas: Soap Opera and the Melodramatic Imagination*. London: Methuen.
Arachi, Diana. 2006. "Foreign Branch Campuses in Malaysia: State Action and Consumer Choices Revisited." In LUP Student Papers, Lund University libraries. https://lup.lub.lu.se/student-papers/search/publication/1326386.
Araki, Mitsuya. 2007. "Japan's Official Development Assistance: The Japan ODA Model That Began Life in Southeast Asia." *Asia-Pacific Review* 14(2): 17–29.
Arif, Imran, and Joshua C. Hall. 2019. "International Flows of People and Institutional Change." *European Journal of Political Economy* 58: 276–288.
Ashbee, Edward. 2023. *Countering China: US Responses to the Belt and Road Initiative*. Boulder, CO: Lynne Rienner.
Atkinson, Carol. 2006. "Constructivist Implications of Material Power: Military Engagement and the Socialization of States, 1972–2000." *International Studies Quarterly* 50(3): 509–537.
———. 2014. *Military Soft Power: Public Diplomacy Through Military Educational Exchanges*. Lanham, MD: Rowman and Littlefield.
Australia, Government of. 2021. "New Colombo Plan." Department of Foreign Affairs and Trade. www.dfat.gov.au/people-to-people/new-colombo-plan/pages/new-colombo-plan.
Bajpaee, Chietigj. 2017. "Dephasing India's Look East/Act East Policy." *Contemporary Southeast Asia* 39(2): 348–372.

Baker, Jayne. 2014. "No Ivies, Oxbridge, or Grandes Écoles: Constructing Distinctions in University Choice." *British Journal of Sociology of Education* 35(6): 914–932.
Baudassé, Thierry, Rémi Bazillier, and Ismaël Issifou. 2018. "Migration and Institutions: Exit and Voice (from Abroad)?" *Journal of Economic Surveys* 32(3): 727–766.
Beine, Michel, and Khalid Sekkat. 2013. "Skilled Migration and the Transfer of Institutional Norms." *IZA Journal of Migration* 2(1): 9.
Bell, Emma. 2016. "Soft Power and Corporate Imperialism: Maintaining British Influence." *Race and Class* 57(4): 75–86.
Bernard, Prosper. 2006. "Canada and Human Security: From the Axworthy Doctrine to Middle Power Internationalism." *American Review of Canadian Studies* 36(2): 233–261.
Bettie, Molly. 2015. "Ambassadors Unaware: The Fulbright Program and American Public Diplomacy." *Journal of Transatlantic Studies* 13(4): 358–372.
Bially Mattern, Janice. 2005. "Why 'Soft Power' Isn't So Soft: Representational Force and the Sociolinguistic Construction of Attraction in World Politics." *Millennium: Journal of International Studies* 33(3): 583–612.
Bing, Ngeow Chow. 2017. "Taiwan's Go South Policy: 'Déjà Vu' All Over Again?" *Contemporary Southeast Asia* 39(1): 96–126.
Botas, Paulo Charles Pimentel, and Jeroen Huisman. 2013. "A Bourdieusian Analysis of the Participation of Polish Students in the ERASMUS Programme: Cultural and Social Capital Perspectives." *Higher Education* 66(6): 741–754.
Bradford, Colin I., and Johannes F. Linn. 2012. "A History of G20 Summits: The Evolving Dynamic of Global Leadership." *Journal of Globalization and Development* 2(2): 1–21.
Bukh, Alexander. 2016. "Russia's Image and Soft Power Resources in Southeast Asia: Perceptions Among Young Elites in Laos, Thailand and Vietnam." *Contemporary Southeast Asia* 38(3): 445–475.
Butcher, Andrew. 2012. "Students, Soldiers, Sports, Sheep and the Silver-Screen: New Zealand's Soft Power in ASEAN and Southeast Asia." *Contemporary Southeast Asia* 34(2): 249–273.
Byrne, Caitlin. 2018. "Finding Australia's Soft Power." *The Strategist*. Australian Strategic Policy Institute. August 27, 2018.
Byrne, Caitlin, and Rebecca Hall. 2013. "Realising Australia's International Education as Public Diplomacy." *Australian Journal of International Affairs* 67(4): 419–438.
Callahan, William A., and Elena Barbantseva. 2011. *China Orders World: Normative Soft Power and Foreign Policy*. Baltimore: Johns Hopkins University Press.
Calleo, David P. 2009. *Follies of Power: America's Unipolar Fantasy*. Cambridge: Cambridge University Press.
Cantwell, Brendan, Sandra G. Luca, and Jenny J. Lee. 2009. "Exploring the Orientations of International Students in Mexico: Differences by Region of Origin." *Higher Education* 57(3): 335–354.
Car, Viktorija, Lidija Kos-Stanisic, and Zrinka Viduka. 2016. "The Limits of Soft-Power Diplomacy: Consumption and Representation of Bollywood Movies Among Croatian Students of Media, Communications and Political Science." *Teorija in praksa* 53(5): 1213–1235.
Cardoso, Fernando Henrique. 1979. *Dependency and Development in Latin America*. Berkeley: University of California Press.
Cassidy, Caitlin. 2022. "Fun, Effective or 'Very Bland'? Advertising Experts Split on Australia's Tourism Mascot Ruby the Roo." *Guardian*, October 12, 2022.
Chadda, Maya. 2014. *Why India Matters*. Boulder, CO: Lynne Rienner.
Chen, Yu-Wen, and Niall Duggan. 2016. "Soft Power and Tourism: A Study of Chinese Outbound Tourism to Africa." *Journal of China and International Relations* 4(1).
Cheng, Xiaohe. 2009. "Education: The Intellectual Base of China's Soft Power." In *Soft Power: China's Emerging Strategy in International Politics*, edited by Mingjiang Li, 103–124. Lanham, MD: Lexington Books.

Chi, Heng-Chang, and Peter Jackson. 2011. "Thai Food in Taiwan: Tracing the Contours of Transnational Taste." *New Formations* (74): 65–81.
Chitty, Naren. 2017a. "Soft Power, Civic Virtue and World Politics." In *The Routledge Handbook of Soft Power*, edited by Naren Chitty, 9–36. London: Routledge.
———, ed. 2017b. *The Routledge Handbook of Soft Power*. London: Routledge.
———. 2019. "Advancing Australia Through Soft Power: Virtue and Virtuosity." *Journal of International Communication* 25(2): 193–205.
———. 2021. "World Propaganda and Personal Insecurity: Intent, Content, and Contentment." In *Research Handbook on Political Propaganda*, edited by Gary D. Rawnsley, Yiben Ma, and Kruakae Pothong, 7–21. Northampton, MA: Edward Elgar.
———. 2023. "Introduction." In *The Routledge Handbook of Soft Power*, 2nd ed., edited by Naren Chitty, Lilian Ji, and Gary D. Rawnsley. London: Routledge.
Chitty, Naren, Lilian Ji, and Gary D. Rawnsley, eds. 2023. *The Routledge Handbook of Soft Power*. 2nd ed. London: Routledge.
Cooper, Andrew F., and Asif B. Farooq. 2016. "The Role of China and India in the G20 and BRICS: Commonalities or Competitive Behavior?" *Journal of Current Chinese Affairs* 45(3): 73–126.
Chu, Yun-han, Yu-tsung Chang, and Min-hua Huang. 2016. "How East Asians View the Influence of United States vs. a Rising China." Brookings Institution.
Cohen, Craig, Joseph S. Nye Jr., and Richard L. Armitage. 2007. *A Smarter, More Secure America*. Washington, DC: Center for Strategic and International Studies.
Cohen, Eliot A. 2016. *The Big Stick: The Limits of Soft Power and the Necessity of Military Force*. New York: Basic Books.
Cooper, Andrew F., and Asif B. Farooq. 2016. "The Role of China and India in the G20 and BRICS: Commonalities or Competitive Behavior?" *Journal of Current Chinese Affairs* 45(3): 73–126.
Crow, David, and Clarisa Pérez-Armendáriz. 2018. "Talk Without Borders: Why Political Discussion Makes Latin Americans with Relatives Abroad More Critical of Their Democracies." *Comparative Political Studies* 51(2): 238–276.
Czaika, Mathias, and Hein de Haas. 2014. "The Globalization of Migration: Has the World Become More Migratory?" *International Migration Review* 48(2): 283–323.
Darchy-Koechlin, Brigitte, and Hugues Draelants. 2010. "'To Belong or Not to Belong?': The French Model of Elite Selection and the Integration of International Students." *French Politics* 8(4): 429–446.
Darian-Smith, Kate, and James Waghorne. 2016. "Australian-Asian Sociability, Student Activism, and the University Challenge to White Australia in the 1950s." *Australian Journal of Politics and History* 62(2): 203–218.
Datta, Monti Narayan. 2014. *Anti-Americanism and the Rise of World Opinion Consequences for the US National Interest*. Cambridge: Cambridge University Press.
De Gracia, Victoria. 2021. "Soft-Power United States Versus Normative Power Europe." In *Soft-Power Internationalism Competing for Cultural Influence in the 21st-Century Global Order*, edited by Burcu Baykurt and Victoria De Gracia, 19–59. New York: Columbia University Press.
de Sola Pool, Ithiel. 1977. "The Changing Flow of Television." *Journal of Communication* 27(2): 139–149.
Deutsch, Karl W. 1966a. *Nationalism and Social Communication: An Inquiry into the Foundations of Nationality*. Cambridge: MIT Press.
———. 1966b. *The Nerves of Government: Models of Political Communication and Control*. New York: Free Press.
Ding, Sheng, and Rey Koslowski. 2017. "Chinese Soft Power and Immigration Reform: Can Beijing's Approach to Pursuing Global Talent and Maintaining Domestic Stability Succeed?" *Chinese Journal of Political Science* 22(1): 97–116.
Donaldson, John A. 2007. "Tourism, Development and Poverty Reduction in Guizhou and Yunnan." *China Quarterly* 190: 333–351.

Doshi, Rush, Judith G. Kelley, and Beth A. Simmons. 2019. "The Power of Ranking: The Ease of Doing Business Indicator and Global Regulatory Behavior." *International Organization* 73(3): 611–643.
Economist. 2002. "Asia: Thailand's Gastro-Diplomacy; Food as Ambassador." 362(8261): 48.
Ellwood, David W. 2012. *The Shock of America: Europe and the Challenge of the Century*. Oxford: Oxford University Press.
Fine, Gary Alan. 2012. *Tiny Publics: A Theory of Group Action and Culture*. New York: Russell Sage Foundation.
Finnemore, Martha, and Kathryn Sikkink. 1998. "International Norm Dynamics and Political Change." *International Organization* 52(4): 887–917.
———. 2001. "Taking Stock: The Constructivist Research Program in International Relations and Comparative Politics." *Annual Review of Political Science* 4(1): 391–416.
Foner, Nancy. 2022. *One Quarter of the Nation: Immigration and the Transformation of America*. Princeton: Princeton University Press.
Foulkes, Nick. 2020. "Takumi Time: The Rise of Japanese Watchmaking." *Financial Times*, October 5, 2020.
Freedom House. 2021. "Freedom in the World." freedomhouse.org/report/freedom-world.
Gallarotti, Giulio. 2010. *Cosmopolitan Power in International Relations: A Synthesis of Realism, Neoliberalism, and Constructivism*. Cambridge: Cambridge University Press.
Gift, Thomas, and Daniel Krcmaric. 2017. "Who Democratizes? Western-Educated Leaders and Regime Transitions." *Journal of Conflict Resolution* 61(3): 671–701.
Gil, Jeffrey. 2017. *Soft Power and the Worldwide Promotion of Chinese Language Learning: The Confucius Institute Project*. Bristol: Multilingual Matters.
Gill, Lesley. 2004. *The School of the Americas: Military Training and Political Violence in the Americas*. Durham: Duke University Press.
Global Firepower. 2023. "Available Manpower by Country." www.globalfirepower.com/available-military-manpower.asp.
Golbert, Rebecca. 2001. "Transnational Orientations from Home: Constructions of Israel and Transnational Space Among Ukrainian Jewish Youth." *Journal of Ethnic and Migration Studies* 27(4): 713–731.
Goldsmith, Benjamin E., and Yusaku Horiuchi. 2009. "Spinning the Globe? U.S. Public Diplomacy and Foreign Public Opinion." *Journal of Politics* 71(3): 863–875.
———. 2012. "In Search of Soft Power: Does Foreign Public Opinion Matter for US Foreign Policy?" *World Politics* 64(3): 555–585.
Goldsmith, Benjamin E., Yusaku Horiuchi, and Terence Wood. 2014. "Doing Well by Doing Good: The Impact of Foreign Aid on Foreign Public Opinion." *Quarterly Journal of Political Science* 9(1): 87–114.
Gonzalez, Roger Geertz. 2017. "Internationalization at a German University: The Purpose and Paradoxes of English Language Master's and Doctoral Programs." *International Education Journal: Comparative Perspectives* 16(2): 49–62.
Graney, Katherine E. 2019. *Russia, the Former Soviet Republics, and Europe Since 1989: Transformation and Tragedy*. New York: Oxford University Press.
Grant, Ruth. 2006. "Ethics and Incentives: A Political Approach." *American Political Science Review* 100(1): 29–39.
Gray, Alex. 2017. "France Becomes the World No. 1 for Soft Power." World Economic Forum. www.weforum.org/agenda/2017/07/france-new-world-leader-in-soft-power.
Grigas, Agnia. 2016. *Beyond Crimea: The New Russian Empire*. New Haven: Yale University Press.
Grix, Jonathan, and Barrie Houlihan. 2014. "Sports Mega-Events as Part of a Nation's Soft Power Strategy: The Cases of Germany (2006) and the UK (2012)." *British Journal of Politics and International Relations* 16(4): 572–596.

Haas, Hein de. 2020. *The Age of Migration: International Population Movements in the Modern World*. 6th ed. London: Macmillan International Higher Education.
Habu, Toshie. 2000. "The Irony of Globalization: The Experience of Japanese Women in British Higher Education." *Higher Education* 39(1): 43–66.
Hall, Ian, and Frank Smith. 2013. "The Struggle for Soft Power in Asia: Public Diplomacy and Regional Competition." *Asian Security* 9(1): 1–18.
Hall, Kenji. 2017. "Monocle's Ranking of Soft Power in Asia." *Nikkei Asia*, November 23, 2017.
Hall, Todd H., and Andrew A. G. Ross. 2015. "Affective Politics After 9/11." *International Organization* 69(4): 847–879.
Havel, Václav. 1985. "The Power of the Powerless (1978)." *International Journal of Politics* 15(3/4): 23–96.
Hayden, Craig. 2012. *The Rhetoric of Soft Power: Public Diplomacy in Global Contexts*. Lanham, MD: Lexington Books.
He, Huifeng, and Josh Ye. 2017. "While Trump Curbs Immigration, China's Giving Out More Green Cards. But Can It Attract More Foreigners?" *South China Morning Post*, February 17, 2017.
He, Lan, and Stephen Wilkins. 2019. "The Return of China's Soft Power in South East Asia: An Analysis of the International Branch Campuses Established by Three Chinese Universities." *Higher Education Policy* 32: 321–337.
Hein, Patrick. 2016. "Reluctant Civilian World Powers? How Nationalism Threatens the Soft Power Image of Japan and Germany." *Asian Journal of German and European Studies* 1(1).
Herpen, Marcel van. 2016. *Putin's Propaganda Machine: Soft Power and Russian Foreign Policy*. Lanham, MD: Rowman and Littlefield.
Hilal, Kholoud T., Safiyyah R. Scott, and Nina Maadad. 2015. "The Political, Socio-Economic and Sociocultural Impacts of the King Abdullah Scholarship Program (KASP) on Saudi Arabia." *International Journal of Higher Education* 4(1).
Hofmeister, Wilhelm, ed. 2011. *G20: Perceptions and Perspectives for Global Governance*. Singapore: Konrad-Adenauer-Stiftung.
Huang, Kai-Ping, and Bridget Welsh. 2017. "Economic Context, Values and Soft Power Competition in Southeast Asia: An Individual Analysis." Asia Barometer Working Paper Series No. 134.
India, Government of. 2001. "Report of the High Level Committee on Indian Diaspora." Ministry of External Affairs. https://mea.gov.in/oia-publications.htm.
Irish, Tomás. 2015. "From International to Inter-Allied: Transatlantic University Relations in the Era of the First World War, 1905–1920." *Journal of Transatlantic Studies* 13(4): 311–325.
Jang, Gunjoo, and Won K. Paik. 2012. "Korean Wave as Tool for Korea's New Cultural Diplomacy." *Advances in Applied Sociology* 2(3): 196–202.
Ji, Li. 2017. "Measuring Soft Power." In *The Routledge Handbook of Soft Power*, edited by Naren Chitty, 75–103. London: Routledge.
Jimenez-Martinez, Cesar. 2013. "Chile's Quest to Improve Its Image Abroad." *Place Branding and Public Diplomacy* 9(4): 279–290.
Jon, Jae-Eun, Jenny J. Lee, and Kiyiong Byun. 2014. "The Emergence of a Regional Hub: Comparing International Student Choices and Experiences in South Korea." *Higher Education* 67(5): 691–710.
Jun, Hannah. 2017. "Hallyu at a Crossroads: The Clash of Korea's Soft Power Success and China's Hard Power Threat in Light of Terminal High Altitude Area Defence (THAAD) System Deployment." *Asian International Studies Review* 18(1): 153–169.
Kaplan, Alice Yaeger. 2012. *Dreaming in French: The Paris Years of Jacqueline Bouvier Kennedy, Susan Sontag, and Angela Davis*. Chicago: University of Chicago Press.
Kapur, Devesh. 2010. *Diaspora, Development, and Democracy: The Domestic Impact of International Migration from India*. Princeton, NJ: Princeton University Press.

Karl, Marion, Christine Reintinger, and Jürgen Schmude. 2015. "Reject or Select: Mapping Destination Choice." *Annals of Tourism Research* 54: 48–64.

Kassim, Azizah. 2014. "Recent Trends in Transnational Population Inflows into Malaysia: Policy, Issues and Challenges." *Malaysian Journal of Economic Studies* 51(1): 9–28.

Kim, Dongbin, and Jin-Young Roh. 2017. "International Doctoral Graduates from China and South Korea: A Trend Analysis of the Association Between the Selectivity of Undergraduate and That of US Doctoral Institutions." *Higher Education* 73(5): 615–635.

Kim, Hyo-Sook. 2018. "The Political Drivers of South Korea's Official Development Assistance to Myanmar." *Contemporary Southeast Asia* 40(3): 475–502.

Kirton, John. 2013. *G20 Governance for a Globalized World*. Surrey: Ashgate.

Koch, Natalie. 2014. "The Shifting Geopolitics of Higher Education: Inter/Nationalizing Elite Universities in Kazakhstan, Saudi Arabia, and Beyond." *Geoforum* 56: 46–54.

Kokas, Aynne. 2017. *Hollywood Made in China*. Oakland: University of California Press.

Kondakci, Yasar. 2011. "Student Mobility Reviewed: Attraction and Satisfaction of International Students in Turkey." *Higher Education* 62(5): 573.

Kounalakis, Markos, and Ambassador Andras Simonyi. 2011. "The Hard Truth About Soft Power." CPD Perspectives on Public Diplomacy, Paper 5, USC Center on Public Diplomacy at the Annenberg School, 51.

Kugiel, Patryk. 2017. *India's Soft Power: A New Foreign Policy Strategy*. London: Routledge.

Kumar, S. Y. Surendra. 2021. "India's Engagement with Its Diaspora in Southeast Asia: A Neglected Diaspora?" In *ASEAN and India-ASEAN Relations: Navigating Shifting Geopolitics*, Routledge Studies on Think Asia, edited by M. Mayilvaganan, 209–223. London: Taylor and Francis.

Kumar, Satish, and Bibhuti Bhusan Biswas, eds. 2016. *Modi's Cultural Diplomacy and Soft Power: Issues and Challenges*. New Delhi: Ansh Book International.

Kurlantzick, Joshua. 2007. *China's Charm Offensive: How China's Soft Power Is Transforming the World*. New Haven, CT: Yale University Press.

Kuznets, Simon. 1934. *A Report on National Income, 1929–1932. Letter from the Acting Secretary of Commerce Transmitting in Response to Senate Resolution No. 220 (72nd Cong.)*. US Government Printing Office. https://fraser.stlouisfed.org/files/docs/publications/natincome_1934/19340104_nationalinc.pdf.

La Pastina, Antonio C., and Joseph D. Straubhaar. 2005. "Multiple Proximities Between Television Genres and Audiences: The Schism Between Telenovelas' Global Distribution and Local Consumption." *Gazette (Leiden, Netherlands)* 67(3): 271–288.

Laifer, Natalie, and Nicholas Kitchen. 2017. "Australia's International Education as Public Diplomacy: Soft Power Potential." *Politics and Policy* 45(5): 813–840.

Lam, Frances. 2019. "How Thai Food Took Over America." *Splendid Table*, January 10, 2019.

Lee, Erika. 2015. *The Making of Asian America: A History*. New York: Simon and Schuster.

Lee, Karl Chee Leong. 2023. "Introduction: Taiwan's International Ostracization and Soft Power." In *Taiwan and Southeast Asia: Soft Power and Hard Truths Facing China's Ascendancy*, edited by Karl Chee Leong Lee and Ying-kit Chan, 1–5. London: Taylor and Francis.

Lemahieu, Herve. 2020. "Soft Power Goes up in Smoke." *The Interpreter*, Lowy Institute. January 25, 2020.

Lepenies, Philipp. 2016. *The Power of a Single Number: A Political History of GDP*. New York: Columbia University Press.

Lesjak, Miha. 2015. "Erasmus Student Motivation: Why and Where to Go?" *Higher Education* 70(5): 845–865.

Li, Mei, and Mark Bray. 2007. "Cross-Border Flows of Students for Higher Education: Push-Pull Factors and Motivations of Mainland Chinese Students in Hong Kong and Macau." *Higher Education* 53(6): 791–818.
Li, Mingjiang, ed. 2009a. *Soft Power: China's Emerging Strategy in International Politics*. Lanham, MD: Lexington Books.
———. 2009b. "Soft Power in Chinese Discourse: Popularity and Prospect." In *Soft Power: China's Emerging Strategy in International Politics*, edited by Mingjiang Li, 21–44. Lanham, MD: Lexington Books.
Lobato, Ramon. 2018. "Rethinking International TV Flows Research in the Age of Netflix." *Television and New Media* 19(3): 241–256.
Lobato, Ramon, Alexa Scarlata, and Stuart Cunningham. 2023. "Conceptualizing the National and the Global in SVOD Original Production." In *Streaming Video: Storytelling Across Borders*, edited by Amanda D. Lotz and Ramon Lobato, 37–53. Cambridge: New York University Press.
Lomer, Sylvie. 2016. "Soft Power as a Policy Rationale for International Education in the UK: A Critical Analysis." *Higher Education* 74(4): 581–598.
Lotz, Amanda D. 2023. "Why SVOD Commissions Matter." In *Streaming Video: Storytelling Across Borders*, edited by Amanda D. Lotz and Ramon Lobato, 18–36. Cambridge: New York University Press.
Lotz, Amanda D., and Oliver Eklund. 2024. "Beyond Netflix: Ownership and Content Strategies Among Non-US-Based Video Streaming Services." *International Journal of Cultural Studies* 27(1): 119–140.
Lotz, Amanda D., Oliver Eklund, and Stuart Soroka. 2022. "Netflix, Library Analysis, and Globalization: Rethinking Mass Media Flows." *Journal of Communication* 72(4): 511–521.
Lotz, Amanda D., and Ramon Lobato, eds. 2023. *Streaming Video: Storytelling Across Borders*. Cambridge: New York University Press.
Louw-Vaudran, Liesl. 2016. *Superpower or Neocolonialist? South Africa in Africa*. Cape Town: Tafelberg.
Lowy Institute. 2021. "Countries—Lowy Institute Asia Power Index." Lowy Institute Asia Power Index 2020. https://power.lowyinstitute.org/countries.
MacDonald, Alistair. 2018. "The Top Soft Powers of 2018: British Council." www.britishcouncil.org/sites/default/files/j119_thought_leadership_global_trends_in_soft_power_web.pdf.
Marlin-Bennett, Renée. 2022. "Soft Power's Dark Side." *Journal of Political Power* 15(3): 437–455.
Matveenko, Veronica Eduardovna, Nataliya Mikhailovna Rumyantseva, and Dina Nikolaevna Rubtsova. 2017. "Migration in the Russian Federation Today." *Teorija in praksa* 54(6): 969–1110.
Mazzarol, Tim, and Geoffrey N. Soutar. 2002. "'Push-Pull' Factors Influencing International Student Destination Choice." *International Journal of Educational Management* 16(2): 82–90.
McAdam, Doug, Sidney G. Tarrow, and Charles Tilly. 2001. *Dynamics of Contention*. New York: Cambridge University Press.
McClory, Jonathan. 2021. "Soft Power 30." https://softpower30.com.
Melnick, Ross. 2022. *Hollywood's Embassies: How Movie Theaters Projected American Power Around the World*. New York: Columbia University Press.
Merritt, Richard. 1966. "Nation Building in America: The Colonial Years." In *Nation Building in Comparative Contexts*, edited by Karl W. Deutsch and William J. Foltz. New Brunswick, NJ: AldineTransaction.
Messaris, Paul, and Jisuk Woo. 1991. "Image vs. Reality in Korean-Americans' Responses to Mass-mediated Depictions of the United States." *Critical Studies in Mass Communication* 8(1): 74–90.

Messer, Dolores, and Stefan C. Wolter. 2007. "Are Student Exchange Programs Worth It?" *Higher Education* 54(5): 647–663.
Migin, Melissa W., Mohammad Falahat, Mohd Shukri Ab Yajid, and Ali Khatibi. 2015. "Impacts of Institutional Characteristics on International Students' Choice of Private Higher Education Institutions in Malaysia." *Higher Education Studies* 5(1).
Migration Policy Institute. 2013. "U.S. Immigration Trends." www.migrationpolicy.org/programs/data-hub/us-immigration-trends.
Mitchell, Tony. 1992. "Mixing Pop and Politics: Rock Music in Czechoslovakia Before and After the Velvet Revolution." *Popular Music* 11(2): 187–203.
Mueller, Milton. 2010. *Networks and States: The Global Politics of Internet Governance*. Cambridge, MA: MIT Press.
Murphy, Ann Marie. 2010. "US Rapprochement with Indonesia: From Problem State to Partner." *Contemporary Southeast Asia* 32(3): 362–387.
Musiani, Francesca, Derrick L. Cogburn, Laura DeNardis, and Nanette S. Levinson. 2016. *The Turn to Infrastructure in Internet Governance*. New York: Palgrave Macmillan.
Nair, Neeti. 2020. "For the First Time, India Is Seeing Secularism Go from a Top-Down Decree to a Street Slogan." *The Print*, January 3, 2020.
———. 2023. *Hurt Sentiments: Secularism and Belonging in South Asia*. Cambridge: Harvard University Press.
Naylor, Tristen. 2019. *Social Closure and International Society: Status Groups from the Family of Civilised Nations to the G20*. London: Routledge.
Netflix. 2020. "Netflix Annual Report 2019 10-K." https://ir.netflix.net/financials/annual-reports-and-proxies/default.aspx.
———. 2023. "Netflix Annual Report 2022 10-K." https://ir.netflix.net/financials/annual-reports-and-proxies/default.aspxhttps://ir.netflix.net/financials/annual-reports-and-proxies/default.aspx.
Nguyen, Van Chinh. 2014. "Confucius Institutes in the Mekong Region: China's Soft Power or Soft Border?" *Issues and Studies—Institute of International Relations* 50(4): 85–118.
Nye, Joseph. 2017. "Soft Power: The Origins and Political Progress of a Concept." *Palgrave Communications* 3(1): 1–3.
Nye Jr., Joseph S. 1990a. *Bound to Lead: The Changing Nature of American Power*. New York: Basic Books.
———. 1990b. "Soft Power." *Foreign Policy* (80): 153–171.
———. 1999. "Redefining the National Interest." *Foreign Affairs*, July/August 1999.
———. 2002. *The Paradox of American Power: Why the World's Only Superpower Can't Go It Alone*. New York: Oxford University Press.
———. 2004a. *Soft Power: The Means to Success in World Politics*. New York: PublicAffairs.
———. 2004b. "Today, It's a Question of Whose Story Wins." *Los Angeles Times*, July 21, 2004.
———. 2011a. "Power and Foreign Policy." *Journal of Political Power* 4(1): 9–24.
———. 2011b. *The Future of Power*. New York: PublicAffairs.
Oakman, Daniel. 2001. "The Politics of Foreign Aid: Counter-Subversion and the Colombo Plan, 1950–1970." *Pacifica Review* 13(3): 255–272.
———. 2010. "Student Sojourners: Museums and the Transnational Lives of International Students." *National Identities* 12(4): 397–412.
Ocampo, José Antonio, and Joseph E. Stiglitz. 2012. "From the G-20 to a Global Economic Coordination Council." *Journal of Globalization and Development* 2(2): 1–16.
Ogunnubi, Olusola, and Christopher Isike. 2015. "Regional Hegemonic Contention and the Asymmetry of Soft Power: A Comparative Analysis of South Africa and Nigeria." *Strategic Review for Southern Africa* 37(1): 152–177.

Onishi, Norimitsu. 2016. "Nigeria's Booming Film Industry Redefines African Life." *New York Times*, February 18, 2016.
Ostrom, Elinor. 2003. "Toward a Behavioral Theory Linking Trust, Reciprocity, and Reputation." In *Trust and Reciprocity: Interdisciplinary Lessons from Experimental Work*, edited by Elinor Ostrom and James Walker, 19–79. New York: Russell Sage.
———. 2005. *Understanding Institutional Diversity*. Princeton: Princeton University Press.
Padoongpatt, Mark. 2017. *Flavors of Empire: Food and the Making of Thai America*. Oakland: University of California Press.
Pang, Zhongying. 2009. "China's Soft Power Dilemma: The Beijing Consensus Revisited." In *Soft Power: China's Emerging Strategy in International Politics*, edited by Mingjiang Li, 125–142. Lanham, MD: Lexington Books.
Park, Elisa L. 2009. "Analysis of Korean Students' International Mobility by 2-D Model: Driving Force Factor and Directional Factor." *Higher Education* 57(6): 741–755.
Patterson, Orlando. 1994. "Ecumenical America: Global Culture and the American Cosmos." *World Policy Journal* 11(2): 103–117.
Pew Research. 2021. "Global Indicators Database." Pew Research Center's Global Attitudes Project.
Pimpa, Nattavud. 2005. "A Family Affair: The Effect of Family on Thai Students' Choices of International Education." *Higher Education* 49(4): 431–448.
Putnam, Robert D. 2002. *Democracies in Flux the Evolution of Social Capital in Contemporary Society*. Oxford: University Press.
Potter, Evan H. 2009. *Branding Canada: Projecting Canada's Soft Power Through Public Diplomacy*. Montreal: McGill-Queen's University Press.
Reilly, Benjamin. 2015. "Australia as a Southern Hemisphere 'Soft Power.'" *Australian Journal of International Affairs* 69(3): 253–265.
Renshon, Jonathan. 2017. *Fighting for Status: Hierarchy and Conflict in World Politics*. Princeton, NJ: Princeton University Press.
Repnikova, Maria. 2022. *Chinese Soft Power*. Cambridge: Cambridge University Press.
Robins, Kevin, and Asu Aksoy. 2001. "From Spaces of Identity to Mental Spaces: Lessons from Turkish-Cypriot Cultural Experience in Britain." *Journal of Ethnic and Migration Studies* 27(4): 685–711.
Rodríguez González, Carlos, Ricardo Bustillo Mesanza, and Petr Mariel. 2011. "The Determinants of International Student Mobility Flows: An Empirical Study on the Erasmus Programme." *Higher Education* 62(4): 413–430.
Rose, Andrew K. 2016. "Like Me, Buy Me: The Effect of Soft Power on Exports." *Economics and Politics* 28(2): 216–232.
———. 2018. "Soft Power, Sanctions, and Exports: Checking the BS in BDS." In *Research Handbook on Economic Diplomacy: Bilateral Relations in a Context of Geopolitical Change*, edited by Peter A. G. van Bergeijk and Selwyn J. V. Moons. Northampton, MA: Edward Elgar.
———. 2019. "Soft Power and Exports." *Review of International Economics* 27(5): 1573–1590.
Roselle, L., A. Miskimmon, and B. O'Loughlin. 2014. "Strategic Narrative: A New Means to Understand Soft Power." *Media, War, and Conflict* 7(1): 70–84.
Rosendorf, Neal M. 2013. *Franco Sells Spain to America: Hollywood, Tourism and Public Relations as Postwar Spanish Soft Power*. New York: Palgrave Macmillan.
Rotaru, Vasile. 2018. "Forced Attraction? How Russia Is Instrumentalizing Its Soft Power Sources in the 'Near Abroad.'" *Problems of Post-Communism* 65(1): 37–48.
Roy, Anjali Gera, ed. 2012. *The Magic of Bollywood: At Home and Abroad*. Thousand Oaks: Sage.
Rui, Yang. 2012. "Internationalization, Regionalization, and Soft Power: China's Relations with ASEAN Member Countries in Higher Education." *Frontiers of Education in China* 7(4): 486–507.

Rutland, Peter, and Andrei Kazantsev. 2016. "The Limits of Russia's 'Soft Power.'" *Journal of Political Power* 9(3): 395–413.

Ryback, Timothy W. 1990. *Rock Around the Bloc: A History of Rock Music in Eastern Europe and the Soviet Union.* New York: Oxford University Press.

Schaefer, David J., and Kavita Karan, eds. 2012. *Bollywood and Globalization: The Global Power of Popular Hindi Cinema.* New York: Routledge.

Schaefer-Wilke, Ute. 2018. "English Language Policy in German Public Sector Higher Education." Dissertation, British Council and St. Mary's University, Twickenham, London. www.teachingenglish.org.uk/sites/teacheng/files/ute_schafer-wilke_st_mary_s_university_twickenham_london_dissertation.pdf.

Scobell, Andrew, and Marylena Mantas, eds. 2014. *China's Great Leap Outward: Hard and Soft Dimensions of a Rising Power.* New York: Academy of Political Science.

Shambaugh, David L. 2013. *China Goes Global: The Partial Power.* New York: Oxford University Press.

———. 2015. "China's Soft-Power Push: The Search for Respect." *Foreign Affairs* 94(4): 99–107.

Shome, Parthasarathi. 2014. *The G20 Macroeconomic Agenda: India and the Emerging Economies.* Delhi: Cambridge University Press.

Shrinivasan, Rukmini. 2012. "Despite Drop, India No. 9 in Number of Immigrants." *Times of India*, March 2, 2012.

Singh, A. K., S. Tiwari, India, and Centre for Joint Warfare Studies, eds. 2010. *Proceedings of Seminar on Leveraging India's Soft Power as a Strategic Resource.* New Delhi: Vij Books India.

Singh, J. P. 2011. *Globalized Arts: The Entertainment Economy and Cultural Identity.* New York: Columbia University Press.

———. 2013. "Information Technologies, Meta-Power, and Transformations in Global Politics." *International Studies Review* 15(1): 5–29.

Singh, J. P., Neslihan Kaptanoglu, and Meng-Hao Li. 2023. "Taking a Soft Power Approach to Cultural Heritage Protection: Toward an Empirical Methodology." In *The Routledge Handbook of Soft Power*, edited by Naren J. Chitty, Ji Li, and Gary D. Rawnsley, 47–69. London: Routledge.

Singh, J. P., and Stuart MacDonald. 2017. "Soft Power Today: Measuring the Effects." British Council.

Snow, Nancy, and Philip M. Taylor, eds. 2009. *Routledge Handbook of Public Diplomacy.* New York: Routledge.

Soba, Joseph Armando. 2015. "Cinema et soft power: L'interventionnisme Africain face aux interets Français et Hollywoodiens" [Cinema and soft power: African interventionism vs. French and Hollywood interests]. *Studia Universitatis Babes-Bolyai. Studia Europaea* 60(3): 203–217.

Sobocinska, Agnieszka. 2013. "Visiting the Neighbours: The Political Meanings of Australian Travel to Cold War Asia." *Australian Historical Studies* 44(3): 382–404.

Spilimbergo, Antonio. 2009. "Democracy and Foreign Education." *American Economic Review* 99(1): 528–543.

Straubhaar, Joseph D. 1984. "Brazilian Television: The Decline of American Influence." *Communication Research* 11(2): 221–240.

———. 1991. "Beyond Media Imperialism." *Critical Studies in Mass Communication* 8: 39–59.

Suryodiningrat, Meidyatama. 2010. "US Rapprochement with Indonesia: From Problem State to Partner—a Response." *Contemporary Southeast Asia* 32(3): 388–394.

Sustainable Development Solutions Network. 2019. "World Happiness Report 2019." https://worldhappiness.report/ed/2019.

Sutter, Robert. 2009. "The Obama Administration and US Policy in Asia." *Contemporary Southeast Asia* 31(2): 189–216.

Swaminathan, Roopa. 2017. *Bollywood Boom: India's Rising Soft Power*. Gurgaon, Haryana, India: Penguin Books.
Taiwan, Ministry of Education, Department of Statistics. 2024. "112 (2023–2024) Annual Report 2023–2024." https://depart.moe.edu.tw/ED4500/News.aspx?n=5A930C32CC6C3818&sms=91B3AAE8C6388B96&Create=.
Takayama, Keita. 2018. "Beyond Comforting Histories: The Colonial/Imperial Entanglements of the International Institute, Paul Monroe, and Isaac L. Kandel at Teachers College, Columbia University." *Comparative Education Review* 62(4): 459–481.
Talaska, Cara A., Susan T. Fiske, and Shelly Chaiken. 2008. "Legitimating Racial Discrimination: Emotions, Not Beliefs, Best Predict Discrimination in a Meta-Analysis." *Social Justice Research* 21(3): 263–396.
Tasci, Asli D. A., and William C. Gartner. 2016. "Destination Image and Its Functional Relationships." *Journal of Travel Research* 45(4): 413–425.
Tettner, Samuel, and Begum Kalyoncu. 2016. "Gastrodiplomacy 2.0: Culinary Tourism Beyond Nationalism." *Ara: Revista de Investigación en Turismo* 6(2): 47–55.
Tharoor, Shashi. 2007. *The Elephant, the Tiger, and the Cell Phone: Reflections on India, the Emerging 21st Century Power*. New York: Arcade Publishing.
Tsang, Eileen Yuk-ha. 2013. "The Quest for Higher Education by the Chinese Middle Class: Retrenching Social Mobility?" *Higher Education* 66(6): 653–668.
Tuccio, Michele, Jackline Wahba, and Bachir Hamdouch. 2019. "International Migration as a Driver of Political and Social Change: Evidence from Morocco." *Journal of Population Economics* 32(4): 1171–1203.
Tulchin, Joseph S. 2004. "Using Soft Power to Enhance Trade Strategies." In *The Strategic Dynamics of Latin American Trade*, edited by Vinod K. Aggarwal and Ralph H. Espach. Washington, DC: Woodrow Wilson Center Press.
UNESCO [United Nations Education Scientific and Cultural Organization]. 2024. "UNESCO Institute for Statistics." data.uis.unesco.org.
Van Oudenaren, John S., and Benjamin E. Fisher. 2016. "Foreign Military Education as PLA Soft Power." *Parameters* 46(4): 105–118.
van Rekom, Johan, and Frank Go. 2006. "Being Discovered." *Annals of Tourism Research* 33(3): 767–784.
Védrine, Hubert, and Dominique Moïsi. 2001. *France in an Age of Globalization*. Washington, DC: Brookings Institution Press.
Vertovec, Steven. 2001. "Transnationalism and Identity." *Journal of Ethnic and Migration Studies* 27(4): 573–582.
Voci, Paola, and Luo Hui, eds. 2018. *Screening China's Soft Power*. London: Routledge.
Vogel, Ezra F. 1980. *Japan as Number One: Lessons for America*. New York: Harper and Row.
Vyas, Utpal. 2011. *Soft Power in Japan-China Relations: State, Sub-State and Non-State Relations*. New York: Routledge.
Wade, Robert Hunter. 2009. "From Global Imbalances to Global Reorganisations." *Cambridge Journal of Economics* 33: 539–562.
Walton, Whitney. 2005. "Internationalism and the Junior Year Abroad: American Students in France in the 1920s and 1930s." *Diplomatic History* 29(2): 255–278.
Wang, Chenjun, and Naren Chitty. 2021. *A Future for the Chinese Diaspora and Australia: Great Story and the Golden Rule*. Stuttgart: Institut für Auslandsbeziehungen.
Wang, Jian. 2011. *Soft Power in China: Public Diplomacy Through Communications*. New York: Palgrave Macmillan.
Wibowo, Ignatius. 2009. "China's Soft Power and NeoLiberal Agenda in Southeast Asia." In *Soft Power: China's Emerging Strategy in International Politics*, edited by Mingjiang Li, 207–223. Lanham, MD: Lexington Books.
Wilson, Ernest J. 2008. "Hard Power, Soft Power, Smart Power." *Annals of the American Academy of Political and Social Science* 616: 110–124.

Wilson, Jeanne L. 2015a. "Russia and China Respond to Soft Power: Interpretation and Readaptation of a Western Construct." *Politics* 35(3–4): 287–300.
———. 2015b. "Soft Power: A Comparison of Discourse and Practice in Russia and China." *Europe-Asia Studies* 67(8): 1171–1202.
———. 2016. "Cultural Statecraft in the Russian and Chinese Contexts: Domestic and International Implications." *Problems of Post-Communism* 63(3): 135–145.
Windle, Joel, and Maria Alice Nogueira. 2015. "The Role of Internationalisation in the Schooling of Brazilian Elites: Distinctions Between Two Class Fractions." *British Journal of Sociology of Education* 36(1): 174–192.
World Bank. 2021. "World Development Indicators DataBank." https://databank.worldbank.org/source/world-development-indicators.
World Tourism Organization. 1960. *International Travel Statistics*. UN Tourism (former IUOTO), Madrid.
———. 1970. *International Travel Statistics*. UN Tourism (former IUOTO), Madrid.
———. 1981. *World Tourism Statistics 1976–1980* 34. UN Tourism (former WTO), Madrid.
———. 1992. *Yearbook of Tourism Statistics*, 44th ed. UN Tourism (former WTO), Madrid.
Wu, Irene S. 2015. *Forging Trust Communities: How Technology Changes Politics*. Baltimore: Johns Hopkins University Press.
———. 2020. "Applying the Soft Power Rubric: How Study Abroad Reveals International Cultural Relations." In *Cultural Values in Political Economy*, edited by J. P. Singh. Stanford: Stanford University Press.
———. 2021. "India and the Soft Power Rubric: The Relevance of Migrants, Students, Visitors and Movies." *India Review* 20(4).
———. 2023a. "Getting to 'We' from 'They': New Ways to Measure Soft Power in International Relations." *Thrēo*. https://thethreo.com/getting-to-we-from-they-new-ways-to-measure-soft-power-in-international-relations.
———. 2023b. "Goal! Soft Power at the Women's World Cup for Soccer ANZ 2023." *SPARC Lighthouse Views*, Macquarie University. www.mq.edu.au/research/research-centres-groups-and-facilities/centres/soft-power-analysis-and-resource-centre/lighthouse-commentary/commentary.
———. 2023c. "The Smithsonian Institution's Contribution to US Soft Power: Applying the Soft Power Rubric." *Journal of Political Power* 15(3): 415–436.
———. 2023d. "Tools for Measuring Soft Power: A Review of Recent Quantitative Analyses." In *The Routledge Handbook of Soft Power*, 2nd ed., edited by Naren Chitty. London: Routledge.
Wu, Shang-Su, and Alan Chong. 2018. "Developmental Railpolitics: The Political Economy of China's High-Speed Rail Projects in Thailand and Indonesia." *Contemporary Southeast Asia* 40(3): 503.
Yamagishi, Toshio. 2003. "Cross-Societal Experimentation on Trust: A Comparison of the United States and Japan." In *Trust and Reciprocity: Interdisciplinary Lessons from Experimental Research*, edited by Elinor Ostrom and James Walker, 352–370. New York: Russell Sage Foundation.
Zeeshan, Muhammad, Sabbar Dahham Sabbar, Shahid Bashir, and Rai Imtiaz Hussain. 2013. "Foreign Students' Motivation for Studying in Malaysia." *International Journal of Asian Social Science* 3(3): 833–846.
Zhang, Juyan. 2015. "The Food of the Worlds: Mapping and Comparing Contemporary Gastrodiplomacy Campaigns." *International Journal of Communication* 9(0): 24.
Zhao, Suisheng. 2009. "The Prospect of China's Soft Power: How Sustainable?" In *Soft Power: China's Emerging Strategy in International Politics*, edited by Mingjiang Li, 247–265. Lanham, MD: Lexington Books.
Zhuk, Sergei I. 2011. "Closing and Opening Soviet Society (Introduction to the Forum)." *Ab Imperio* 2011(2): 123–158.

Index

Afghanistan, 100
Africa, 25, 74, 89, 105, 117–118, 137, 139, 155, 173
African Americans, 59.
Afrobarometer, 39. *See also* Data
Aid, 21, 22, 24, 42, 110, 125
Albania, 32, 183
Algeria, 59, 151, 180, 182
Altbach, Philip G., 89
Altruism, 13
Americas, 4, 9, 27–28, 34, 48, 91, 123, 173
AmericasBarometer, 38. *See also* Data
Amnesty International, 12
Anderson, Benedict, 14, 51, 76
Ang, Ien, 47–48, 53,
Anime, 65, 168
Archigos dataset, 34
Argentina, 34, 104, 184, 189
Arif, Imran, 58
Armed Forces, 155–156
Armenian community, 140
Army Command, 37
Army War College, 37
ASEAN (Association of Southeast Asian Nations), 4, 105, 123–140
Asia, 40–41, 62, 65, 74, 79, 81–84, 88–92, 113, 117, 124–140, 141–143, 165–167
Asia Barometer, 124–125, 136. *See also* Data
Atkinson, Carol, 5, 25, 36–37, 41, 88–89, 151, 161
Audience, 5, 8, 11, 14–17, 20–22, 40, 42–43, 47–49, 56, 64–65, 70, 74, 76–78, 93, 121, 160–162, 164
Australia, 18, 40–43, 60, 62, 72–73, 79–85, 89–90, 97, 117, 126, 131, 144–148, 166–168, 177–191

Austria, 50, 104, 147–148, 153, 177–178, 180–182, 184–189
Azerbaijan, 139, 187

Baker, Jayne, 86
Baker, Josephine, 58
Baldwin, James, 58–59
Baltic states, 111
Bangladesh, 95–96, 100, 131, 135
Baudassé, Thierry, 40
Bazillier, Remi, 40
BBC GlobeScan survey, 29. *See also* Data
BBC World Service, 25
Beatles, 1
Beijing, 69, 125
Beine, Michel, 38
Belarus, 188
Belgium, 39, 104, 148, 177–178, 184–190
Berlin Wall, 1, 111
Bially Mattern, Janice, 12, 14, 20, 161
Biswas, Bibhuti Bhusan, 92
Blood libel, 11
Bollywood, 92
Bouvier, Jacqueline, 57–61, 63, 66, 86
Brazil, 65, 75, 86, 93, 102–4, 150, 187, 190
Bretton Woods, 103
Bukh, Alexander, 126
Bulgaria, 176, 182, 185
Bush, George W., 26–27
Byrne, Caitlin, 90

CAFSA, 116–117, 121
Calleo, David P., 16
Cambodia, 34, 124, 140
Canada, 4, 64, 86, 97, 102–104, 117, 144–146, 148, 150, 171–172, 178–191

Canberra, 90
Cantonese, 120
Car, Viktorija, 40
Cardoso, Fernando Enrique, 64–65
Central Asia, 100, 111
Ceylon, 81
Chad, 99
Chadda, Maya, 92
Chaiken, Shelly, 17
Chang, Yu-tsun, 125
Chen, Yu-Wen 118
Cheng, Xiaohe, 117
Chi, Heng-Chang, 139
Chicago, 62
Chicago Council, 25
Chile, 34–35, 99, 185, 187, 190
Chimes of Freedom, 1
China, 4, 16–17, 19–20, 61, 64–65, 69, 72–73, 84–87, 93–97, 100, 102–104, 107–108, 109–127, 131, 135–136, 140, 150–157, 164–166, 182, 184, 187–191
Chinese, 18, 53, 84, 86, 88, 109, 113, 117–121, 124, 126, 140
Chitty, Naren, 14–16, 18, 20– 23, 27, 44, 53, 85, 90, 161
Chu, Yun-han, 125
Cingranelli-Richards, 36. *See also* Data
Coca-Cola, 28
Coercion, 10, 15, 16, 137
Cold War, 1–2, 15, 19, 79, 81–83, 137, 150
Colombo Plan, 79–83, 85, 90, 126, 166
Colonial history, 29, 36, 50–51, 82, 153
Communication, 4–5, 12–15, 20–21, 40, 47, 49–54, 161–162, 168, 173
Communications technologies, 76, 78, 146, 150, 166
Communities, 2, 7–8, 11–16, 18, 47, 49–51, 53, 61–62, 66–68, 70, 84, 86, 89–90, 96, 105, 123, 135, 138, 159–160, 162–164, 168–169
Confucius Institutes, 109
Constructivism, 16
Contentment, 15, 22–23
Cooperation, 3–4, 6, 11, 23, 26–27, 33, 46–47, 51–56, 161–163
Core-periphery, 3, 57, 64–65, 89, 140, 165
Cosmopolitan power, 10, 16, 86, 160
Covid-19, 5, 95, 105, 107, 117, 148, 174
Crimea, 103
Crow David, 38–39
Cuba, 150, 180, 182, 185
Cuisine, 61, 92, 101, 123–24, 139
Culinary cultures, 138–139
Culture, 6, 8, 10, 12, 23, 30, 47–52, 61–69, 76–79, 88–89, 92, 96, 98, 107, 136, 144, 146, 150, 157 163, 168, 169; institutions, 5, 7, 30–31, 49, 85, 110; programs, 21–22, 53, 56–57, 76–77, 83, 85, 124, 163

Cultural Revolution, 116, 121
Cyprus, 61, 67, 164, 182, 185
Czaika, Mathias, 87
Czech Republic, 117, 185, 187, 190
Czechoslovakia, 1

Dallas, 47–48, 53
Data: Afrobarometer, 39; AmericasBarometer, 38; Asia Barometer, 124–125, 136; BBC GlobeScan survey, 29; Cingranelli–Richards Index, 36; Ease of Doing Business Index 143, 146, 157; Freedom House Freedom in the World Index, 25, 33, 143; Gallup International Iraq Poll and Post–War Iraq Poll, 25, 31; Global Firepower, 3, 156, 159; Good Country Index, 31; Happiness Index, 143; Lowy Asia Power Index, 92, 136, 143; Monocle, 141; Moroccan government ministry survey, 39; Pew Global Attitudes Poll, 25, 143; Polity IV Index, 36, 40; Press Freedom Index Score, 146; Program on International Policy Attitudes, University of Maryland, 29; Soft Power 30, 5, 18, 55, 85, 92, 136, 141–147, 151, 156–158, 167; UNESCO (United Nations Educational, Scientific, and Cultural Organization) Institute of Statistics, 8, 33, 56, 70–74, 77–81, 93–94, 97–98, 106, 108, 116–119, 121, 130, 134, 137–140, 149, 152, 155, 171–175; United Nations Demographic Yearbook, 108, 174; United Nations Development Program (UNDP) Gender Equality Index Score, 146; United Nations Population Division, 8, 56, 95–96, 100–101, 106, 108, 112–115, 130, 134, 149, 151, 154–155, 174; United Nations World Tourism Organization (UN Tourism), 8, 19, 40, 94, 108, 118, 130, 134, 140, 149, 152 155, 171, 175; World Bank, 19, 25, 87, 99, 104, 108, 143–144, 156, 157; World Values Survey, 39; Zogby International, 28
Datta, Monti Narayan, 5, 27–28, 33, 40
Davis, Angela, 58–60, 63, 66, 86
de Sola Pool, Ithiel, 65
Democracies, 5, 18, 30–38, 43, 92, 110, 124, 155, 161
Denmark, 104, 107, 145, 165, 178, 184, 187, 190
Destination, 5, 7, 38–39, 57, 60, 62–64, 66, 80, 83, 85, 90, 97, 118, 127, 131, 137, 140, 146, 150, 154, 162–166, 172
Destination image, 7, 57–58, 62–64, 66, 139–140, 163, 165, 168–169

Deutsch, Karl W., 5, 50, 53
Diaspora, 4, 18, 92, 98–99, 113, 125, 135
Diplomacy, 10, 53, 81–82, 89, 92, 103, 125, 144
Diplomats, 28, 53, 56, 163
Discrimination, 17, 60, 66, 85, 117–118, 125, 163
Disempowerment, 10, 160, 168
Dominican Republic, 32
Doshi, Rush, 157
Duggan, Niall, 118
Dylan, Bob, 1

East Berlin, 1, 45
Eastern Europe, 1, 2, 28, 100, 137
East Hollywood, 140
Economy, 3, 9, 19, 36, 43, 46, 49, 54, 76, 87, 102–105, 110, 117, 143, 155, 159
Economics, 30, 52, 54, 56, 76, 91, 121, 125, 161
Economic power, 9, 11, 12, 16, 18, 20, 93, 102, 105, 111, 141, 156, 164
Economic production, 5, 19, 31, 46, 54–55, 87, 110
Ecuador, 99
Education, 4, 33, 35, 60–61, 63, 67–69, 82, 85–87, 89–90, 109–110, 117, 120–121, 126, 135–136, 144, 150, 163–164
Education hub, 85, 90, 109, 140, 166
Education sector, 3–4, 14, 41, 66, 85, 97, 117, 126, 137
Egypt, 173, 178–180, 182
Eklund, Oliver, 75–76
El Salvador, 150, 185
Ellwood, David W., 27
Emigrants, 2–4, 8, 21–22, 38–39, 40, 42, 87, 97–98, 101, 107–108, 113, 154, 159
Emotions, 6, 16–18, 62, 64, 161
Empires, 82
Empowerment, soft, 160, 168
Emulation, 4, 14–17, 67, 161
Endearment, 4, 14–17, 22–23, 67, 161
Engagement, 5, 10, 77–78, 92, 144, 160
English, 17, 86, 97, 120–121, 137
Epistemic communities, 12–13
ERASMUS program, 80, 82
Ethics, 23, 27, 67, 161
Europe, 1–4, 16, 28–29, 41, 58, 61–64, 74, 77, 79–80, 82–83, 88, 100, 103–104, 111, 137, 153, 162, 166
European Union, 10, 30–31, 45, 80, 103
Eurovision, 111
Exports, 25, 29–30, 65 139

Faith, 6, 23, 47, 51, 125, 163
Families, 2, 24, 38–39, 40, 43, 48, 55, 60–61, 64, 66, 78, 85–87, 89, 97, 155, 159
Fans, 53, 69, 77

Films, 8, 11, 53, 63–65, 69–70, 73, 78, 119, 166, 175
Financial crisis, 10, 102–3, 124
Fine, Gary Alan, 23, 53
Finnemore, Martha, 23, 53
Fiske, Susan, 17
Foner, Nancy, 41
Foreign aid, 24–25, 27, 30, 125, 161
Foreign audiences, 42, 72–73, 76, 93, 173
Foreign countries, 2–3, 6–7, 24–25, 46–47, 60, 62, 85–86, 92, 110, 113, 157, 159–160, 166–170
Foreign degrees, 66
Foreign development assistance programs, 173
Foreigners, 2–6, 17–18, 24–25, 27, 37, 42–43, 46–47, 61, 67, 70, 85, 88, 91–96, 101, 105–109, 112–113, 119–121, 136, 143–44, 146, 153, 161–162, 164–166, 168–169
Foreign movies, 2, 6, 70, 78, 107, 159, 166
Foreign policy, 4, 7, 10, 12, 22–27, 31–32, 42 63, 68, 78–79, 83, 89, 107–110, 124, 137, 165, 167, 169
Foreign public opinion, 24–27, 32–33, 41–42, 151, 161, 167
Foreign students, 18, 37, 41, 55, 79–82, 84–85, 87–90, 94–95, 105–7, 113, 116–17, 121, 126, 135, 137–138, 140, 146–147, 150–151, 152–153, 157, 162, 166–167, 171–174
Foreign universities, 7, 79–80, 86, 96–97, 127, 134, 137, 150, 153
Foreign visitors, 6, 8, 77, 90–91, 94–95, 105, 107, 117–118, 120 , 146–147, 150–151, 153, 164–167, 171–172, 174–175
Foulkes, Nick, 18
France, 4, 9, 19, 32, 57–60, 61–66, 72–73, 75, 80–82, 86, 88, 91, 93, 103–107, 141–148, 151–153, 166–167, 171–172, 177–191
Franco, Francisco, 40, 63
Freedom, 1, 31, 33, 36, 58–60, 124
Freedom House, 25, 33, 143. *See also* Data
Friendships, 18, 82, 89, 90, 169
Fulbright Program, 82

G20, 101–103
Galbraith, John Kenneth, 45–46
Gallarotti, Giulio, 10–11, 14, 16–17, 20, 23, 62, 160–161, 168
Gallup International, 25, 31. *See also* Data
Gambia, 183
Gandhi, Mahatma, 11, 92
Gastrodiplomacy, 123, 139–140, 166
GDP (gross domestic product), 2–3, 6, 9, 11, 25, 28, 30, 33, 45–46, 54–56, 103–105, 108, 143, 155–159

208 Index

Geithner, Timothy, 102
General Staff College, 37
Georgia, 185
Germany, 4, 9, 39, 41, 45–46, 59, 72–75, 80, 82, 103–4, 108, 113, 117, 120, 137, 142–154, 166–167, 171–173, 184–191
Gift, Thomas, 34, 36–37
GlobeScan, 25
Global Firepower, 3, 156, 159. *See also* Data
GNP (gross national product), 4, 45
Goldsmith, Benjamin E., 4, 24–27, 31–33, 151
Good Country Index, 31. *See also* Data
Gorbachev, Mikhail, 1
Grandes Écoles, 88
Graney, Katherine E., 111
Grant, Ruth, 16, 23, 26–27, 161
Great Bridge approach, 18
Great Britain, *See* United Kingdom
Great Stories approach, 18
Great Wall approach, 18
Greece, 104, 178–182, 187, 189
Grigas, Agnia, 12, 110–11
Gross domestic product. *See* GDP
Gross national product. *See* GNP
Guangxi, 126
Gulf, 39

Habu, Toshie, 86
Hafez's poetry, 53
Hall, Joshua C., 40
Hall, Todd H., 17, 62
Hallyu, 65
Hamdouch, Bachir, 39
Happiness Index, 141. *See also* Data
Hard power, 10, 11, 19, 109, 111, 124, 154, 157, 160, 167
Harry Potter, 72
Havel, Vaclav, 1
Hayden, Craig, 14, 20, 53
Hofmeister, Wilhelm, 105
Honduras, 180
Hong Kong, 75, 86, 117–121, 124, 131, 153, 187, 189–191
Horiuchi, Yusaku, 4, 24–27, 31–33, 151
Host countries, 30, 33–34, 78, 82, 88–90, 99, 101, 108, 151
Hosting, 20, 22, 87, 90, 95, 105, 107, 110, 131, 155, 166, 171, 173
Hu Jintao, 10, 109
Huang, Kai-Ping, 124
Huang, Min-hua, 125
Humboldt Park, 62
Hungary, 1, 180–184, 187, 190

Imagined community, 51, 76
Immigrants, 18, 40–43, 61, 64, 78, 82, 84–87, 90–91, 94–96, 99, 105–108, 112–115, 120–121, 125, 132, 135–136, 146–147, 150–153, 164–169, 171–174, 177–190
Immigration policy, 41, 68, 82–83, 95, 155
India, 60, 72–76, 83–87, 91–108, 113, 124–25, 153, 156–157, 165–166, 173
Indonesia, 83, 93, 104–105, 124–126, 136, 140, 187
Institute for International Education, 28
Institutions, 3, 12–13, 31–38, 40, 48–49, 52–53 60, 77, 116, 160–161
Integration, 1, 50–51, 102, 111, 159
Interactions, 2–4, 6–7, 13–14, 22–25, 33, 42–43, 46–47, 49–51, 53–54, 56, 61, 76, 78, 88–89, 91, 107, 112, 136, 146, 159, 164–165, 168
International Criminal Court (ICC), 31–32, 44
International education, 4–5, 7, 28, 37, 57, 59–60, 71, 73, 78, 79–90, 161, 163–164, 166–167
International student mobility, 8, 33, 86
International students, 5, 30, 43, 60, 69, 84, 88, 113
International system, 15, 17, 23, 43, 47, 124, 133, 142, 158, 167
International Union of Official Travel Organisation, 175
Internet, 10–11, 13, 19, 30, 48, 51, 148
Iran, 34, 53, 104, 187, 190.
Iraq, 10, 19, 26, 31–32, 150
Ireland, 153, 180, 182, 184, 187, 190
Israel, 29, 104, 148, 178–180, 187
Issifou, Ismaël, 40
Istanbul, 136
Italian culture, 105
Italy, 39, 93, 103–7, 147–48, 153, 165, 171–72, 177–178, 180–191

Jackson, Peter, 135
Japan, 9–10, 16, 18–19, 52, 59–60, 66, 69, 75, 83–86, 103–104, 117, 20, 124–126, 131, 141, 144–145, 148, 150, 154, 163–164, 177–78, 182–191
Jim Crow, 58–59

Kalyoncu, Begum, 136
Kaplan, Alice, 60, 62, 64, 86
Kapur, Devesh, 97, 99
Karan, Kavita, 92–93
Kazakhstan, 99, 153, 184, 187, 190
Kelley, Judith G., 157
Kennedy, Jacqueline. *See* Bouvier
Kenya, 178
Kokas, Aynne, 64–65
Korea, North, 29
Korea, South, 34, 36, 40, 65, 75, 85–88, 104, 123–126, 139, 150, 182, 185, 187, 189
Kos-Stanisic, Lidija, 40

Krcmaric, Daniel, 34, 36–37
Kugiel, Patryk, 92
Kuczynski, Jürgen 45
Kumar, S.Y. Surendra 125
Kumar, Satish, 92
Kuznets, Simon, 45 54–56
Kyrgyzstan, 185

Language, 14, 29–30, 51, 61, 79, 86, 89, 105, 126, 137
Laos, 126, 140
Latin America, 34, 38, 65, 88, 139
Latvia, 185, 187
Lavrov, Sergei, 110
Lebanon, 148, 178–180, 190
Libraries, 8, 68, 74–76, 89, 103
Libya, 39
Lithuania, 185
Little Armenia, 136
Lomer, Sylvie, 89
London, 44, 61, 66
Los Angeles, 61, 123, 138, 140
Lotz, Amanda 74–76
Louw-Vaudran, Liesl, 155
Lowy Asia Power Index, 92, 136, 143. *See also* Data

Macao, 86, 117, 187, 190
MacDonald, Stuart, 5, 31, 33
Macedonia, 183
Mail, postal 50–51
Malawi, 99
Malaysia, 60, 123–126, 135–138, 140, 153, 189–191
Mali, 36
Malta, 185
Mao Zedong, 113
Marine Corps University, 37
Marlin-Bennett, Renée, 11, 14, 20, 167
Marshall Plan, 46
Martinique, 58
Marxist-Leninist ideology, 111
Maryland, 29
Mazzarol, Tim, 60
Media, 7, 8, 22, 32, 40, 42–43, 47, 65, 69, 76–78, 93, 109–111, 126, 166, 168, 173; social, 8, 47–48, 70, 76, 78, 166, 173
Merritt, Richard, 50, 53
Messaris, Paul, 40
Metapower, 14, 48, 161
Mexico, 88, 100, 102–104, 113, 150, 178–180, 184, 189
Middle East, 28, 53, 74, 133–135, 171
Migrants, 8, 37–39, 66, 87, 101, 106, 108, 162–163
Migration, 2, 4–8, 37–38, 40, 42, 46, 57, 59–60, 65–66, 69, 71, 73, 76–78, 86–87, 99, 159, 162–163, 169

Military, 3, 6, 12, 15, 20, 24, 30, 37, 44, 89, 111, 113, 125, 139, 141, 145, 153–158
Military officers, 36–37, 88–89, 161
Military power, 3, 11, 20, 141, 155–157, 159, 167
Minute associations, 23, 51
Miskimmon, A., 49
Modi, Narendra, 92, 125
Monocle ranking, 141. *See also* Data
Montesquieu, 15
Morocco, 39–40, 153, 173, 180, 182
Movies, 1–8, 14, 40–42, 46, 53–78, 92–94, 110, 119–121, 126, 131, 163–168, 175
Murphy, Ann Marie, 126
Museums, 62, 77
Music, 1–2, 61–62, 77, 101, 126, 168
Muslim, 28, 125, 131, 136, 138
Myanmar, 124–25, 131, 135, 139–140, 182

Nair, Neeti, 92
Nalanda University, 125
National Defense University, 37
National income, *See* GDP and GNP
Nationalism, 50–51, 139
National Socialism, 153
NATO, 1
Naylor, Tristen, 102
Neighbors, 61, 66, 78, 83, 85, 125, 155
Nehru, Jawaharlal, 92
Netflix, 71, 73–7
Netherlands, 39, 48, 99, 104, 145, 180–182, 184–87, 189
Networks, 10, 13, 24, 31, 43, 50, 77, 84, 109–110, 113, 121, 123, 142, 161
New Colombo Plan, 85
News, 13, 32, 110, 117
New South Policy, 126
Newspapers, 50–51, 76
New York City, 63
New Zealand, 84, 97, 126, 180, 182, 184, 187, 190
Nicom, Henrietta, 58
Nigeria, 69, 73, 93, 103, 135
Nogueira, Maria Alice, 86
Norms, 12–14, 21–22, 36–37, 160, 162, 168
North American, 53, 88
North American students, 88
North Atlantic, 82
Northeast Asia, 28, 125
North Korea, 29
Norway, 104, 185, 190
Nottingham, University of, 134
Nye, Jr., Joseph S., 6, 9, 10–15, 19–23, 49, 55, 69, 150–153, 166, 173–175

Oakman, Daniel, 82–83
OECD (Organisation for Economic Co-operation and Development), 38, 142, 144

Olympics, 14, 20, 77, 110, 146
Oman, 187, 190
Openness, 1, 2, 5–6, 12, 31, 39, 42–44, 53, 61, 63, 68, 83, 107–113, 121, 143, 146, 157, 164–165, 169, 172
Organisation for Economic Co-operation and Development, *See* OECD
Ostrom, Elinor, 23, 25, 51–53
Ozyegin University Department of Gastronomy and Culinary Arts, 139

Padoongpatt, Mark, 123, 138–140
Pakistan, 96, 135, 153
Pandemic, 6
Papua New Guinea, 83
Paraguay, 36
Paris, 57–59, 66
Paseo Boricua, 62
Patterson, Orlando, 77
People's Liberation Army, 88
People-to-people interactions, 3, 67, 107, 125, 158; direct, 2, 159; observing, 47, 162
People-to-people relationships, 55, 107, 140, 165–166
PEPFAR (President's Emergency Plan for AIDS Relief), 24–25
Pérez-Armendáriz, Clara, 38–39
Peru, 123, 139
Petty, William, 45
Pew Global Attitudes Poll, 143. *See also* Data
Pew Research Center, 25, 28, 143
Philippines, 32, 85, 124, 127, 136, 150, 178–180, 182
Pimpa, Nattavud, 86
Pikachu, 69
Pinjar, 40
Pizzagate, 11
Place identity, 57–58, 62–64, 66, 140, 163, 166, 168–169
Poland, 104, 148, 151, 153, 180–184, 187, 189
Polity IV Index data on quality of institutions, 36, 40. *See also* Data
Popular culture, 1, 4, 7, 18–19, 63, 69, 71, 73, 75, 77, 168
Portland, 157
Portugal, 36, 104, 117, 153, 178, 180, 182–184, 187, 190
Postal system, 51
Pot, Pol, 34
Powell, Colin, 27
Power resources, 11, 20, 161; converting soft, 161; economic, 3, 159; soft, 3, 92, 107, 160, 165
President's Emergency Plan for AIDS Relief (PEPFAR), 24–25

Press Freedom Index Score, 146. *See also* Data
Producers, 14–15, 20–22, 42–43, 47–49, 63, 65, 73, 76, 93, 162–164
Producer country, 17, 21, 33, 41–43
Public diplomacy, 7, 12, 18, 49, 53, 157, 160, 168
Public health program, effective, 24
Public opinion, 4, 21–22, 24–27, 29, 32, 42, 63, 136
Puerto Rico, 62, 67, 150, 164
Push-pull, 57, 59, 60, 85–86, 165, 169; push, 1, 3, 59–60, 85, 169; pull, 1, 3, 60, 85, 94
Putin, Vladimir, 12, 110–111
Putnam, Robert D., 53

Qatar, 187, 190

Race, 17, 59, 66, 83, 155
Radio, 69, 93, 173
Rankings, 40, 54, 54, 85, 136–137, 141–158, 164, 167, 172
Reciprocity, 15, 54
Refugees, 95–96, 108
Reggae, 77
Religion, 7, 36, 61, 92, 111, 124, 173
Renshon, Jonathan, 140, 157
Repnikova, Maria, 109–110, 117
Respect, 15–17, 22, 36, 110
Réunion, 190
Rock music, 1
Romania, 99, 182, 185, 187, 189
Rose, Andrew, 29–30, 33
Roselle, Laura, 49
Rosendorf, Neal M., 63
Ross, Andrew 17, 62
Rotaru, Vasile, 110
Russia, 4, 12, 29, 61, 72–73, 100–104, 109–122, 123, 126, 137, 142, 146–148, 151, 154, 164, 166, 171–172, 182–191; Soviet Union, 1, 10, 16, 19, 45, 93, 100, 110–111, 113, 116, 121, 126
Rutland, Peter, 111

Sanctions, 10, 29–30, 52
Satellite television, 61, 70, 71, 76
Saudi Arabia, 75, 82, 101, 104, 113, 131, 148, 150, 173, 182–191
Schaefer, David J., 92–93
Schaefer-Wilke, Ute, 137
Scotland, 102
Security Council, 101–102
Seiko, 18
Sekkat, Khalid, 38
Serbia, 185
ShahidVIP, 75
Shome, Parthasarathi, 102

Sikkink, Kathryn, 12–13
Simmons, Beth A., 157
Simonyi, András, 1
Singapore, 83, 124, 131, 136, 140, 148, 178–182
Singh, JP, 30, 33, 48–49, 53, 76
Slovakia, 185
Slovenia, 185
Smith, Frank, 83, 125
Smithsonian Institution, 77
Social capital, 13, 18, 46–47, 51–54, 157, 161–62, 169
Social interactions, 3–4, 6–7, 45–47, 50, 54, 56, 67–70, 77–78, 90–92, 101, 105, 107, 163–166
Social media platforms, 49, 51, 78
Soft Power 30, 5, 18, 55, 85, 92, 136, 141–147, 151, 156–158, 164, 167. *See also* Data
Soft Power Rubric, 100–102, 104, 106–108, 110, 112, 116, 118, 136–147, 150–151, 154–161, 163–169, 172–173, 177–178
Somalia, 99
Sontag, Susan, 58–60, 63, 66, 86
Soroka, Stuart, 74–75
Soutar, Geoffrey N., 60
South Africa, 102–5, 125, 154–157, 167, 184, 187, 189
South Asia, 100, 125, 131, 135–137
Southeast Asia, 4, 28, 76, 103, 105, 123–127, 131, 135–137, 139
South Korea. *See* Korea, South
Soviet Union. *See* Russia
Spain, 39–40, 63, 72–73, 104, 142, 147–148, 156, 171–172, 178–191
Spilimbergo, Antonio, 33–37, 41, 151, 161
Sport, 7, 66, 77, 124, 155
Springsteen, Bruce, 1
Sri Lanka, 81
Starbucks, 28
Status, 6, 11, 36, 56, 60, 85, 99, 103, 118, 140, 142, 166
Stiglitz, Joseph, 103
Strategic Narrative, 49
Straubhaar, Joseph, 93
Students, 1, 4–8, 14, 18–43, 57–61, 69, 79–101, 105–110, 116–140, 144–153, 157, 161–167, 171–191
Suryodiningrat, Meidyatama, 126
Sutter, Robert, 126
Sweden, 104, 144–145, 187–188, 190
Switzerland, 18, 30, 50, 104, 141–145, 148, 177–182, 184–187, 189

Taiwan, 110, 123–27, 139, 166
Tajikistan, 185
Takayama, Keita, 89
Talaska, Cara, 17
Taoyuan, 135
Tarrow, Sidney G., 13
Taylor, Philip M., 53, 108,
Technology, 8, 10–11, 13–14, 48–49, 51, 64–66, 70, 73, 78, 83, 87, 93
Telegraph, 70, 76
Telenovelas, 65
Television, 1, 47–48, 51, 61, 64–65, 71, 76–78, 83, 93, 126, 166, 173
Tettner, Samuel, 139–140
Thai Americans, 61, 123, 138–140
Thailand, 61, 104, 123–126, 136, 138–140, 166, 187–189
Thailand's destination image, 140, 166
Thai people, 86, 123, 126, 140, 166
Thai restaurants, 123, 139
Tharoor, Shashi, 92
Tiny publics, 23, 51
Tocqueville, Alexi, 23, 51
Togo, 180
Tokyo, 141
Tourism, 4, 7–8, 28, 41, 57, 62–63, 80, 118, 121, 138–140, 168
Tourists, 5, 27, 31, 33, 62–63, 66, 94, 123, 144, 146, 153, 161
Trade, 4, 16–17, 22, 24, 27, 29–30, 33, 42–43, 124–125, 153, 161
Trade negotiations, 3, 20, 159
Trading partners, 33
Transnational, 3, 7–8, 13, 38, 60–61, 66–67, 78, 86, 101, 146, 166, 172
Transnational companies, 64
Transnational culture, 47, 163
Transnational engagement, 124
Transnational family, 39– 39
Transnational identities, 7, 57–58, 61, 66, 86, 135, 137, 165–166
Travelers, 57, 64, 76, 147, 160, 163
Trust, 6–7, 13, 23, 25–26, 46–47, 51–53, 160, 162–163
Trust communities, 7, 13, 51, 70, 76
Tsai Ing-wen, 125
Tsang, Eileen Yuk-ha, 86
Tuccio, Michelle, 39
Tunisia, 151, 183
Turan, Ilan, 105
Türkiye (formerly Turkey), 32, 61, 67, 104–105, 146, 148, 151, 164, 171–172, 180–187, 189–191

UAE (United Arab Emirates), 101, 148, 171–72, 189–91
Uganda, 178–180
Ukraine, 100, 111, 120, 147, 187–189
UNESCO (United Nations Educational, Scientific, and Cultural Organization) Institute of Statistics. *See* Data

Union of European Football Associations (UEFA), 111
United Arab Emirates. *See* UAE
United Kingdom, 31, 50, 59–60, 72–75, 89, 97, 104, 117, 127, 131, 142–148, 151–153, 166–167, 171, 177–191; British, 17, 23, 30, 36, 60–61, 82–83, 89, 125, 137, 141, 153–155; Great Britain, 4, 9, 11, 17, 28, 58, 84, 117, 137
United Nations Demographic Yearbook, 108, 174. *See also* Data
United Nations Development Program (UNDP) Gender Equality Index Score, 146. *See also* Data
United Nations Population Division. *See* Data
United Nations World Tourism Organization (UN Tourism). *See* Data
United Nations, 4, 10, 12, 56, 69, 102, 113, 143
United Nations Educational, Scientific, and Cultural Organization, Institute of Statistics. *See* Data
United States, 3–4, 9–11, 16–17, 23–28, 31–32, 38–41, 43–45, 50–60, 63–65, 69–74, 120, 124–26, 125–127, 135–136, 150–151, 153–155, 166–169, 177–186, 188–191; immigration, 108, 116, 117, 147, 150; military, 24, 34, 36–37, 44, 81, 82, 88; movies, 5, 4, 55, 64–65, 70–72, 75. 78, 93, 131; universities, 36–37, 43, 46, 60, 78–79, 81–86, 89, 97, 99, 116–117, 120–121, 137, 140

Védrine, Hubert, 27
Venezuela, 53
Video gamers, 23, 51, 77
Video streaming, 71
Viduka, Zrinka, 40
Vietnam, 32, 85, 124, 126–127, 136, 140, 150
Virtue, 4, 14–15, 22, 27, 42
Virtuosity, 4, 14–16, 22, 42, 67, 161
Visitors, 55, 61, 63, 69, 77, 101, 106–108, 117–118, 120–121, 131, 135–136, 150, 153, 164–165, 168, 171–173, 177–191

Vogel, Ezra, 9, 18

Wagenführ, Rolf, 45
Walker, James, 52
Walton, Whitney, 89
Wang, Chenjun, 18
Washington Consensus, 110, 124
Watchmaking, 18
Welsh, Bridget, 124–25
Western Europe, 23, 48, 117
White Australia, 40–41, 79, 82, 83, 90, 166–167
White House, 58, 62
Wibowo, Ignatius, 124, 136
Wilkins, Stephen, 126
Wilson, Ernest J., 1560
Wilson, Jeanne, 17, 21
Windle, Joel, 86
Woo, Jisuk, 40
Wood, Terence, 25
World Bank, 19, 25, 87, 99, 104, 108, 143–144, 156–157. *See also* Data
World Economic Forum, 141, 143
World Trade Organization, 64
World Values Survey, 39. *See also* Data
World War I, 81–82
World War II, 9, 34, 40, 45–46, 63, 82, 125, 153
World Tourism Organization, *See* United Nations World Tourism Organization
Wright, Richard, 58
Wu, Irene S. 7, 13, 51, 53, 70, 76–77, 86, 91, 96, 153, 169
Wu, Shang-Su, 125

Xinhua, 110

Yamagishi, Toshio, 52
Ye, Joseph, 95, 113
YouTube, 71
Yunnan, 126, 139

Zambia, 99
Zamroni Salim, 105
Zimbabwe, 187
Zogby International, 28. *See also* Data

About the Book

SOFT POWER TYPICALLY GETS SHORT SHRIFT IN FOREIGN policy strategy because it is considered difficult to measure. To what degree do student-exchange programs matter to international politics? How exactly does a diaspora network affect a country's influence abroad? What are the foreign policy implications of hosting the Olympics? Can hit movies solidify alliances?

In response to this conundrum, Irene Wu has developed the Soft Power Rubric, an innovative framework that allows soft power to be quantified, as GDP is, supporting country comparisons, historical analysis, and global rankings. Composed of four indicators with publicly available data—immigration, study abroad, travel, and movies—the rubric identifies which countries in the world have the most soft power by the breadth and depth of their people-to-people relationships abroad.

Irene S. Wu is a lecturer at Georgetown University and senior economist at the US Federal Communications Commission.